LONG HISTORY, DEEP TIME

DEEPENING HISTORIES OF PLACE

Aboriginal History Incorporated

Aboriginal History Inc. is a part of the Australian Centre for Indigenous History, Research School of Social Sciences, The Australian National University, and gratefully acknowledges the support of the School of History and the National Centre for Indigenous Studies, The Australian National University. Aboriginal History Inc. is administered by an Editorial Board which is responsible for all unsigned material. Views and opinions expressed by the author are not necessarily shared by Board members.

Contacting Aboriginal History

All correspondence should be addressed to the Editors, Aboriginal History Inc., ACIH, School of History, RSSS, 9 Fellows Road (Coombs Building), Acton, ANU, 2601, or aboriginal.history@anu.edu.au.

WARNING: Readers are notified that this publication may contain names or images of deceased persons.

LONG HISTORY, DEEP TIME

DEEPENING HISTORIES OF PLACE

Edited by Ann McGrath and Mary Anne Jebb

Australian
National
University

PRESS

Published by ANU Press and Aboriginal History Inc.
The Australian National University
Acton ACT 2601, Australia
Email: anupress@anu.edu.au
This title is also available online at http://press.anu.edu.au

National Library of Australia Cataloguing-in-Publication entry

Title: Long history, deep time : deepening histories of place /
              edited by Ann McGrath, Mary Anne Jebb.

ISBN: 9781925022520 (paperback) 9781925022537 (ebook)

Subjects: Aboriginal Australians--History.
              Australia--History.

Other Creators/Contributors:
              McGrath, Ann, editor.
              Jebb, Mary Anne, editor.

Dewey Number: 994.0049915

Cover design and layout by ANU Press. Cover photograph by Kartikeya Sharma.

Printed by Griffin Press

Contents

Illustrations

Foreword

For all the methodological innovations that the discipline of academic history has seen since its birth in Europe in the late-eighteenth and early-nineteenth centuries, historians have on the whole, in deciding what constitutes historical evidence, clung to the idea of the primacy of the written word, of textual sources, and have been satisfied to leave the business of dating and interpreting ancient artefacts and material remains of human civilisations to prehistorians and archaeologists. While it has to be granted that these boundaries have occasionally been breached in some areas, such as in ancient Roman or Greek histories or in art history, debates in the historical profession over issues raised by the evidence of memory, personal experience, and legends and myths, have once again highlighted the 'value' of written sources. True, historians now acknowledge that history is only one way among many of telling the past, but the idea of the archive – a repository of written sources – is still central to how historians think of what constitutes the activity called 'research'. We imagine prehistorians and archaeologists as people who go digging around, literally, in unfamiliar places to find their treasure-troves of evidence; when we speak of historians, we still think of a group of people prepared to suffer the consequences of prolonged exposure to the dust that usually collects over 'old' documents. The French once used to say, 'no documents, no history'; the moral rule among historians still seems to be: 'no sniffles and sneezes, no history!'

This present collection is evidence of how this presumed primacy of the written, textual evidence that historians have for generations taken for granted is now coming to be challenged. The sources of this challenge are multiple: clearly, indigenous histories, long narrated in stories and storied performances, have been troubled by this question for some decades now. Another source of this challenge has been the realisation on the part of some gifted scholars that graduate training of future historians – thanks to the relative abundance of written sources for the last hundred years or so – has often come to focus on ever shorter periods of time, and that even the tendency to go 'global' in world history has not been able to rectify this tendency sufficiently. History has remained, for the purpose of graduate training at least, a discipline parcelled up into regions and periods. It is out of this sense of profound dissatisfaction that arguments have arisen for 'big' and 'deep' histories, accounts of human pasts that go far, far beyond the few hundred years – or even the few millennia – that historians of globalisation or world history deal with. Some 'big' historians seek to incorporate human history into the history of the universe – and see this as the new 'creation myth' that an increasingly connected and globalised humanity needs – while other 'deep' historians want to go at least as far back as the time when humans developed the 'modern', big brain that enabled them to create symbolic systems and thus cooperate in the interests of abstract and larger identities such as the group or the nation, or even 'humanity' itself.

The current planetary environmental crisis that often goes by the name of climate change has made us only more aware that humans exist and work today, not only as differentiated members of rich and poor classes and societies, but also as a species, united by their shared dreams of development and prosperity that end up making increasing demands on what the planet and its biosphere produce. Whatever may be the sides that historians choose to pick in debates to do with climate change and the growing human consumption of energy, no one can neglect the fact that the perennial question of the place of humans in the natural order of things has emerged as one of the most urgent and insistent questions of our time, especially for scholars in the humanities. It is important therefore that historians who work on relatively short and more recent periods of human history speak to scholars and scholarship in the historically minded fields of archaeology, prehistory and evolutionary biology. *Long History, Deep Time* is precisely a step in this direction. It does not devalue the work that historians do in the archive; but it equally values historians who have long attempted to supplement the written word with the materials furnished by memory and oral history; and it now seeks to extend the conversation by including in it the work of those who deal with deep time, the time of prehistory and human evolution. Australia, with its rich tradition of Indigenous pasts and distinctive history of human occupation of the continent, provides an excellent site for the staging of this conversation that is of undeniable global importance today.

Needless to say, it is still early days for such conversation to happen across the disciplines represented in this collection. This book remains an experiment. But it is a timely experiment that needs to be welcomed. One just hopes that many other and similar conversations will follow. I, for one, feel particularly pleased that the conversation has now begun in real earnest, and congratulate the editor and the contributors to this volume for what they have collectively achieved.

Dipesh Chakrabarty
Canberra
July 2015

Preface: 'The gift of history'

In June 2013, at the invitation of Ann McGrath and her colleagues, I spent a week in Canberra and had a chance to attend the Deepening Histories of Place Symposium. Such opportunities to share ideas with colleagues over more than just a few days are rare and precious. For me, it was a life-changing experience, offering a chance to learn about a world of scholarship and knowledge of which I was hitherto but dimly aware. Along with the exhilaration, though, came the troubling realisation that the idea of deep history, for all its logic and for all the good it might do, contains unresolved contradictions. The problem I confronted during the symposium and in conversations with colleagues before and after is encapsulated in an anecdote related in this volume by Martin Porr. The anecdote arose from a reported exchange between an anthropologist and a group of young Indigenous men. 'The scientists said that Aborigines only arrived in Australia 50,000 years ago, but our elders have told us that we have *always been here*.' Contributions in this volume by Julia Torpey Hurst, Jeanine Leane, and others reveal a concern about the potentially disabling effects of taking a deep historical perspective on time and history. The gift of history, it seems, is not a gift that everyone is eager to receive, especially when it has negative implications for identity.

Deep history has a profound political agenda. This is not in the least surprising; as Harry Allen observes in this volume, archaeology and history are guided by a significant political task. As he suggests, the fields have not always done a good job confronting the political agendas inherited from older approaches. One of the political goals of deep history has been to join with other critical viewpoints in exposing the operation of those agendas in the histories of nations and civilisation. Viewed through the lens of this critique, these histories appear as elements in a powerful marketing campaign that emerged in Europe and elsewhere a century and more ago, at a time when history was subservient to the task of inventing nations and justifying colonialism. To treat the history of our species as *history* and not only as biology or archaeology is one way for us to provincialise both Europe and modernity.

Another and perhaps more salient goal of deep history has been to restore historicity to the peoples without history. In my own case, as a citizen of the United States, it seems patently obvious to me that 'history', as a curricular structure and a framework for organising the past, should embrace Native American and First Nation peoples by acknowledging that North America has a history that antedates 1492. This kind of deep historical move means folding archaeology, history, and all the other disciplines concerned with the human past into a single field. In doing so, we can reduce methodology to its proper and subordinate role, that of being a tool in the service of explanation. Calling this 'history' is just a convenience, and is not meant to imply that history, as conventionally defined, is somehow sovereign in the resulting ménage.

But here is the rub, for the act of extending the embrace of history, however well intentioned, carries with it the necessity of accepting the very idea that being in history is a Good Thing. Among other things, rendering the past as history seems to demand that everyone share a similar stance toward time itself: namely, the belief that the events of the human past can be arrayed on a scaffolding of time. Not everyone sees time this way. To those who do, a long and datable history may seem to empower those who possess it. But as Ann McGrath reminds us, this works only if you accept the mode of determining power that matters to the white population.

The concern expressed here raises the legitimate question of whether time's scaffolding has an objective reality. To a geologist and an archaeologist, the answer to this may be straightforward. But other disciplines might have a different response. As Peter Riggs's contribution suggests, no physicist will accept that there is any such scaffolding, given the fact that light travels at a finite rather than an infinite speed. When archaeologists and historians suppose that we can thread a skewer between Europe and America in 1066, and claim that certain events were unfolding in Cahokia at the same time that other events were unfolding in England, we are claiming a synchronicity of timelines that could not be claimed for events unfolding in the Andromeda Galaxy and the Milky Way.

The lesson is worth pondering. If and when humans settle planets in the Andromeda Galaxy, we will be forced, once and for all, to abandon the idea that history can be written as if events everywhere unfold on a universal scaffolding of time. The likelihood of humans ever colonising planets in the Andromeda Galaxy is exceedingly remote, of course, but it is not non-existent. That being the case, perhaps now is a good time to rethink any commitments we might have to the understanding of what time is. We can allow ourselves to think of time's scaffold as an intellectual convenience or a habit of thought rather than a description of any physical reality.

The time dilation between Cahokia and Hastings being miniscule, these observations about time amount to little more than playful philosophical ruminations, and perhaps we should simply ignore the physics of time and accept the pastness of the deep past. But even if we do, there are good reasons to join with scholars of material culture in believing that the past is not only past. The past is also present with us on the 'temporal wave', the term Rob Paton uses to represent Indigenous time. Once you stop and think about it, the point seems obvious. When I work with a medieval European manuscript, for example, I am working with something that is old. I know it is old because, like all the documents I happen to work with, it has a date, and the possibility of it being a forgery are next to nil. But although it is old, it is nonetheless *present*. Moreover, the manuscript has changed in the nearly 600 years since it was first compiled. I can barely read the words on certain areas of many of its pages for all the damage caused by damp and mould and book lice. On many pages, chemical reactions have caused the ink, once black, to turn brown. In addition to these material changes, the manuscript's purpose in life has changed dramatically from the time it was compiled to the time in which I use it. Where it was once a living thing, a register of legal contracts, it has now become a symbolic artefact.

We can push this insight further. The date found on the manuscript is an attribute that attaches to only one of the many components of the register, namely, the writing. Other components have different temporalities. The paper from which the register was made, for instance, was compiled from linen fibres that circulated in the previous generation as tablecloths, bed sheets and shifts. The oak galls from which the ink was made came from trees that were even older. Scattered through the register are fragments of DNA left by the book lice, the mould, the linen, the sheep from whose hide the cover was made, and of course all the archivists and historians who have used it. All that DNA was made following patterns that are immeasurably old. If I were a scientist sequencing the genome of the book louse rather than a historian studying medieval household inventories, I would have a very different idea about the chronological horizons of the sources for my data. The medieval register, in short, is entangled in many different chronologies. It 'punctures' the present, to use Karen Hughes's lovely term.

To say that the manuscript is coeval with me is not to deny that the date it carries is both real and interesting to historians like me. Similarly, I do not doubt that Mungo Lady lived around 42,000 years ago. Nor do I have any doubt that the archaeological traces found in the central Mungo lunette can be used to provide a framework for writing an account of human settlement in the Willandra Lakes area, even if, as Nicola Stern's contribution shows, erosion and other processes render the landscape a palimpsest that is hard to read. The potential power of such dates is revealed in Bruce Pascoe's choice to emphasise the antiquity of the Brewarrina fish traps, a choice that springs from justified pride. The fact that it is possible to date the events of the past is one of the lessons of physics. By way of another philosophical excursus, imagine that intelligent beings in the galaxy of Andromeda have invented a telescope with infinite resolution. Imagine that the telescope is trained on the Willandra Lakes area. Several million years from now, by our time line, the photons recording the events of Mungo Lady's life and death will arrive in the field of that telescope.

Dates, in short, do have a kind of objective reality. They become problematic, in history and archaeology, only when they become attached so firmly to events that they 'lock' those events in time. Objects and artefacts are native time travellers, carried along on the face of the temporal wave. Objects have some of the same qualities of *Tjukurpa* as described by Diana James, having existence at every moment of their biographies. This observation holds even more forcefully for practices or behaviours. There is no such thing as 'medieval' acts of violence, let alone a 'palaeodiet', unless we also admit that these habits are simultaneously modern.

To say that the first Australians arrived on the continent 45,000 to 60,000 years ago, then, is not to say that the defining feature of Indigenous culture is that it is really, really old. Whatever the culture of the Indigenous Australians may be, it is present in the here and now. The amazing archaeological evidence of Australia that has accumulated in the last half century, surveyed here by Allen and others, shows that Indigenous culture has moved in the currents of change. This being so, it makes little sense to speak of anything we might be tempted to call 'tradition'. In this volume, Luke Taylor explains very clearly why we should not accept the idea that some artefacts represent a timeless tradition while others have been contaminated by the cultural decline of the present day. The point has been made before, but Taylor adds a delicious irony in pointing out how Baldwin Spencer suppressed certain bark paintings that engaged enthusiastically with the present day. As we know, and as Peter Read reminds us, the concept of tradition becomes especially problematic when it is tied to identity. Once the two are linked, losing the one means losing the other.

In this sense, we can choose to think with dates as long as we do not think of them as anchors that prevent things from travelling in time. But this does not yet respond to the question of whether the elders were telling the truth about 'always being here'. I was intrigued by Porr's creative solution to this thorny problem. Trends sweeping through the biological sciences these days now point to the idea that there is no such thing as an organism without a niche. An organism makes a niche and in turn is continually shaped by the niche it inhabits. In a sense, the object of inquiry can never be singular. We need to think instead about a composite meshwork, where the organism-and-niche is simply one of those meshworks. Alongside this is the idea, now emerging in the field of microbiomics, which proposes that your body, however much it may seem to be a product of your DNA, is in fact a coral reef composed of many different life forms, ranging from mitochondria to gut bacteria. We have never been individuals. As evolutionary theorists compile what is known as the 'Extended Evolutionary Synthesis', they have challenged the idea that the identity of any organism lies solely in its genome. In place of this, they propose giving pride of place to the gene regulatory networks, some of which reside in the niche that controls gene expression. Translated into the realm of history and culture, what this means is that we cannot leave Australia, the place, out of any definition of the people. Indigenous Australians have always been there, perhaps, because they were not Australian before arriving in Sahul. The Indigenous peoples made Australia, and Australia, returning the favour, made them.

This is an idea that is good to think with. Whether it is acceptable to indigenous peoples all over the world is not for me to decide. Here, all I would observe is that it does not violate any commitments that are characteristic of a scientific approach to understanding the past. Yet there remains an obstacle to the prospect of thinking about Australia in the light of deep history. The very wording of the expression sets up an apparent contrast between a deep history and a thin or shallow history, thereby inadvertently creating two time-spaces for peoples old and new. It may be that Indigenous Australians are able to cross this conceptual gap with ease, as Malcolm Allbrook and McGrath suggest in their conclusion. But Leane's contribution points in a different direction, for she implies that we ought to be careful about deploying any language of gaps or, for that matter, deep and shallow time spaces. Perhaps above all, we ought to think carefully about whether these spaces are *time* spaces.

Herein lies the unresolved and perhaps unresolvable tension that ran through the symposium and runs through these contributions. Despite what I once thought, the gift of deep history is not necessarily an appropriate solution to the politically disempowering state of being 'historyless'. Faced with this paradox, what shall we do with the very idea of deep history? Though I have no persuasive solutions to the conundrum, I would begin facing up to it by observing that whatever the problems with the formulation of 'history', people like me, and the cultures we inhabit, are stuck with it. If history is about meaning-making, then I will stick by my claim that the truncated history we retail in classrooms in the United States and elsewhere offers our children a thin and insubstantial understanding of what it means to be human. As a cultural actor, I am free to think with deep history, and I can choose to make meaning with all that we have learned and are learning about the long-ago from fields such as archaeology. To this extent, the most important thing to emerge from the Deepening Histories of Place Symposium, and the extraordinary volume that has emerged from it, is not that people like me should query our commitments to deep history. The lesson, instead, is that we should always be careful about making gifts.

Daniel Lord Smail
Harvard University
June 2015

Acknowledgements

The editors are grateful for the many people and organisations who made this book possible. Firstly, we thank The Australian National University and the Australian Institute of Aboriginal and Torres Strait Islander Studies (AIATSIS) and our many colleagues at the Australian Centre for Indigenous History, including Maria Nugent and Jeanine Leane. We thank the Australian Research Council (ARC) for funding the 'Deepening Histories of Place: Exploring Indigenous Landscapes of National and International Significance' project through a Linkage grant, LP100100427. We are appreciative of the expertise, the vision, enthusiasm and ongoing backing of our partners: The National Film and Sound Archive, AIATSIS, Parks Australia, The NSW Office of Environment and Heritage, Ronin Films, and Sydney University. The Northern Territory Government also provided significant funding. We also benefited from another ARC grant, DP110103193 on Australia's Ancient Past, which enabled research into the deep history of Lake Mungo and the Willandra Lakes. David Ritchie was also a valuable supporter, and we also appreciated the support of the then Attorney General the Hon. Mark Dreyfus who launched our Deepening Histories website. Andrew Pike, filmmaker and historian, and Managing Director of Ronin Films, assisted at many levels, especially as Partner to the Deepening Histories project and as Co-Director and Producer of the film *Message from Mungo*.

People who have assisted along the way with our wider project include Toni Makkai, Sean Downes, Doug MacNicholl, Stella Armstrong, Margaret Harding, and the many ANU staff who work in finance and in school administration, including Stella Armstrong, Karen Smith, and photographer Stuart Hay. We thank photographer Kartikeya Sharma for his wonderful cover image.

Along with co-editor Ann McGrath, who was lead Chief Investigator, other Chief Investigators on the project included the talented Peter Read, who was then working at the University of Sydney. Shino Konishi and Luke Taylor provided important advice on ethical protocols and visual representations. Indigenous IP lawyers Terri Janke and Lucinda Edwards played an important role in developing best practice intellectual property protocols for this multimedia research project.

Malcolm Allbrook played an exceptional role as researcher and project manager on the Mungo project, and in co-convening and bringing the symposium together. Jason Ensor assisted with many things digital, including the design of innovative history tools and the website, and he provided many insights and breakthroughs in forging the ground for history's digital future.

The project gained a talented complement of doctoral students funded by the ARC: Julia Torpey, Shannyn Palmer and Rob Paton. They each brought special strengths to the project and developed truly collaborative approaches to working with Indigenous communities. They also became very savvy in new digital recording techniques, editing and in historical data management. Rob Paton was especially generous in sharing his archaeological experience and assisting whenever required.

We thank the Board of Aboriginal History, and especially its monograph editor, Rani Kerin. The manager of ANU Press, Lorena Kanellopoulos, had the vision to encourage us in developing this digitally enhanced volume.

Some of those who participated in the Deepening Histories of Place Symposium but who were not able to provide chapters for this volume, contributed significantly to our thinking. These include Paul Taçon of Griffith University, Tom Griffiths, and astrophysicist Lisa Kewley of The Australian National University, along with colleagues Charlie Lineweaver and Ray Norris. Matthew Spriggs and a range of audience members offered incisive comments and discussion. We greatly valued the contributions of the Mutthi Mutthi, Ngyiampaa and Paakantji (Barkindji) peoples from Willandra who participated at the symposium and recorded their views on history and heritage in the film *Message from Mungo*. Along with the staff of National Parks New South Wales, they expressed sustained interest in our symposium and shared their ideas of long and deep history. Among those we would like to thank are Darryl Pappin, Leanne Tobin, Tanya Charles, Joan Slade, Mary-Anne Marton and Peggy Thomas, Beryl and Roy Kennedy, Eric and Maureen Taylor, Sam Wickman, Marie Mitchell, Lottie Mitchell, Ricky Mitchell, Jo Gorman, Richard Mintern and Warren Clark. Many more people also assisted during our visits to Lake Mungo, and they are credited in our film *Message from Mungo* (Ronin Films 2014).

In the preparation stages of the manuscript, Maria Haenga Collins and Alycia Nevalainen provided high-quality assistance, making the trickiest tasks seem easy. Geoff Hunt provided the model of a congenial, interested and conscientious copyeditor.

Ann McGrath is particularly appreciative of her family — Milton, Venetia and Naomi Cameron — for tolerating her through many solid chunks of work. Of special benefit to the development of this volume was my membership of the School of Social Sciences at the Institute of Advanced Study, Princeton, for which I wish to thank the Director Didier Fassin and faculty members Joan Scott and Danielle Allen, as well as my fellow members. Staff at the school's library were amazing. My residency at the Rockefeller Center, Bellagio, was also beneficial, introducing me to a range of amazingly supportive and talented people, including Pat Mitchell, Jacqueline Novagratz, Chris Anderson,

Brian English, Pilar Pallacia, and others whose company I continue to look forward to beyond Bellagio. Without my colleague Mary Anne Jebb, who did a phenomenal job of getting the Deepening Histories project off the ground, supporting the students, liaising with partners, and enabling our project to achieve goals beyond expectations, it is difficult to imagine a book at all. Finally, I have been inspired by the work, generosity and collegiality of David Armitage of Harvard University and Dipesh Chakrabarty of the University of Chicago.

Mary Anne Jebb would like to thank her co-editor and colleague Ann McGrath for the opportunity to join the Deepening Histories of Place research team at the Australian Centre for Indigenous History at ANU. Thanks to Ann's leadership, the centre provided the innovation and interdisciplinarity necessary for deepening histories of place.

Special thanks to the custodians of the Australian landscape and for their contribution to this volume.

A Gentle Warning

The photographs, films and sound recordings in this webpage contain the images and voices of deceased people. To avoid unintentional distress, people should be aware of this when they download material, or if they view the website in the presence of people who may be affected.

Sponsors

Contributors

Malcolm Allbrook is employed in the School of History at The Australian National University as Managing Editor of the Australian Dictionary of Biography. He was previously (2011 – January 2014) Research Associate to Professor Ann McGrath on her ARC Discovery Project 'Australia's Ancient and Modern Pasts: A History of Lake Mungo'. His interests include British colonial histories and family biographies in the Indian Ocean region, and Indigenous community histories. He has recently published *Henry Prinsep's Empire: Framing a Distant Colony* through ANU Press. He has previously collaborated with prominent Kimberley elder John Darraga Watson to produce *Never Stand Still: Stories of Life, Land and Politics in the Kimberley* (2012) and in 2012 co-curated a historical exhibition 'Burlganyja Wanggaya' in Carnarvon, Western Australia, which was awarded the MAGNA prize for best permanent exhibition.

Harry Allen is a Research Fellow in the Department of Anthropology at the University of Auckland, and a Research Associate at Melbourne Museum and in the Archaeology Programme at La Trobe University. His archaeological research began at ANU with his doctoral studies of Lake Mungo and the Willandra Lakes carried out between 1969 and 1972. Since that time he has conducted research in western Arnhem Land, Central Java and New Zealand. More recently he has embarked on a material culture study of Australian Aboriginal spears. His publications include two edited volumes, *Australia: William Blandowski's Illustrated Encyclopaedia of Aboriginal Australia* (2010) and, with Caroline Phillips, *Bridging the Divide: Indigenous Communities and Archaeology into the 21st Century* (2010).

Karen Hughes is a Senior Lecturer in Indigenous Studies at Swinburne University of Technology. She formerly taught at Monash University and the University of South Australia, and in 2011 was a Visiting Fellow at University of Paris 13. Her research focuses on intimate and gendered histories of the contact zone in New World settler-colonial societies, incorporating transnational perspectives. She is currently working with Victoria Grieves and Catriona Elder on the ARC-funded project 'Children of War'. Her research pursues decolonising methodologies through a partnership approach to ethnography. She is also involved in an intergenerational study with the Ngukurr community of south-east Arnhem Land and a cross-cultural collaborative project with Indigenous communities in south-eastern Australia and the United States.

Diana James is a Senior Research Associate in the School of Archaeology and Anthropology at The Australian National University. She has worked as an anthropologist and bilingual interpreter in the areas of philosophy, art and culture since 1975. Her research focus is on the dynamic visual and auditory performance space of the art, song and story of the Western Desert peoples of central and western Australia. Increasingly the multimedia tools of recording available to ethnographic and visual anthropological research have enabled a more dynamic exploration of the many cultural expressions of Indigenous kinship to country and holistic sense of place.

Her publications include *Painting the Song* (2009) and *Ngintaka* (2014). She is currently a lead investigator and coordinator of the ARC Linkage Project 'Songlines of the Western Desert'. This collaborative research project initiated by elders, artists, dancers and singers of the Anangu Pitjantjatjara Yankunytjatjara, Ngaanyatjarra and Martu Lands is investigating Aboriginal peoples' oral song-poem tradition; the *songlines* that are the foundational cultural routes of Australia.

Mary Anne Jebb is a Research Fellow at the Australian Institute of Aboriginal and Torres Strait Islander Studies. Previously, she was the Research Associate and Project Manager for the ARC Linkage project 'Deepening Histories of Place' at The Australian National University. She researches and writes in areas of Australian history, medical history, women's history and Indigenous history. She has particular interest in the recording and use of spoken histories and sound for increasing understanding and participation in Australian history. Her books, sound productions and exhibitions include 'Across The Great Divide; Gender Relations On Australian Frontiers' with Anna Haebich (1992), *Emerarra: A Man of Merarra* (1996), *Blood Sweat and Welfare* (2002), *Mowanjum* (2008), 'Noongar Voices' with Bill Bunbury (2010), 'Burlganyja Wanggaya' (2012) and 'Singing The Train' (2014). She is working on a monograph biography and analysis of the visual narrative artworks of deceased Aboriginal artist and historian Jack Wherra.

Jeanine Leane is a Wiradjuri scholar from south-west New South Wales. Formerly a Research Fellow at the Australian Institute of Aboriginal and Torres Strait Islander Studies, she is currently a research fellow in the Australian Centre for Indigenous History at The Australian National University. She is an award-winning poet and novelist. In 2013 Jeanine received a Discovery Indigenous Award to examine the way the David Unaipon Award for Indigenous writing impacts on Australian literary history and culture.

Ann McGrath is Professor of History and Director of the Australian Centre for Indigenous History at The Australian National University. She is a Fellow of the Academy of Social Sciences and was awarded an Order of Australia Medal for services to history, especially Indigenous history. She has published widely on the history of gender and colonialism in Australia and North America. She was awarded an Honorary Doctorate at Linneaus University in Sweden, has advised various government enquiries and produced two documentary films, *Frontier Conversation* (2006) and *Message from Mungo* (2014). Her publications include *Born in the Cattle: Aborigines in Cattle Country* (1987) and *Contested Ground: Aborigines under the British Crown* (1994). She wrote, with Ann Curthoys, *How to Write History that People Want to Read* (2011). She was a Member of the Institute for Advanced Study, Princeton, 2013–14, and was awarded a Bellagio Residency for 2014. She serves on the board of the journal *Aboriginal History*.

Bruce Pascoe is a Bunurong/Tasmanian Yuin man and winner of the Australian Literature Award 1999 (*Shark*), Radio National Short Story 1998, FAW Short Story 2010, Prime Minister's Award for Literature (Young Adult) 2013 (*Fog a Dox*) and published and edited *Australian Short Stories* magazine 1982–99. His books include *Night Animals, Fox, Ruby Eyed Coucal, Shark, Ocean, Earth, Cape Otway, Convincing Ground, The Little Red Yellow and Black Book*. His most recent books are *Bloke* (2009), *Chainsaw File* (2010), *Fog a Dox* (2012) and *Dark Emu. Dark Emu*, a the history of Aboriginal agriculture, was published in 2014 (reprinted four times since March) and shortlisted in the Victorian Premiers' Literary awards in 2014. He is a board member of the Aboriginal Corporation for Languages and First Languages Australia, and past Secretary of the Bidwell-Maap Aboriginal Nation. Bruce lives in Gipsy Point, Far East Gippsland, with his wife, Lyn Harwood, and their two children and three grandchildren.

Rob Paton has been a professional archaeologist for 30 years, working throughout Australia and overseas, for museums, government agencies, universities and as a consultant. Rob has been published in books, journals and written reports in the disciplines of archaeology, anthropology and history. He is also a long time board member for the journal *Aboriginal History* (since 1992) where he holds the positions of Public Officer and Treasurer. Presently he is a doctoral scholar with the ARC Linkage project 'Deepening Histories of Place', in the Australian Centre for Indigenous History at The Australian National University. Rob is researching Aboriginal trade and exchange networks in the Top End of the Northern Territory. His research shows how Aboriginal people can shape their histories through elegant mechanisms that leave material traces dating back several thousand years.

Martin Porr is Associate Professor in Archaeology at the University of Western Australia and a member of the Centre for Rock Art Research Management. He has published widely on Palaeolithic art and archaeology as well as general theoretical aspects of archaeological research. He is co-editor of *The Hominid Individual in Context: Archaeological Investigations of Lower and Middle Palaeolithic Landscapes, Locales and Artefacts* (with CS Gamble, 2005) and *Southern Asia, Australia and the Search for Human Origins* (with R Dennell, 2014). He is currently engaged in research projects into the Indigenous art of the Kimberley, north-west Australia, the Early Upper Palaeolithic art of Central Europe and the impact of postcolonial approaches on the understanding of human origins.

Peter Read is Adjunct Professor, Australian Centre for Indigenous History, at The Australian National University. From 2009–13 he was Australian Research Professor, Department of History, University of Sydney and Director of the website historyofaboriginalsydney.edu.au. He was also a Chief Investigator on the 'Deepening Histories of Place' team. He is the author of several books on the history of Aboriginal Australia, including *Charles Perkins: A Biography* (1990) and *Tripping Over Feathers: Scenes from the Life of Joy Janaka Wiradjuri Williams* (2009).

Peter J. Riggs is a Visiting Fellow in the Research School of Physics and Engineering at The Australian National University. He has held teaching and research positions at a number of Australian universities, including the Universities of Melbourne, La Trobe, Adelaide and Queensland. His research currently focuses on the nature of time and the foundations of physics. Dr Riggs's publications include *Quantum Causality: Conceptual Issues in the Causal Theory of Quantum Mechanics* (2009), *Whys and Ways of Science: Introducing Philosophical and Sociological Theories of Science* (1992), and the edited volume *Natural Kinds, Laws of Nature and Scientific Methodology* (1996).

Nicola Stern is a Senior Lecturer in Archaeology in the Department of Archaeology, Environment and Community Planning at La Trobe University, with a long-standing interest in the contribution that archaeology makes to our understanding of the narrative and dynamics of human evolution. She has studied the earliest archaeological traces in East Africa and the late Pleistocene record in Australia with a view to understanding the way in which time and site formation processes structure the archaeological record and the behavioural information that can generated be from it. She currently leads an interdisciplinary research project in the Willandra Lakes region.

Luke Taylor is currently an Adjunct Professor with the Research School of Humanities and the Arts at The Australian National University. Until recently he was Deputy Principal at AIATSIS. He has published his research with Aboriginal artists in *Seeing the Inside: Bark Painting in Western Arnhem Land* (1996), with Peter Veth edited *Aboriginal Art and Identity* (a special volume of the AIATSIS Journal, 2008), edited *Painting the Land Story* (1999), and is co-editor with Jon Altman of *Marketing Aboriginal Art in the 1990s* (1990). As a Visiting Research Fellow at the Institute in 1987–89, he prepared the first edition of the National Aboriginal and Torres Strait Islander Visual Artists Database (electronically published by Discovery Media). He is a Chief Investigator on the ARC Linkage project 'Deepening Histories of Place' at The Australian National University.

Julia Torpey Hurst is completing her PhD, 'History in the Making: Re-imagining Heritage, Identity and Place across Darug and Gundungurra Lands', at the University of Sydney. She is a member of the ARC Linkage project 'Deepening Histories of Place'. Growing up in Ocean Grove, Victoria, Julia's Indigenous family heritage is from the Sydney region. She has completed a Bachelor of Arts from the University of Melbourne majoring in Indigenous and Development Studies and a Masters of Urban Planning also from Melbourne. She has worked as a social and cultural planner and social researcher. Her interests lie in storytelling, social justice and the arts, and she has successfully merged these projects over the years on main stage and community theatre projects, including *Urgent* – first a book (Random House, 2004) and then a theatre production developed for young people to learn about, and engage with, the living stories of young Aboriginal women. This production was a joint initiative of the Courthouse Arts Centre and Wathaurong Aboriginal Co-operative and was performed in Geelong and La Mama Theatre in 2008 as part of the Next Wave Festival. Most recently she produced the 'Our Music, Performing Place, Listening to Sydney' Aboriginal Music Day at the Sydney Conservatorium of Music.

1. Deep Histories in Time, or Crossing the Great Divide?

Ann McGrath

Long History, Deep Time asks whether it is possible to enlarge the scale and scope of history.[1] If so, the vast shape-shifting continent of Australia may be a good place to start. It hosted a very long human history that endured through the great climatic epochs of the Pleistocene and Holocene. Rising and falling seas carved out new islands and coastlines, creating the larger Ice Age continent of Greater Australia that was connected to current-day New Guinea and Tasmania. Over time, its edges and internal waterways facilitated different kinds of travel, and its people created worlds of their own making.

Reliant upon measurable units of time to order its pasts, academic history tends to divide itself up according to place and time-period. Here, we consider how historians, humanities scholars and Indigenous knowledge custodians might combine to tackle an epoch of immense, arguably history-defying duration. Although the field of history is fluid and inclusive, it currently lacks a worldview commodious enough to encompass this trajectory. Unspoken limits pertain not only to history's timescale, but also to its geographic centre and scope, and to its range of human subjects.

In this volume, we consider history's temporality, and ask how it might expand to accommodate a 'deep time' sequence. We reflect upon the need for appropriate, feasible timescales for history, pointing out some of the obstacles encountered in earlier efforts to slice human time into thematic categories. History as a discipline has made strides towards producing environmental histories, but new strategies are needed to cross the great divide that blocks the peopled Pleistocene from the peopled present.

In the absence of other suitable terms, 'deep history' is used in this volume as a helpful term to distinguish it from periods of more recent history. However, it is still worth thinking about alternatives; perhaps our enterprise is really 'big history' rather than deep. Or perhaps we should call it multi-millennial history. When we do use 'deep', we use it as expansively as possible, with critiques and complexities in mind. It is difficult to find the right adjectives to describe an epoch of 40,000 years, probably 60,000 years of modern human time. Is it deep, distant, ancient, long history or prehistory? Modern history links past to

---

1   Aslanian et al. 2013.

present, whereas these metaphors distance the viewer, reinforcing that past as too long ago, and too far away. Too remote to be included in ancient history, it remains the 'pre' — an era before history proper began. Lacking an obvious fit with existing historical narratives of rather short pasts that self-consciously lead up to the modern present, the deep past becomes an incommensurable past. As if history ran out of room, Australia's 60 millennia of human occupation poses a major stumbling block for world history.[2]

This volume ponders how the discipline of history might deal with a chunk of time so voluminous that change itself seems too slow, even imperceptible. The history discipline's expectations regarding the *pace* of history — of its anticipated speed and slowness may need to change to accommodate this period. We do not necessarily know where we are going. *Slow history* may take us more deeply inside history, or simultaneously throw us outside history as we know it. Methodology and theory will need to be rethought. New tools and techniques will be required.[3]

Even experts in the migration of *Homo sapiens* out of Africa, and in the biological and cultural evolution of modern humans, are thrown out by the Australian dates, for the continent's modern human occupation is seen as 'too early'. Yet, the idea of relegating this time span outside of History with a capital H — that researched and written about in scholarly forums — makes no sense. And there can be no such thing as a 'people without history',[4] let alone one whose descendants live today, some actively exploring such questions inside and outside the academy. Unless, that is, history wishes to concede that disciplinary limitations make this impossible.

Historians currently leave this field to archaeologists. Their energetic research and the burgeoning knowledge of Australia's past cultures is exciting indeed. However, since the 1980s, as dating and related sciences became more technical and complex, archaeologists have tended to publish their findings as scientific reportage around distinctive sites rather than as peopled, connected histories in a contextualised landscape.[5] Popular science journalism reports the new discoveries, but does not necessarily explain how they fit into the broader picture.[6] Historians have the capacity to pose different questions, and to develop analytically informed narratives in accessible language for wide audiences.

---

2   For an excellent discussion on this theme, see Douglas 2010; Griffiths 1996: 42–62; Griffiths 2001: 2–7.
3   Chakrabarty 2009.
4   Wolf 1982.
5   The archaeology discipline in Australia has adopted an increasingly scientific style of technique and analysis. See, for example, the journal *Australian Archaeology*. Some recent works adopt a more narrative, coherent approach in the humanities style of writing. For example, Smith 2013; Hiscock 2008.
6   For a discussion on collaboration, see Colwell-Chanthaphonh and Ferguson 2008. Chip Colwell is also engaged in a new venture to create a more accessible website for archaeology news.

Nonetheless, in recent decades, few historians have attempted to bridge the gap at all, let alone to collaborate in formulating research questions.[7] Nor have they attempted to critique and integrate archaeological findings as evidence for any larger history.[8] In order to tell the story of a peopled landscape story of long duration,[9] diverse kinds of research teams, forms of evidence collection, narration and analysis are required. If historians are interested in joining such teams, they will need to develop a different orientation, new training, and a change of gear.

Thinking about the longer epoch of Australia's past as *deep history* raises many and varied questions. Even finding suitably expansive metaphors is difficult. Depth – the deep – can be a dangerous place. Ideas of 'depth' and 'time' vary culturally and within culture. When astrophysicists discuss their work, they speak of deep space and ultra-deep space. Due to distance and the speed of light, they study objects remote in time and space. What they actually *see* through their telescopes is the ultra-deep past. This is something they work with every day, and theories of space-time remain central to their practice. Yet, physicists concede that the existence of time cannot exactly be proven.

When a surgeon talks about something 'deep', they refer to organs further inside the body. When geologists talk of deep time, they refer to millions of years before humans stepped foot on the earth. Transdisciplinary insights shift our sensibilities. Next time you crunch on dry grassland, consider what it once was. In the case of the track I use for my morning walk, I find that this place had once been in a steamy tropical rainforest with bubbling volcanoes. More astonishing was that the earth's surface was then several kilometres *above* the altitude of the present day. 'Deep' suggests the past is underneath – a vertical drop, yet 'deep' can mean below the earth – or in outer space, high above it.

The idea of 'deep' history probably mirrors northern hemisphere archaeology, where deep excavations became the standard technique to research several thousand years of human time. In searching for visualisations of vague categories like time and space, humans often imagine them as tangible and material. Timescales suggest horizontal lines, measurement and written traditions. Containing evidence of how places were different climatically, ecologically and

---

7   Trained in ancient history and classical archaeology, in the late 1960s, scholars such as John Mulvaney established a disciplinary bridge between these fields in the subject called 'prehistory'. Mulvaney's *The Prehistory of Australia* (1969) was later followed by a popular Penguin paperback, published in 1975. Jack Golson and John Mulvaney believed that the desire of Aboriginal people to control human remains caused a research hiatus. See also Pike and McGrath 2014 (henceforth *Message from Mungo,* 2014).

8   The relationship between the disciplines of history and archaeology in Australia is a topic that requires far more attention than I could give it here. The disciplines have increasingly veered away from each other in approach and style. Only in 'historical archaeology' or studies of coloniser history are historians working with archaeologists.

9   See David and Haberle 2012. Recent advances in the field including Robin 2013: 329–340 and Blainey 2015.

socially, the physical stratigraphy of geological layers evokes the complexity of multiple-time history in the one site. Even the earth's magnetic forces may have been different.[10] Yet, portraying such pasts as always 'deep' is misleading, for it implies that this past is something that has to be dug up. Very ancient artefacts can appear on the surface too. All the current metaphors risk prescribing uniform directions and dimensions.

The notion of 'deep history' can be jarring for other reasons, because many Indigenous Australians hold a sense of the past as an immediate part of a living contemporary landscape. By the same token, due to colonising ruptures, the linguistic, spiritual connections and knowledge held by Indigenous people are not necessarily 'deep' in the sense of deriving from a multi-generational ongoing association.[11] In many Aboriginal languages,[12] there is an expression to convey the concept of 'long, long ago' — a zone that also converges with the 'dreaming', creation-time, which is actually not a discrete time at all, but an ongoing process. In Central Australian languages such as Arrernte, the closest term for 'deep' is *iperte*, which translates as 'hole'; it can also convey 'down', 'under' or 'inside'. In many groups, the past is represented in orientational terms, according to the body of the speaker. It is not a case of past/behind us, but past/in front of us. The deep past is akin to 'in front, before'.[13] The logic is explicit: you can actually *see* the past, not the future, which is out of sight, behind us. Astrophysicists say the same thing; they can see stars and galaxies of the deep past in present time.

In order to accommodate such long, long ago histories, the geography of global history may need realignment. In many accounts of ancient lives, the southern hemisphere is 'down under' — a telescope and an ocean too far away. When considered at all, Australian history is understood as white, modern, and lacking antiquity.[14] Similarly, North American history is generally restricted to the centuries since the 'discoverers' arrived — a history defined by Europe transatlantic ship and human arrivals. Both nations have histories that repeatedly allude to foundational 'arrival' narratives resting upon the technologies of European modernity.[15] Perhaps many people like to look back to a relatively recent familial and familiar ancestral past that connects with their own lives. In settler-coloniser societies, history remains contested ground. National parks and world heritage materials categorise 'historical heritage' as evidence of what happened after imperial arrivals. Indigenous evidence or association with heritage landscapes are described as 'cultural heritage' or 'prehistoric',

10 An event called the Mungo excursion was observed in a fireplace. See Jacobs 1995: 94–97.
11 Byrne 1996.
12 Koch and Nordlinger 2014; Evans and Wilkins 1995.
13 Harold Koch and David Nash, pers. comm. to author, 6–9 August 2014.
14 A useful analysis is contained in Veracini 2007.
15 Guldi and Armitage 2014.

reinforcing a status as history's outsiders. As history scholarship in the academy has been content to portray a short past, in 'short history' volumes, this is hardly surprising.

This chapter uses 'Crossing the Great Divide' to refer to deep history, cultural and transdisciplinary divides. The term holds special resonance in Australian coloniser history. We may immediately think of the Great Dividing Range, a vast range running along Australia's east coast, in which each mountain has dual names – first one or more Indigenous names, superimposed with an English one. The range's rugged heights presented a great barrier for coloniser expansion and land takeover. 'The First Crossing' to be memorialised was that of the Blue Mountains near Sydney, which came to symbolise how the authorised white explorers Blaxland, Lawson and Wentworth had overcome a major obstacle.

This collection, *Long History, Deep Time,* attempts to subvert the coloniser trope of 'firstness', and its coloniser 'crossings' by suggesting crossings over a lengthy period that should rightly come under the umbrella of history. The crossings of this chapter title suggest journeys in multiple directions, and along quite different routes. The human crossings 'out of Africa' and the journeys via Asia, or the continental crossings from north to south, present other potential beginnings for a Greater Australia.

By the same token, searching for a 'deep nation' could easily become another colonial appropriation by anxious colonisers.[16] Given the colonising power relations that have shaped the worlds in which many of us now live, any venture into Indigenous histories carries the danger that this might become another precinct for acquisition and appropriation. Yet, for historians to ignore the people who lived in Australia prior to 1788 is arguably a more disturbing, if not unethical position. Neither history writing, nor its interpretation or representation, is the domain of the coloniser alone. In this collection, we hope to prepare the way for crossings that rely upon collaborative knowledge exchange, with clear benefits for participants outside the academy.[17]

But, can humanities scholars even imagine how they might step outside this truncated world of short coloniser-time history? Is it possible for history's latitude and longitude to be expanded across time and space? Without Europe as reference point, is the deep temporal and geographic field of Greater Australia even pertinent to global history? And without ornaments, text and monumental buildings, how can this be researched and classified? Furthermore, without

---

16   Byrne 2003.
17   See Preucel 2012; Preucel and Mrozowski 2010.

a sense of chronology, can we have history at all? In order to make a start, we will first need to consider ways to think outside the usual constraints of historicised time.[18]

Australian Aboriginal people hold a sense of a much longer history that challenges the western historical imagination. They have a quantitatively and qualitatively different ambit of connection to the past. It is worth noting that narrative, metaphoric and visual frameworks of Indigenous history-telling vary regionally, according to people's lifeways and educational experiences, and according to the overall impacts of colonialism. Yet, both urban and remote dwellers often portray a historical ontology that works around an intricate folded-in place/time landscape. Time is multi-layered and mutable. Many view the recent and ancient past as something personal, familial, geological and omnipresent. The nature of this 'long ago past' stretches time beyond short timeframes. It is matched by narratives, in art and other enactments, that give prominence to the connectedness between human and other living beings, and in which the earth itself is a living force. Indigenous teachers explain a non-enumerated, undated, multi-layered 'now', with living spirits present and walking around, conducting themselves in the everyday.[19] Many Indigenous Australians do not sense any great chasm dividing the present from the past.

In this schema, specific places, people and landscapes are living archival repositories. They are not open access, for the level of revelation depends upon an individual's relationship to place, age, gender and their level of authority in the community. Through different methods of reconnecting with sites – including moments of physically being there, and of walking the ground, and through story, song, dance and ritual, people in the present keep place, spirit and ancestral memory alive. Similarly, untended history sites can die. Places contain connective routes – with songlines and storylines linking tracts and groups far and wide.[20] As Diana James, Karen Hughes and Rob Paton expand in their insightful chapters, Indigenous ontologies hold complex, entangled, subversive notions of what history might be. These gesture beyond measured scientific time towards an omnipresent, where the spirits of past peoples continue to affect the everyday now. Stories of place and of creation dreamings,[21] along with ongoing ancestral action, provide a sense of a very long but enduring epoch, an elongated now/then.

---

18 The postcolonial movement challenged European-centred narratives. It allowed for different readings of history and its explanatory framings – the cross-cultural logic suggested in the provincialising of Europe. Post-modern approaches challenged the ways we argue, and think about truth – or at least to rethink history's objectivity and subjectivity. See Chakrabarty 2000; Hokari 2014.

19 Wolfe 1991.

20 There is a rich historical and cultural studies literature on place which we do not expand on here. Tim Ingold's work is valuable, for example, Ingold 2000.

21 For more discussion of the meaning of dreaming, see Stanner 1979.

Time immemorial?

European accounts have glossed Aboriginal history as 'timeless'. If time is lacking, of course, there would be no need for history. Did timelessness reflect a response to the apparent slowness of the pace of change compared with modern times, or was it its location *outside* modernity? This view mirrors Aboriginal people's own accounts of this past, which often give primacy to *continuity* over change. The Willandra Lakes custodians often become frustrated with the scientists' obsession with dating – a field where findings differ, and are constantly challenged and debated.[22] Some Aboriginal elders proclaim that they do not see the relevance because they knew 'we have always been here'.[23] Other academics and elders see the political uses of 'having a date', for they prove lengthy occupation in a mode that matters to the white population and to the ruling powers.[24]

Settler-coloniser nations use a confection of anniversary dates to celebrate the beginnings of white, European pasts. Ceremoniously staged in the Australian Federal Parliament by the Prime Minister Kevin Rudd, the Apology of February 2008 gestured towards a different Australian history of global relevance. He proclaimed: 'That today we honour the indigenous peoples of this land, the oldest continuing cultures in human history.'[25] The idea of being the 'oldest', of being 'continuing' and of being described as 'cultures' at once locates the Australians into stasis and inserts them into '*human history*'. Rudd's words were a welcome and long overdue recognition for a people who had suffered two centuries and more of racism, where they were classed as backward, and as lacking the historical achievements for which Europeans took credit. The phrase the 'oldest continuing cultures' is frequently echoed in official public statements these days. Yet, it holds the potential to dismantle and enrich current thinking, or to become an additional burden for Indigenous Australia.[26] 'Old' has no date; so is it more a state of mind?

Chronological sequences are intrinsic to history; they govern its thinking. The nation begins when European time arrived. Its starting gun is fired when Captain Cook's ship *Endeavour* drops anchor on the seabed of Australia's north-east coast, and in the south-east at Botany Bay in 1770. Soon after January 1788, shiploads of expelled British felons came ashore under marine guard. Explorers and white settlers follow. Maps are marked with new names and places. History

---

22 See for example, Grün et al. 2000; Grün et al. 2011; Gillespie 1998; Gillespie and Roberts 2000.
23 Lottie Mitchell, appearing in *Message from Mungo*, 2014.
24 See also Marcia Langton, appearing in *Message from Mungo*, 2014.
25 'Kevin Rudd's sorry speech', *Sydney Morning Herald*, 13 February 2008, www.smh.com.au/news/national/kevin-rudds-sorry-speech/2008/02/13/1202760379056.html.
26 See McKenna 2014; McGrath 2011.

writings repeated the dates of the white pioneering 'firsts', which served to expunge the 'firstness' of First Nations peoples and the validity of their prior histories.[27] As mediaevalist Kathleen Davis has pointed out in her wonderful study *Periodization and Sovereignty*, periodisation is power.[28] By not challenging the datelines, even 'postcolonial' and 'decolonising' histories inadvertently validate imperial and coloniser sovereignties.[29] For imperial and settler-coloniser contexts outside Europe, the markings and datings of European arrival are ubiquitously memorialised in texts and monuments. In nations like Australia, imperial timelines are recycled as the key means of carving up time.

Other influences preceded maritime imperialism and colonialism. As Daniel Lord Smail, the historian of mediaeval Europe and of deep time has pointed out, the chronological range of history has generally been restricted to 'sacred time' and specifically to Biblical chronology.[30] Divinity scholars often led European intellectual traditions, including the rise of the university system. The Irish intellectual, Bishop Ussher's dating system for the time of the earth's creation left a lasting legacy. Although the old markers of 'BC' – before Christ – are less used, being replaced by 'BP' – before the present – sacred time continues to foreshorten histories that stretch too far beyond modern nations. Historians have been loathe to venture outside the epoch of 4,000 BC. Even the calendar we use for dating the present is handed down by Pope Gregory.

Historians of the 1970s onwards challenged the Anglocentric narratives, the 'great Australian silence' that had omitted the Aboriginal past from history books. Other historians argued that there was no text-based evidence for writing Aboriginal people into history, but this has been proven resoundingly false. In decades of growing civil rights action, historians made a concerted effort to tackle colonising power relations. Their studies highlighted racism, oppression and other injustice, and signalled a hoped-for redress and reconciliation.[31] With new legislation and entitlements following in their wake, a major backlash followed, with ongoing, well-publicised and highly politicised controversies vaunted as 'the History wars'. In North America, the 'culture wars' were raging simultaneously, focusing especially around new histories of race and national identity. Inevitably, histories of colonial invasion and post-invasion reinforce the image of Aboriginal people as victims of conquest, while their enduring history of survival across dramatic climatic and geographical change suggests alternative, even empowering, plotlines.

---

27 O'Brien 2010.
28 Davis 2008.
29 McGrath 2014.
30 Smail 2008; Shryock and Smail, et al. 2011.
31 McNiven and Russell 2005. On reconciliation, see Chakrabarty 2001.

Today, the game-changer of a new climatic era, the Anthropocene, is encouraging historians to consider longer time spans beyond nation and the transnational.[32] History as a discipline has stressed identifiable change over time, tracking and accounting for its processes, its stories, patterns, causes and effects. As it stands, however, certain times, places and peoples receive more historical attention than others. Despite projects to the contrary, the greater Europe of the western imagination still stands at history's heart, carving out standardised chronologies and reference points often associated with the rise and fall of 'civilisations' or nations.[33] The ancient history sections of European and North American bookshops and libraries contain studies of the Middle East (even this term derives from a European vantage point), and Imperial era museums hold their treasures. Native peoples, on the other hand, are not part of 'ancient history'. Rather, they are displayed in natural science and older-style museums as exemplars of hominid biology – either in skeletal form or in the now objectionable 'Stone Age' dioramas.[34] In Europe, Aboriginal Australians are still ranked, in many instances, as the fossil primitive – historyless – at least until Europeans came. By this logic, they did not – and cannot now – make history.

One answer to the problem of such selective human exclusion is to think about our common humanity, and to think bigger. At a time when leading scholars are starting to contemplate the question of scale in history, much is at stake. In play are the discipline's methodology, conceptualisation, and the politics of developing a history practice that speaks to the present. Historians such as David Armitage and David Christian[35] have called for 'big history' – more ambitious, broader history projects. After rejecting the grand narratives still popular up to the mid-twentieth century, historians turned to micro history, but now they are making a return to the French Annales school. In 1958, Ferdinand Braudel theorised and took up the *longue durée* approach, arguing for the importance of the texture of the everyday, as well as the less noticeable, slowly evolving, environmental structures. With the sea as a key agent of history, Braudel's three volume work, *La Méditerranée et le Monde Méditerranéen a l'époque de Philippe II* (1949) explored the relationship between people, travel, weather and ecology.

32 Smith 2005.
33 Chakrabarty's *Provincializing Europe* (2000) challenged this with timely effectiveness. It not only interrogates the intellectual roots and logics of western academe, but opens a path to consider the logic of historical causality and the possibilities of other ontological framings.
34 See Russell 2001, 2012.
35 Christian 2004; Armitage 2012.

Braudel advocated interdisciplinary richness – with outreach 'to all the sciences of man' with history to be 'totale'.[36] The *longue durée* may thus prove useful for our purposes, as it argues for attention to both change and continuity.

Of late, historians have started to reconsider optimal size – that is, on what scale of geomorphic time can we do history best, or most usefully? In the annual Conversation section of the *American Historical Review* this problem was explored at length.[37] Big questions need big thinking. Exactly where and when on the planet should we start – with that of the universe or planet before human time, or perhaps with our human precursors, the earlier hominids? Or should it be with modern humans? Are any of our framings of time and space stable? On what scale might we measure 'stable' anyway? Will an overstretched historical imagination become too weak to work properly?

As David Armitage and Jo Guldi argue in their upbeat tome, *The History Manifesto* (2014),[38] the return to the *longue durée* 'is now both imperative and feasible: imperative, in order to restore history's place as a critical social science, and feasible due to the increased availability of a large amount of historical data and the digital tools necessary to analyse it.'[39] The *longue durée* is 'intimately connected to changing questions of scale. In a moment of ever-growing inequality, amid crises of global governance, and under the impact of anthropogenic climate change, even a minimal understanding of the conditions shaping our lives demands a scaling-up of our inquiries.' Furthermore: 'The moral stakes of *longue-durée* subjects – including the reorientation of our economy to cope with global warming and the integration of subaltern experience into policy – mandates that historians choose as large an audience as possible'.[40]

Having aimed at analytical depth in neatly or broadly contextualised analyses, the discipline of history has perhaps become too confined by its own stylistic and encultured sense of scholarly rigour, with its contextualised time zones and micro-studies.[41] Possibly historians are still trained to be overly cautious;

---

36 Lee 2012: 2. With new scientific knowledge, historical interpretation is being modified. For example, the environment, and the climate are no longer understood, as Braudel's time frame allowed, as constant, unchanging elements. Lee's other works critique nineteenth-century assumptions about knowledge, and argue against the two cultures of science versus the humanities. For example, see Lee et al. 2005.

37 Aslanian et al. 2013.

38 This has triggered vigorous debate. See, for example, *American Historical Review* 2015 – 'AHR Exchange: On The History Manifesto': Introduction; Cohen and Mandler 2015; Armitage and Guldi 2015.

39 Cited in Guldi and Armitage 2014: 84–85; Braudel 1958, cited in Wallerstein 2009. See also Armitage and Guldi 2014: 1.

40 Guldi and Armitage 2014: 85, 84.

41 Guldi and Armitage 2014, Chapter 2: 38–60.

too narrow in their temporal and spatial specificity.[42] Additionally, with the exception of environmental historians, they became increasingly concerned with human action as something separate from nature – from plants, animals, things, geology and climate. Furthermore, historical scholarship dealt with philology, with the eras of writing and the manufacture of letters, newspapers and print media. Indeed, as Daniel Smail explains, leading historians such as Vico and Ranke argued 'that writing made the past knowable ... Writing ... actually put civilization on the move and created history out of the historyless Paleolithic.'[43] So it was that history was proscribed from reaching further back than a few millennia. Yet, in the future, the new environmental and climatic turns potentially ally social science and humanities scholars more closely with biological and natural scientists. Noting that humans are not alone as agents of history, some scholars, particularly in sociology and anthropology, are arguing for a rebalancing of agency, and a decentring of the role of humans in the world.[44] What is characterised as 'evidence', as object, may not be passive at all; remains can be 'actants' or agents of history too.[45]

Bones

Can bones speak? Daniel Smail and Andrew Shryock have argued for a reappraisal of history's beginnings, and a reunion with our ancient ancestors. By appreciating the history and propensities of the hominids that preempted our living *Homo sapiens* selves, we gain insights into the forces of human history. Not only the decisions of great men and women, but embodied hominid

---

42 Armitage 2012. Today's history profession prides itself on being modern in its approach, and accordingly, it has been particularly concerned with *modernity*. It has been particularly concerned with modern nations and empires. Its techniques teach careful scouring of evidence, predominantly in text form. It is never static, responding to challenges, key questions, philosophical and political trends of that ever-changing era that we call the present. Over the twentieth century, it switched and reconfigured its scale by favouring a positivist 'scientific' practice, an emphasis on storytelling, and an emphasis on narrative. History has generally argued its case in clear language. It has deployed categories of power – to do with economics, race, gender, class, religion, and to pluralise by considering culture, or to make more tangible by considering environment. It valued the rational dismantling of decision-making processes. It has also been a discipline that tells stories to varied audiences – it creates tales to satisfy or to challenge national imaginings. In this, history's strokes have potential impact upon framing the future. For a summary of developments in the practice of history over time, see Curthoys and Docker 2006.

43 Smail 2008: 35.

44 Concerns for future human survival raises complex philosophical questions. Sociologists, led by Latour, ask whether humanity has given itself too much pre-eminence over geography, geology, animals, plants and even over the making of the universe itself. Animals, plants, the climate, even things like boats, shrimp and computers are actants too, however unconsciously they may have reshaped the world.

45 Schmidgen 2015.

drives, longings and motivations underpin the currents of human history.[46] In a scientific turn, mediaeval experts such as Patrick Geary and Michael McCormick are collaborating with scientists specialising in stable isotopes and the human genome to consider isotopic and DNA evidence as data for European history. In settler-coloniser societies, however, palaeoanthropology or research into skeletal remains takes on a very different dimension, sparking profound anxiety and contestation. To Indigenous Australians, human remains are not 'scientific evidence' to be controlled by outsiders, but something personal. They are relatives, ancestors. By reactivating their relationships with the long dead, they reassert Indigenous connection with landscapes and legacy, fulfil social obligations, and enact their sovereignty and law. Their work with the ancient dead revives kinship and living relationships.

Scientists understand ancient human remains as an invaluable archive offering potential clues to knowledge of human history. To prehistorian John Mulvaney, this is also part of a discrete history of a continent of which he believes all Australians should be proud.[47] However, debates over the repatriation and reburial of remains of people who lived in the Pleistocene remain deeply contentious, not least because of the legacy of trauma left behind by nineteenth and twentieth-century collectors, who robbed graves and sold remains to metropolitan museums in the Imperial centres such as London, Berlin, Paris, Sweden and elsewhere. Significant finds that resonate as iconic individuals include Kennewick Man in Washington State in the United States, and Lady Mungo and Mungo Man in south-western New South Wales, Australia. Their fate has been at the centre of repatriation negotiations between scientists and Indigenous peoples. Recent histories of coloniser massacre, theft of land, and state-induced family separations through boarding schools, adoption and other institutions, mean that few Indigenous people trust the state and its entwined scientific and historical practices.[48]

---

46 As Andrew Shryock and Daniel Smail's *Deep Histories* (2011) has powerfully demonstrated, a history that explores hominin time before the *Homo sapiens* promises to tell us more about the way humans think and have made history through our bodies as well as our minds. Outside the obsession with the fast pace of modernity and rapid change, the mediaevalists lead the way in new, scientific directions for historical evidence and thinking. Daniel Smail's works, for example, represent major breakthroughs for the history profession. In an open-ended way, and in close collaboration with a range of scientific experts, *Deep Histories* urges us to engage with the long evolutionary history that made *Homo sapiens* what we are today. He argues that our hominid instincts, urges and needs may be crucially responsible for making history. Perhaps more important than the ideas and thoughts of 'great men'. Patrick Geary of the Institute of Advanced Study, Princeton, is involved in important work with leading European scientists tracing isotopic evidence to ascertain the movements of European tribes and thus critiquing accepted accounts. Through the chemistry of disease, Monica Green is tracking histories of diseases and plagues that cannot be known through documents.
47 John Mulvaney articulates this stance in *Message from Mungo*, 2014.
48 McGrath 2014.

Scientific removal of people's remains from their long resting places brought anxiety and spiritual harm. Many Indigenous people saw these remains as worth fighting for. Whether genetically related, terribly ancient or not, they wish to fulfil their duty to ensure that the dead are undisturbed. At the same time, they assert their right over this tangible link to, and power over, their history. They are often fascinated by what science can reveal, and collaborate with archaeologists, palaeoanthropologists and earth scientists on archaeological projects, some of which require access to human remains. By being involved, they gain some control and, under Australian heritage laws, are entitled to ensure that respectful practices are followed. Although dialogues over human remains become sites for highlighting historical hurt, they also open paths to possible redress, and for cultural and national recuperation. And, as elucidated in Wailoo, Nelson and Lee's edited collection, *Genetics and the Unsettled Past: The Collision of DNA, Race and History*, in many instances, breakthroughs and increasing use of DNA research can play a role in reconciliation.[49]

Ethical practices should be central to the research process. At the Deepening Histories of Place Symposium held at The Australian National University in Canberra, many Aboriginal people were in attendance. Consequently, Daniel Smail sought advice as to whether to show an image of a prehistoric European burial in his keynote address. Some researchers ask, some do not. But the right to say 'no' presents a conundrum. When scientists and Indigenous custodians cannot reach agreement on proposed projects, this effectively compromises future knowledge gathering. Yet the issues are incredibly complex and enmeshed in wider and localised politics. Whether certain research goes ahead or is blocked, in either instance, it is not clear-cut who loses most.

In an age where science and economics seem preeminent, scholars of the humanities call for more traction for their own disciplines in explaining the world. They can only achieve this, however, if they embrace 'epistemic diversity' – that promise of enrichment when people work across disciplinary and cultural ontologies.[50] The project of deep history calls for serious and sustained cross-cultural and interdisciplinary collaboration. In order to engage with Pleistocene history, historians need to learn the research languages and techniques of disparate disciplines; they will need to understand and critique the ways they use evidence and analyse data. They will not be able to bypass the politics.

---

49 Wailoo et al. 2012.
50 The Harvard Initiative for the Science of the Human Past is making strides in this direction.

Diving into the digital deep

Digital visualisation and interactive maps offer useful ways of advancing studies of history, and of handling complex interacting agents over great spans of time. Historians are starting to experiment stylistically with different writing and multimedia presentation techniques, including digital formats for history telling. Digital history is often narrowly understood as using the digitised archive and reference library. Certainly, an enormous amount of historical data, including climatic and geological information, can be searched, stored and cross-referenced; and it has a profound search capability. But there is more to it. Biographical analytics have the capacity to reveal astonishing social networks that can be interpreted almost instantaneously by desktop computers.[51] Universities are investing in supercomputers that have optimal storage and fast analytic capacity. New technologies and scientific insights, such as 3D scanners, more sophisticated dating technologies, advances in neuroscience, DNA and isotopic research, all offer breakthroughs in data analysis, and new ways of researching history and science. Additionally, new apps provide tools for quantitative and qualitative analysis, and innovative research tools are constantly being developed. Digital platforms enable wider circulation of the traditional monographs, edited collections and journal articles, and they enable historians to present history in a multitude of other ways. Increasingly accessible tools allow people to develop DIY (do-it-yourself) history websites, edited videos and films, animated history-scapes and tours, virtual exhibitions, and blogs.

Digital innovations deliver exciting interpretative and methodological directions now, and as yet unmapped possibilities in the future. New kinds of evidence, expanded storage and expedited data analysis, creates expanded possibilities for novel questions to be asked of the past.[52] Humanities scholars should play a role in developing the tools for both analysing and presenting history-specific visual, textual and aural data and findings. Interactive time and place maps — for example, featuring geological and ecological change and human, animal and plant mobility — are possible. Affect-driven web interfaces, and other creative programs will change the way we conduct our digital work. For example, we might create visualisations to convey multi-temporal histories, to connect up geological and seasonal maps of bush food, and to develop trade route maps that track ochre and stone manufacture and ceremonial exchange. We might analyse the nuances of multi-vocal representations of an event or a sequence of events.

---

51 For example, the Australian Dictionary of Biography runs an Obituaries database with capacity to map out human networks.
52 The American Historical Association has been especially proactive in this regard, appointing digital history developers and discussing the future of digital collections at its meeting in 2013.

Experimenting in a basic way with ANU Press' digital platform, *Long History, Deep Time* integrates links to aural, visual and multimedia content throughout. We take you, or hyperlink you, to places where you can find more. Although no more than a modest step forward, this digitally enhanced volume anticipates some of the potential of digital modes of delivering history.

A space-time project?

As indicated, this book arises from a symposium held in 2013, which in turn was part of a larger project entitled 'Deepening Histories of Place'. The aim was to consider the historical theme of deep history in spatial contexts, and to try some new directions in digital history. The project, which commenced in 2010, attempted to address the limitations of the short time span of Australia's history.

We wondered if we could provide another kind of history tour. As you drive up the highways that connect Australia's key cities, you will be using roads named after European explorers of the nineteenth century, such as the Sturt and Stuart Highways, and you will notice the monuments and memorials of white, usually European-born pioneers. The road to the Blue Mountains, for example, is memorialised by towns along the route named after the explorers who were attributed as the pioneers of the first successful crossing: Lawson, Blaxland and Wentworth.[53] When you visit North Queensland, you will encounter islands and towns first named in the journal of the British navigator Captain James Cook in 1770.[54] You will also find statues and memorials to soldiers who died in northern hemisphere wars. Again, it would appear that Australian history is contingent upon being made by the European-born or their descendants, including those who travelled to fight in Europe or the Middle East. Memorialisation expunged the time and people that preceded their arrival. Europe certainly had a big role in making the modern nation of Australia, but so too did Aboriginal people. For one thing, they shaped the landscape over thousands of years.

By looking towards less visible layers of time and place, our project aimed to scour beneath the surface of short history as currently understood. We thought we might be able to do this by focusing upon discrete places – sites of both recent and 'deep' history and of historical entanglement. We hoped to uncover stories written into selected landscapes, most of which were located in areas classified as national parks and World Heritage areas. In order to achieve this, we developed a partnership funded by an Australian Research

53 The Old Great North Road, built by convicts, is a World Heritage walk, www.nationalparks.nsw.gov.au/dharug-national-park/old-great-north-road-walking/walking.
54 Carter 1987.

Council Linkage grant through The Australian National University. We paired with the University of Sydney, gaining the insights of the renowned historian of landscapes of belonging and of Aboriginal Australia, Peter Read. We also partnered with organisations that specialise in multimedia collections and with research bodies, including the Australian Institute of Aboriginal and Torres Strait Islander Studies, the National Film and Sound Archives and Ronin Films. They contributed funding support, expertise and collections resources. Partnerships with Parks Australia and National Parks New South Wales enabled us to pay close attention to World Heritage areas, which often had joint management arrangements with local Indigenous custodians. The Aboriginal Advisory Committees of these organisations provided opportunities for the team to negotiate formal permission to undertake research, to suggest and inform people about proposed projects, and to agree on mutually acceptable research protocols. The Northern Territory Government also joined us, being particularly interested in the project's potential for Indigenous training and tourism. Investigators included Peter Read, Luke Taylor, Denis Byrne, Shino Konishi and myself, as well as a range of representatives from partner organisations. We held a series of multimedia and archaeological training workshops for students and community participants. As well as producing scholarly journal articles and this edited collection, we aimed to connect with digital users and younger generations, and to ensure the participants themselves received useful outcomes. Some were not particularly interested or schooled in using scholarly books, but were keen on websites and DVDs.

The Deepening Histories of Place project used versatile delivery modes that would be part of an integrated research platform. This required development of a new interactive architecture for historical research, some of which would become public. Humanities scholar Jason Ensor was engaged to build a digital history research platform on which the team could store, edit and develop their material in high quality formats for future preservation. In consultation with Australia's top Indigenous Intellectual Property (IP) lawyer, Terri Janke, the project devised sets of ethical protocols and templates aimed to protect Indigenous IP. Intended for use by researchers and participants, they are also open to all scholars to use: www.deepeninghistories.anu.edu.au/ethical-protocols/. Intellectual property protection and control was integrated into the design of the digital history platform.

The project developed a website which would serve as the front end of the history database. Once approved and polished for public consumption, we posted the downloadable and web-based histories. We also developed a large collection of raw files, stored in the highest quality possible, to form an archive of history data. Research Associate and project manager, historian Mary Anne Jebb, expertly managed a great deal of complexity – not only keeping all these balls in the air, but also achieving key goals. Three doctoral students – Rob Paton, Julia Torpey and Shannyn Palmer – were trained in multimedia data management, undertaking video editing and creating digital history products in website and downloadable formats.

A visitor to the project website can click to discover many different layers of historical interpretation – in text articles, still images, voice/audio, moving footage, edited short films and maps. This web and data design process allowed us to reflect upon the multiple layerings of historical time and interpretation and its potential to present many voices. In preparing content, we did not wish to lose the sense of the visual, tactile and spiritual nature of people's engagement with history. Wherever possible, we filmed and recorded participants in situ – in the deeply storied landscapes that they selected. We thought it was important not to lose the specificity of the relevant landscape, or the positionality of speakers. In this style, they could often stand 'on country' and speak for it. The Deepening Histories project – www.deepeninghistories.anu.edu.au – thus explored multiple possibilities for new ways of researching, documenting, archiving, presenting and storytelling. This platform and the website continues to evolve, with more to be posted once the students complete their doctoral projects.[55]

As indicated earlier in this introduction, disciplinary and knowledge limitations seem to be preventing us from doing 'deep history'. So whereas we may agree that it is *timely* to do such histories, *how* might we do them? Our aims for the June 2013 Symposium were threefold: firstly, to consider some fresh approaches that might expand the possibilities of 'history' by diving into 'the deep'; secondly, to consider how we might 'deepen history' by having a transdisciplinary conversation about time and history; and thirdly, to exchange ideas cross-culturally with Indigenous custodians of knowledge about new understandings and approaches relating to time, and history as lived, living and enacted experience. Our project aimed to make steps towards epistemic diversity – to use an enriching practice incorporating insights from different knowledge regimes.[56]

We knew that this would not be easy to achieve, as Aboriginal people are not necessarily interested in the academy, and scientists are pressured to research and publish within the discrete knowledge systems and economies of their own disciplines. The symposium's keynote speaker, Daniel Smail, along with Andrew Shryock, have pioneered a form of 'deep history' that is collaborative across the disciplinary spectrum; in an open-ended way, it works on history questions with researchers in neuroscience, biology, psychology and evolutionary science.[57]

---

55 We hope we can keep this live, as long-term access is a major issue for both databases and web-based histories.
56 Wylie 2002, 2006. Bohman and Roth 2008. See also Dawid et al. 2011; Wylie 2010.
57 Shryock and Smail 2011; Smail 2008.

The paper that Smail presented at the symposium argued for taking the 'Pre' out of Prehistory, with the full article now published in *American Historical Review*.[58]

Inviting scholars from the 'hard sciences' of geology, geomorphology and palaeoanthropology, the symposium stepped outside the humanities and social science departments. In order to think about history in more expansive ways, we reconsidered some basic concepts – time and space-time being the most fundamental and the most complex of all. Although historians deal with time, few of us really reflect upon what constitutes time itself. Astrophysicists Lisa Kewley and Charlie Lineweaver from the Mt Stromlo Observatory provided compelling insights into how physicists understand the universe, which is all about measuring time. Suddenly, the time breadth we hoped to tackle seemed minuscule.

Certain scientists are already crossing the barrier between scientific and Indigenous knowledge. With the promise of thinking about time and history together, the symposium shared conversations across Indigenous knowledge, archaeology, anthropology, geography, geomorphology, history, prehistory and museology. We had discussions with physicists, astrophysicists, literary experts and novelists. It was exciting to be in the room with so many accomplished experts from multiple fields and we are pleased to bring some of that to you in this collection. Astrophysicists such as Ray Norris are working with Indigenous peoples to collect stories and to assess rock art and engravings that contain detailed predictive astronomical, ecological and climatic information about the past.[59] They conclude that scientific knowledge may not be so modern and western after all. As the astrophysicists were unable to contribute papers to this collection, we invited physicist and philosopher Peter Riggs to share his expertise on the conceptualisation of time in a special chapter. The space-time theories of contemporary physics raise the question of that unsolved conundrum of time itself – does it actually exist?

About 30 Indigenous people – custodians of the Willandra Lakes and Blue Mountains and Sydney regions – participated in the Deepening Histories of Place Symposium. They offered valuable insights across the breadth of academic disciplines.[60] Aboriginal people do a lot of history, using mediums that include autobiography, autofiction, fiction, art, dance and musical. Some interpretations of history through musical performances in many genres are showcased on our project website and also available for download – as a free iBook at www.deepeninghistories.anu.edu.au/at-the-heart-of-it/ and as a website at dhrg.uws.edu.au/at-the-heart-of-it/. As Jeanine Leane explained, many Aboriginal people see scholarly history and writing as too constraining, and we hope that these accounts of landscape connection are more accessible.

---

58   Smail and Shryock 2013.
59   Norris 2009.
60   See also Nabokov 2002.

Figure 1.1: Visitors and friends from the Willandra Lakes World Heritage region at The Australian National University in June 2013.

From left to right: Ann McGrath, Darryl Pappin, Leanne Mitchell, Tanya Charles, Joan Slade, Dawn Smith, Robyn Bancroft, Beryl and Roy Kennedy, Eric and Maureen Taylor, Warwick Clark (at rear), Sam Wickman (at rear), Marie Mitchell, Lottie Mitchell, Ricky Mitchell, Richard Mintern, Warren Clark.

Source: Photograph by Monica Conaghan.

The Willandra Lakes Community of south-western New South Wales was represented at the symposium by a full complement of elders who held authority to speak on behalf of the Mutthi Mutthi, Ngyiampaa and Paakintji (Barkindji) peoples. We had not expected such a large turnout, not only because they are not employed as academics, but because they had to travel more than eight hours by bus to get there. Among the younger people were National Parks officers employed as Discovery Rangers, who present public educational tours about the deep history of the World Heritage area. One of the Mutthi Mutthi present, Darryl Pappin, works as an archaeological fieldworker, while others regularly supervise archaeological work. Participants in the Willandra panel discussion included Marie Mitchell, Ngyiampaa elder Roy Kennedy and World Heritage and National Parks officer Richard Mintern.[61] Significantly, the Deepening Histories of Place Symposium coincided with some very important Willandra cultural business – supervision of the DNA research into ancient ancestral remains still held at The Australian National University.[62]

---

61   We recorded audio of this discussion for our database. The film *Message from Mungo* elucidates the story of the 'discovery' and 'surfacing' of Lady Mungo and the relationship between scientists, parks officers, pastoralists and Indigenous custodians of the landscape. For another take on these debates, see Tuniz et al. 2009.

62   The research was being conducted by Michael Westaway and Dave Lambert of Griffith University.

A few weeks before the symposium, in order to facilitate a 'Yarning about Willandra Lakes History' event, Malcolm Allbrook and myself had visited Lake Mungo, near the site where the ancient Pleistocene remains of Lady Mungo and Mungo Man remains had appeared in 1968–69. Rather than discussing the deep past, which the locals and the parks authorities tend to categorise as 'culture' rather than history, the group expressed an interest in recalling their own lives, especially the impacts of state intervention and racism. We recorded their memoirs in professionally filmed interviews on country, and they received copies of these.[63] Again, at the symposium, there was strong interest in discussing the coloniser era, especially child removal, which had an especially painful and damaging impact. History, as they had been taught – history with a capital 'H' – was European coloniser time: massacre time, autobiographical, state-surveillance and rupture time. They valued having a space to be heard, and demanded wider public awareness of what they had endured. Older people laughed at the irrelevancy of school lessons proclaiming that European navigators had discovered Australia. But they lamented the denial that Aboriginal people had any history before whites arrived, for this denigrated their grandmothers and past generations. I wondered whether we were wrong-headed to have spent so much attention researching the deep past. Were these recent experiences of history of greater direct relevance, and therefore in need of more urgent community and national attention? Historians may think the Prime Ministerial Apology has happened, the commission of enquiry and Sorry Days happened, but many stories remain untold and these legacies of injustice continue to eat away at people.

Perhaps there is another explanation for the fact that the 'deep history' concept as imagined in the academy lacks draw-card appeal. People from the three tribal groups of the Willandra Lakes did not refer to the ancient ones as occupying a 'deep past', because they do not distinguish recent and ancient pasts; all are 'recent' in a sense, as ancestors are present in the landscapes of the here and now, and their pasts are immanent and observable. Past actors represent not 'history', but culture, their ancestral legacies standing outside time. In public forums like these, the deep past is political and its continuity is what they choose to embody and re-enact. 'History' is colonising rupture and pain. Opening up the many layers of mutual historical understanding may open up different routes for understanding projects of value for the present and future.[64]

In recounting their histories for the Deepening Histories research project, many of the Willandra and Blue Mountains people shared what their parents and grandparents told them. This underlined how listening and telling stories are

---

63 This took place on 14 and 15 May 2013.
64 McGrath 2014.

deeply meaningful, cherished activities that connect them to an ancient past. In considering what historians currently describe as deep history, the fact that Willandra elders do not necessarily consider that there is any great depth to dive into, may provoke fresh ways to think about the past. The documentary *Message from Mungo* (2014) conveys this feeling about the past.

The symposium presented an opportunity to obtain feedback on the near-final version of this documentary feature film that Andrew Pike and I had been developing with the Willandra community since 2006. Attendees at its screening included some of the researchers, the Aboriginal interviewees, parks officers and a much-respected archaeologist who worked with the community in the 1970s and 80s, Isabel McBryde. The trailer of the final film, *Message from Mungo*, which explores several contrasting perspectives on the world heritage of human remains, can be found here: www.youtube.com/watch?v=JOuHgVss9Wk. A shorter sampling is posted here: www.youtube.com/watch?v=nLF6TwhJhAY. A discussion of the making of the film, which also touches on the significance of deep history, is available at this site: www.youtube.com/watch?v=qGM3jzOWv8c. The film presents contrasting perspectives, for example the scientific 'discovery' versus the Indigenous 'surfacing' of Lady Mungo, and the often tense exchanges that led up to the repatriation ceremonies that followed in 1992.

It is worth recalling the emphasis on 'discovery' in the historical narratives of settler-coloniser nations like the United States, Canada and Australia, who asserted sovereignty on the basis of discovery, conquest and land takeover. These performative enactments involved planting flags, toasting kings and delivering speeches on behalf of European monarchs – all of which took place on lands of long Indigenous connection, where ancestral remains stood as proof of successions of inter-generational connection. Coloniser governors required ink markings as proof of discovery – the journals of navigators and explorers were printed and circulated, followed by printed sets of laws pertaining to land, civic and criminal matters. Colonisers and descendants later compiled and published written histories of exploration and pioneering settlement that offered enduring encores to earlier European performances. Australia was *terra nullius*, a wasteland or occupied by 'no one'. If noticed at all, the long occupation of Aboriginal Australians was depicted as 'timeless', and certainly outside modernity. According to imported intellectual traditions, these were a people 'outside time', and outside of the national future. The logic of literacy and its lack became another key justification for the exclusion of the pre-European past from the study of history.

New questions might be asked by research consortiums comprising such expertise as archaeologists, geomorphologists, geographers and geologists. The big dating experts, the time lords of carbon dating and photoluminescence, the isotopic and DNA experts will be essential to such an enterprise. If we could start to write this mass of relatively unknown world history into a convincing, more detailed historical entity, this would help transform the way we think about global history. Possibly, too, it could change the way historians think about Europe, as well as potentially transforming the practice of history itself.

Although history has fruitfully grown out of western intellectual traditions, our ontology and practice requires modification. To research and present the ambitious history that finds an appropriate place for the *longue durée* of Australia's human past in world history, mutual exchanges with Indigenous knowledge holders are essential and enriching.

To sum up, the Deepening Histories of Place project aimed to think about a deeper chronology for a Greater Australia that cut beyond the European anniversary dates. We had started to consider 'deep' as something usefully witnessed in the landscape – in a kind of material and human ecology evident in the present. Such histories adopt a revived interest in place, in geography, and a collaborative practice where historians work with archaeologists and other scientists. But how else to go about 'deepening histories of place'? A deep history evokes longer, more meaningful association with histories of place. This plays out somewhat uniquely so in Australia, as Indigenous people occupied the continent for 60,000 years. Scholars are only beginning to appreciate what might be called 'ancient memory' – the ways in which this sense of a long-enduring past are carried and held in living memory.

What becomes clear in our engagement with Indigenous modes of historical practice is that the 'deep past' does not fit neatly, if at all. Australian Indigenous concepts of time are already expansive. The Central Australian languages of Kattetye, Anmatyerr and Arrernte refer to 'long ago' as *arrwekele*, which means in front, before and in the past. An ancestor, too, can be seen in front – this 'one from before' can be seen ahead of you. As earlier discussed, the future sits behind a person, sight unseen.[65] The past sits in front, known, or at least knowable.

By the same token, Indigenous culture has been rocked by coloniser regimes, and many people struggle to hold onto language, let alone to visit country that has been sold off, fenced off, turned into tourism businesses, farms, towns or into big cities like Sydney. For Indigenous people, from the nineteenth century through until the 1970s, government reserves, missions, child removal, assimilation/urbanisation severed multi-generational association with place. Yet, in video interviews, many people testify to deep spiritual associations with place.

---

65   Koch and Nordlinger 2014.

Even when 'shallow' in length of past visitations, association with place could be 'deep' in terms of identity and in a more spiritual sense: www.deepeninghistories. anu.edu.au/at-the-heart-of-it/.

The paper run

In order to take a fresh look at the concept of time and history, the papers in this collection begin with Diana James' chapter 'Tjukurpa Time' – the embodied and emplaced sense of time held by the Anangu Pitjantjatjara Yankunytjatjara peoples of the Western Desert of central Australia. Tjukurpa time resides in the living, the dead, in the landscape and in spaces beyond and below the earth. Integrating anthropological and linguistic insights, Diana James provides fresh perspectives into an Indigenous ontology that stretches time and space. Actors converge in landscape; whether living or dead, everything and everyone is, or could be, concurrent. In accessible language, Peter Riggs' chapter provides an up-to-date, solid empirical framework of time and space through the perspectives of western science, particularly physics. Further, his chapter explores approaches to time through western philosophy, and elaborates on how physics and philosophy have histories of their own.

In his research with Indigenous people in the Top End of the Northern Territory, archaeologist and historian Rob Paton finds not only that time and space can be mutable, but also that, in order to heal a community suffering a deep trauma, the past can be ritually reconfigured. Dreamings were crafted into material objects that stand for something beyond themselves, creating powerful effects, and rearranging history itself, as well as its epic stories. Readers can also witness this through the interactive sites posted on this website: www.deepeninghistories. anu.edu.au/sites/pelican-dreaming/. The Pelican Dreaming module includes historical footage, maps, analysis and discussion of the repatriation or return to country of images and videos, much of which prompted further re-remembering with Aboriginal participants and descendants. Historian Karen Hughes' illustrated chapter describes Aboriginal women's storytelling practices at Ngukurr in the north-west of the Northern Territory of Australia. Acutely aware of its power in the real politic, local women revealed how ancestral histories dynamically changed past landscapes. The process is encapsulated in her useful revival of the term 'iruptions of dreaming'. This kind of deep time pierces the earth's surface from beneath, changing the present.

Through the lens of Arnhem Land artists' bark painting and its rich iconography, anthropologist Luke Taylor dismantles and critiques the notion of 'old' and 'new' art. Art is a form of history making, which simultaneously negotiates the space between tradition and modernity. The art business reminds us how the market is often more interested in Indigenous stasis – in an imagined 'authentic' culture frozen in time – than in one of real dynamism and change. In a contrasting example, Peter Read rejects the view that people from the highly urbanised, early colonised Sydney region and surrounds are only authentic if they had continuous residency or custodianship. He stresses the legitimacy of acknowledging *disconnection*. Spiritual ties can be visceral and immediate – even recent – rather than enduring over continuous generations. Eora scholar Julia Torpey probes the immediate, embodied nature of belonging, as materialised in a variety of landscapes – wilderness, rural and urban. In one of her digital histories, an artist takes control of directing the film of her story on site, on the local rubbish tip, where she makes sculptures that express her identification with ancient stories of connection. In her much-cherished Blue Mountain locale, she creates a visually delightful telling here: www.deepeninghistories.anu.edu. au/at-the-heart-of-it/.

Wiradjuri literary scholar, poet and novelist Jeanine Leane examines Alexis Wright's rich novel *Carpentaria,* in which the whites are befuddled at the wild moods of the monsoonal, cyclone-prone and ever-changing far northern coastline. Its local Aboriginal characters anticipate many more environmental turns, and it is these, and not necessarily coloniser time, that created the most drastic changes in the *longue durée* past. They are conscious of a seamless, intensely storied and ever-disputed landscape where human transgressions can engender past and future change and transformation. Because of the protagonists' confidence in local and enduring Indigenous knowledges, the authority of science or the process of 'scientifying' information is treated sceptically, as a newfangled fad. Presenting a world in active negotiation with its ancient past, *Carpentaria* cracks history's borders. In such an inspirited landscape, with long past actions alive in memory, people of the past and present jostle to speak, argue and fight with each other. The landscapes themselves are principal actors capable of changing everything.[66] In this world it is the whites, the non-Indigenous Australians who are the 'historyless people'.

In his chapter, the prize-winning Tasmanian/Pallawah Aboriginal author Bruce Pascoe argues for Indigenous dynamism and achievement. When he discusses the long-overlooked technological innovations of Aboriginal Australia, he takes us away from the scientific emphasis on burials and stone tools, debunks historical stereotypes, and reveals his ancestors as modernisers and innovators. Much recent Indigenous literary, oral and multimedia storytelling examines the complexities of history-time with wit and insight. Historical scholarship is in dire need of such eye-opening perspectives.

---

66   Wright 2006.

So too is an examination of the epistemologies of the western disciplines, the 'scientifying' that we often take for granted as common sense. Archaeologist Harry Allen provides a detailed account of the now-entrenched scientific taxonomies of human progress. Consequently, it was remnants of stone tools, ceramics and metals that provided the evidence to create a classificatory system for 'prehistory'. These relied upon the happenstance of their resilience in geology. Based upon a narrow European view of the development of discrete technologies, prehistory encountered difficulty accounting for other cultural and social practices. Such formulations have enduring intellectual legacies. Even the assertion that Aboriginal people had the 'oldest continuing cultures' – currently understood as a positive spin that is empowering of Aboriginal identity – could reinforce entrenched notions of the 'oldest' as unchanging and backward. Physical anthropologist Martin Porr expounds the theme of the 'exceptional primitive'. Examining the practices of molecular genetics in relation to the origins of modern humans, he considers the controversial politics of bioanthropological research in contemporary Indigenous spaces and knowledge regimes.

Archaeologist Nicola Stern explains how a meticulously applied grid approach to surface archaeology will lead to more exact and reliable data about changing technologies, societies and economies at Willandra Lakes. Malcolm Allbrook and Ann McGrath outline the historical and archaeological significance of that region, explaining how a collaborative history-sharing approach is recording the region's past. The evolving twists in the relationship between scientists, parks officers, pastoralists and Indigenous custodians of the landscape are being explored in sustained conversations and on film.[67]

Probing the connections between deep time, present time, place and history will allow for many future conversations, but we will need all the right people in the room. To be good historians, we must challenge the presentism of our everyday assumptions, while at the same time acknowledging that our historical questions are framed within sets of intersecting cultures moulded by histories of the present, immediate and longer past. Furthermore, we will need to address audiences located in the imminent future. In this collection, we listed some of the diverse ontologies that promise to expand history's horizons. Witnessing how scientists think in different registers about time, distance and the pace of change provided a shake-up. Critiquing historical methodology and concepts with Indigenous knowledge holders equally so.

If it is possible to join these 'partners in time', and to gesture towards future collaborations, historians will need to deploy new digital and multimedia platforms for historical research, interpretation and presentation. We hope that

---

67 *Message from Mungo*, 2014.

this volume displays some of the many layers of history that might be explored and complemented by such techniques, as well as hopefully prompting some better ideas.

We aim at a capacious history – one that can travel the surface, and the deep. As well as the shallow soil that was once deep below, we hope to embrace the ground of history that we can no longer see – that was once above where we stand – that ubiquitous surface of now. The 'we' refers to all those people currently occupying the earth's surface in the present. Such an elongated house of history might host far-sighted eyes and telescopes looking out and in. The landscape of history can be as big as we are – or as small.

One of the possible approaches is to develop a chronology for the deep past that is beyond the climatic, and that also looks beyond the stone tool. We can only grapple with these issues if we acknowledge how imperialism is implicated in all that we do – our disciplines, and even the global measurement of time. Space and time might be one entity, but there is much more thinking to be done around both. Perhaps widening history's temporal and spatial hemispheres will be a step towards producing integrated historical perspectives with room for all.

We hope that reading, viewing and listening to *Long History, Deep Time* will challenge some of the ways we think about ourselves, about time, place and history – both what we can see in front and what we cannot see behind us. We hold out hope for new histories that can generate ripples that change the climate of history towards greater inclusion and equity. These might be connected with modern *national* futures, but also integrated into global analyses.

Chasms and mountainous obstacles still pose a great divide between the deep past and the present. But in ways not so distant; these times happened in the same places, if not upon the same ground, where we can walk around today. Experts, passers-by and descendants witness tangible human presences in landscape and objects left behind. As well as the horizontal linearity that we might equate with the term 'long history', we also know that history can be buried. The past's stratigraphy is both horizontal and vertical – long and deep. The earth and its past spirits wake us up to a deeper sense of place as history – an ever-present site of change and continuity that emanates the present and the presence of the past. Ultimately, we would like this book to help spark the possibilities of what the inclines and the expanses of history's places might be.

Bibliography

American Historical Review 2015, '*AHR Exchange*: on *The History Manifesto*', scholar.harvard.edu/files/armitage/files/ahr_exchange.pdf.

Armitage, David 2012, 'What's the big idea? Intellectual history and the longue durée', *History of European Ideas*, DOI:10.1080/01916599.2012.714635.

Armitage, David and Jo Guldi 2014, 'The Return of the *Longue Durée*: An Anglo-Saxon Perspective', forthcoming in *Annales. Histoire, Sciences sociales* 70(2) (April–June 2015), scholar.harvard.edu/files/armitage/files/rld_annales_reply.pdf.

Armitage, David and Jo Guldi 2015, '*The History Manifesto*: A Reply to Deborah Cohen and Peter Mandler', *American Historical Review* 120(2): 543–554.

Aslanian, Sebouh David, Joyce E Chaplin, Ann McGrath and Kristin Mann 2013, AHR Conversation: 'How size matters: the question of scale in history', *American Historical Review* 118(5): 1420–1472.

Blainey, Geoffrey 2015, *The Story of Australia's People: The Rise and Fall of Ancient Australia*, Penguin, Melbourne.

Bohman, James and Paul A Roth (eds) 2008, 'Selected Papers from the Philosophy of Social Science Roundtable', *Philosophy of the Social Sciences* 38(1).

Braudel, Fernand 1949, *La Méditerranée et le Monde Méditerranéen a l'époque de Philippe II*, three vols, Colins, Paris.

Braudel, Fernand 1958, 'Histoire et Sciences sociales: La longue durée', *Annales, Histoire et Sciences sociales* 13(4): 725–753.

Byrne, Denis 1996, 'Deep nation: Australia's acquisition of an indigenous past', *Aboriginal History* 20: 82–107.

Byrne, Denis 2003, 'Nervous landscapes: race and space in Australia', *Journal of Social Archaeology* 3: 169–184.

Carter, Paul 1987, *The Road to Botany Bay: An Essay in Spatial History*, Faber & Faber, London.

Chakrabarty, Dipesh 2000, *Provincializing Europe: Postcolonial Thought and Historical Difference*, Princeton University Press, Princeton.

Chakrabarty, Dipesh 2001, 'Reconciliation and its historiography: some preliminary thoughts', *Cultural Studies Review* 7(1): 6–16.

Chakrabarty, Dipesh 2009, 'The climate of history: four theses', *Critical Inquiry* 35(3): 197–222.

Christian, David 2004, *Maps of Time: An Introduction to Big History*, University of California Press, Berkeley.

Cohen, Deborah and Peter Mandler 2015, '*The History Manifesto*: a critique', *American Historical Review* 120(2): 530–542.

Colwell-Chanthaphonh and Thomas John Ferguson 2008, *Collaboration in Archaeology Practice: Engaging Descendant Communities*, AltaMira Press, Lanham, MD.

Curthoys, Ann and John Docker 2006, *Is History Fiction?*, University of New South Wales Press, Sydney.

David, Bruno and Simon Haberle (eds) 2012, *Peopled Landscapes: Archaeological and Biogeographic Approaches to Landscapes*, ANU E Press, Canberra.

Davis, Kathleen 2008, *Periodization and Sovereignty: How Ideas of Feudalism and Secularization Govern the Politics of Time*, University of Pennsylvania Press, Philadelphia.

Dawid, Philip, William Twining and Mimi Vasilaki (eds) 2011, 'Critical distance: stabilizing evidential claims in archaeology', in William Twining, Philip Dawid, and Dimitra Vasilaki (eds), *Evidence, Inference and Enquiry*, Oxford University Press, Oxford, 371–394.

Douglas, Kirsty 2010, *Pictures of Time Beneath: Science, Heritage and the Uses of the Deep Past*, CSIRO Publishing, Collingwood, Victoria.

Evans, Nick and David Wilkins 1995, 'The Inside Story of Under: A Strange Case of Regular Polysemy in Australian Languages', handout, Max Planck Institute for Psycholinguistics, Nijmegen.

Gillespie, Richard 1998, 'Alternative timescales: a critical review of Willandra Lakes dating', *Archaeology in Oceania* 33: 169–182.

Gillespie, Richard and Richard G Roberts 2000, 'On the reliability of age estimates for human remains at Lake Mungo', *Journal of Human Evolution* 38: 727–732.

Griffiths, Tom 1996, 'In search of Australian antiquity', Tim Bonyhady and Tom Griffiths (eds), *Prehistory to Politics: John Mulvaney, the Humanities and the Public Intellectual*, Melbourne University Press, Melbourne, 42–62.

Griffiths, Tom 2001, 'Deep time and Australian history', *History Today* (UK), November 2001, 2–7.

Grün, Rainer, Nigel Spooner, Alan Thorne, Graham Mortimer, John Simpson, Malcolm McCulloch, Lois Taylor, and Darren Curnoe 2000, 'Age of Lake Mungo 3 skeleton, reply to Bowler & Magee and to Gillespie & Roberts', *Journal of Human Evolution* 38: 733–741.

Grün, Rainer, Nigel Spooner, John Magee, Alan Thorne, John Simpson, Ge Yan, and Graham Mortimer 2011, 'Stratigraphy and chronology of the WLH 50 remains, Willandra Lakes World Heritage Area, Australia', *Journal of Human Evolution* 60: 597–604.

Guldi, Jo and David Armitage 2014, *The History Manifesto*, Cambridge University Press, Cambridge, DOI: dx.doi.org/10.1017/9781139923880.

Hiscock, Peter 2008, *The Archaeology of Ancient Australia*, Routledge, New York.

Hokari, Minoru 2014, *Gurindji Journey: A Japanese Historian in the Outback*, University of New South Wales Press, Sydney.

Ingold, Tim 2000, 'The temporality of the landscape', in Tim Ingold, *The Perception of the Environment: Essays on Livelihood, Dwelling and Science*, Routledge, London.

Jacobs, John Arthur 1995, *Reversals of the Earth's Magnetic Field*, Cambridge University Press, Cambridge, 94–97.

Koch, Harold and Rachel Nordlinger (eds) 2014, *The Languages and Linguistics of Australia: A Comprehensive Guide*, The World of Linguistics vol. 3, de Gruyter Mouton, Berlin.

Lee, Richard E 2012, *The* Longue Durée*, and World-Systems Analysis*, Suny Press, New York.

Lee, Richard E, Immanuel Maurice Wallerstein and Vokan Aytar 2005, *Overcoming the Two Cultures: Science versus the Humanities in the Modern World System*, Paradigm, Boulder.

McGrath, Ann 2011, 'Taking charge of the offspring of mixed frontier unions', in Ulla Ratheiser and Helga Ramsey-Kurze (eds), *Antipodean Childhoods*, Cambridge Scholars Press, Cambridge.

McGrath, Ann 2014, 'Is history good medicine?', *Journal of Australian Studies* 38(4): 396–414.

McKenna, Mark 2014, 'Tokenism or belated recognition? Welcome to Country and the emergence of Indigenous protocol in Australia, 1991–2014', *Journal of Australian Studies* 38(4): 476–489.

McNiven, Ian and Lynette Russell 2005, *Appropriated Pasts: Indigenous Peoples and the Colonial Culture of Archaeology*, AltaMira Press, Lanham, MD.

Mulvaney, John 1969, *The Prehistory of Australia*, Thames & Hudson, London.

Nabokov, Peter 2002, *A Forest of Time: American Indian Ways of History*, Cambridge University Press, New York.

Norris, Ray 2009, *Emu Dreaming: An Introduction to Australian Aboriginal Astronomy*, Emu Dreaming, Sydney.

O'Brien, Jean 2010, *Firsting and Lasting: Writing Indians out of Existence in New England*, University of Minnesota Press, Minneapolis.

Pike, Andrew and Ann McGrath 2014, *Message from Mungo*, Ronin Films, Canberra.

Preucel, Robert 2012, 'Indigenous archaeology and the science question', *Archaeological Review from Cambridge* 27(1): 121–141.

Preucel, Robert W and Stephen A Mrozowski 2010, *Contemporary Archaeology in Theory: The New Pragmatism*, Malden, Chichester.

Robin, Libby 2013, 'Histories for changing times: entering the Anthropocene?', *Australian Historical Studies* 44(3): 329–340.

Russell, Lynette 2001, *Savage Imaginings: Historical and Contemporary Constructions of Australian Aboriginalities*, Australian Scholarly Publishing, Melbourne.

Russell, Lynette 2012, 'Remembering places never visited: connections and context in imagined and imaginary landscapes', *International Journal of Historical Archaeology* 16(2): 401–417.

Schmidgen, Henning 2015, *Bruno Latour in Pieces: An Intellectual Biography*, trans. by Gloria Custance, Fordham University Press, New York.

Shryock, Andrew and Daniel Smail, et al. 2011, *Deep History: The Architecture of Past and Present*, University of California Press, Berkeley.

Smail, Daniel Lord 2008, *On Deep History and the Brain*, University of California Press, Berkeley.

Smail, Daniel Lord and Andrew Shryock 2013, 'History and the "pre"', *American Historical Review* 118(3): 709–757.

Smith, Mike A 2005, 'Paleoclimates: an archaeology of climate change', in T Sherratt, Tom Griffiths and Libby Robin (eds), A Change in the Weather: Climate and Culture in Australia, National Museum of Australia Press, Canberra, 176–186.

Smith, Michael 2013, Archaeology of Australia's Deserts, Cambridge University Press, Cambridge.

Stanner, William Edward Hanley 1979, White Man Got No Dreaming, Australian National University Press, Canberra.

Tuniz, Claudio, Richard Gillespie and Cheryl Jones 2009, The Bone Readers: Atoms, Genes and the Politics of Australia's Deep Past, Allen & Unwin, Crows Nest, New South Wales.

Veracini, Lorenzo 2007, 'Historylessness: Australia as a settler colonial collective', Postcolonial Studies 10(3): 271–285.

Wailoo, Keith, Alondra Nelson and Catherine Lee (eds) 2012, Genetics and the Unsettled Past: The Collision of DNA, Race, and History, Rutgers, New Brunswick.

Wallerstein, Immanuel 2009, 'Braudel on the longue durée: Problems of conceptual translation', Review 32(2): 155–170.

Wolf, Eric 1982, Europe and the People without History, University of California Press, Berkeley.

Wolfe, Patrick 1991, 'On being woken up: the Dreamtime in anthropology and in Australian settler culture', Comparative Studies in Society and History 33(2): 197–224.

Wright, Alexis 2006, Carpentaria, Giramondo, Sydney.

Wylie, Alison 2002, Thinking from Things: Essays in the Philosophy of Archaeology, University of California Press, Berkeley, CA.

Wylie, Alison 2006, 'Introduction: when difference makes a difference', Episteme: A Journal of Social Epistemology 3(1–2): 1–7.

Wylie, Alison 2010, 'Archaeological facts in transit: the "eminent mounds" of central North America', in Peter Howlett and Mary S Morgan (eds), How Well do 'Facts' Travel? The Dissemination of Reliable Knowledge, Cambridge University Press, Cambridge, 301–322.

2. *Tjukurpa* Time

Diana James

Introduction

Before it was written it was told and sung; this ancient land resounded to the language of its first peoples. The Indigenous history and creation ontology of Australia has been continuously retold in story and song, and performed in dance passed down through countless generations, before ever lines on a page tried to fence it into the timeline of written history or authoritative text. The Anangu Pitjantjatjara Yankunytjatjara peoples of the Western Desert refer to their history as a continuum of ancestral to present time in their country – one that is both spiritually and physically remembered. Anangu locate both creation ancestors and their intergenerational history within the continuity of *Tjukurpa* time. The *Tjukurpa* is not relegated to a past 'Dreamtime', but rather is an active continuous time.

> *Tjukurpa iriti ngaringi munu kuwari wanka nyinyangi.*
> *Tjukurpa* has existed from a long time ago and is alive today.[1]

This sense of nonlinear time challenges the western conceptual framework that divides time into prehistory, history, present and future.

History written in the land

Nganyinytja, a Pitjantjatjara woman of elder high degree, learned to read her people's history written in the land. As she stated in 1988:

> We have no books, our history was not written by people with pen and paper. It is in the land, the footprints of our Creation Ancestors are on the rocks. The hills and creek beds they created as they dwelled in this land surround us. We learned from our grandmothers and grandfathers as they showed us these sacred sites, told us the stories, sang and danced with us the *Tjukurpa* (the Dreaming Law). We remember it all; in our minds, our bodies and feet as we dance the stories. We continually recreate the *Tjukurpa*.[2]

---

1 Nganyinytja Ilyatjari, Senior Pitjantjatjara Law Woman, pers. comm. 1990.
2 James 2005: 272.

The Anangu concept of history is here described as inseparable from their creation ontology of *Tjukurpa*, which tells of the creation of the rocks, hills, waterholes, plants, animals, people and the law of the Anangu Pitjantjatjara Yankunytjatjara (APY) lands. This creation story is written in the land; the marks of the ancestors' footprints are clear to see for those who have memorised the long song sagas that recount the ancestors' activities at sites along their travelling routes. A trained eye notes the subtle signs of the human hand in the clearing of vegetation around sacred sites, stone arrangements, engraved or painted marks on rocks or cave walls. The cultural landscape is not one of constructed temples and monuments, but rather the land itself is imbued with religious significance. The interconnectivity of humans and the sentient land is celebrated in song, story and dance. The land comes alive as the places, food and water sources created by the ancestors are re-energised through caring for *Tjukurpa* in place and spirit.

Western Desert peoples lived lightly on the land, their only possessions those that they could carry as they traversed the land seasonally. The desert environment is characterised by low rainfall with cycles of plenty followed by long droughts, cycles of boom and bust.[3] Survival for humans depended on high mobility and knowledge of water and food sources across vast tracts of country. People constructed transient windbreaks or shelters at the end of each day. During the dry season, when the ephemeral waters across the plains had evaporated, they returned every year to more substantial campsites located near semi-permanent waterholes. By adding spinifex to the bare bones of mulga-branched domes, shelters at these campsites could be revived. People travelled in tune with the seasonal cycles of 'hot time' *waru*, 'cold time' *wari* and 'springtime' *priyakutu*, always following the spatial distribution of rain.

Family groups returned annually to *ngura walytja*, their homeland or 'country of my spirit'.[4] This return was part of a cycle of relationship renewal to kin-country; renewal of relationship with *Tjukurpa* ancestors and the spirits of forbears who have passed into the rocks and trees of their home-country. Returning to country with *nguraritja*, people belonging to that place, is like walking into the land as a multi-dimensional text. Through their eyes and voice the spirit of place comes alive. When she located remnants of her mother's *wilytja* that she had not seen for 40 years, it was as if Nganyinytja, aged 63, was transported to her childhood. The weathered mulga stumps of a once comfortable spinifex shelter were redolent with memory and the history of her family hunting, gathering food, living and loving in this place. Her husband Ilyatjari explained the intimacy of people's connectivity to place, explaining

---

3   Robin et al. 2009.
4   Downing 1988.

how the imprint of a body on the ground where a person slept holds both the physical and spiritual memory of that person.[5] The desert winds, rain and harsh sun may erase physical traces of humans in this landscape over time, but the spiritual imprint of their soul is absorbed into the land, and remains there. In the Western Desert, it is not the built environment that marks and holds people's history; rather it is the land itself that holds the history of creation and the people who have walked upon it. The *tjina* footprints of the creation ancestors and the grandparent generations can be read by those who tell their stories and sing their songlines alive.

The challenge for people who rely on written texts is to lift their eyes from the page and attune their aural senses to other ways of knowing history through song and poetic prose, and the visual performative arts of sand and body painting, dance and drama. These are the aural and visual arts of history and religious storytelling in which the Indigenous people of Australia excel. Their sense of history is one embedded in an intimate spiritual and physical sense of place.

Nganyinytja's account of learning her people's history is told in terms of a past, present and future tense of experience that takes place within the continuous time of *Tjukurpa*. Her way of knowing history and place arises from the holistic Anangu ontology of *Tjukurpa*, the Dreaming Law, that explains the past creation and present continuous existence of all things. To appreciate this concept of time and history, this chapter discusses the key concept of *Tjukurpa* Dreaming Law, then it explores how this elucidates Anangu concepts of time and history, using versions of *Tjukurpa* stories, songs and the visual arts that are 'open' to discussion with a wider public.[6]

Tjukurpa time: Dreamtime

The metaphysical aspects of Tjukurpa, *the Dreaming, need to be understood as central to Anangu ontology – as the first principle of things, which include concepts of being, knowing, substance, essence, cause, identity, time and space. Tjukurpa is an unfolding mystery in Western Desert society, the meaning of which has to be acquired throughout one's lifetime, where individuals earn the right to progress through stages of initiation into ever more complex layers of cultural knowledge. Outsiders looking into this metaphysics of being can only partially understand its complexity. However, the publicly shared songs, stories and art provide a valuable pathway into some of the meaning and understandings of* Tjukurpa.

---

5   Charlie Ilyatjari, Senior Pitjantjatjara Law Man, pers. comms, 1994.
6   *Tjukurpa* includes both secret sacred law restricted to senior men or women and also versions of creation stories, songs and performance open to men, women, children and the outside wider community. Only knowledge of the sacred that has been shared in an open context is discussed here.

The translation of the term *Tjukurpa*, and related terms in Western Desert dialects, as 'the Dreamtime' or 'Dreaming' historically arose from the ethnographic tradition established by early anthropologist Baldwin Spencer and Frank Gillen in their pioneering publication in 1899 on the Aboriginal peoples of central Australia.[7] Frank Gillen was the Alice Springs postmaster and sub-Protector of Aborigines from 1892 to 1899, and also a keen amateur anthropologist with a particular interest in local Aboriginal languages. In his notes in the 1896 Horn Scientific Expedition to Central Australia Report, Frank Gillen glossed the Arandic term *Alcheringa* as 'dream-times'.[8] Spencer and Gillen's use of 'Dreamtime' to denote the mythic primordial times of Aboriginal religion established the precedence for all anthropological literature in Australia since 1899. Elkin reported that during his fieldwork from 1927 onwards he found that Aboriginal people had adopted the English term 'Dreaming' to refer to their totemic ancestors, 'in southern, central, north-western and northern regions of Australia, whatever the term, it was the "Dreaming"'.[9] The veracity of this original translation and the now ubiquitous use of the term 'Dreamtime' or 'Dreaming' have been thoroughly critiqued elsewhere by linguists and anthropologists.[10] It is not my current purpose to argue for or against the use of these terms, but rather to expand the understanding of *Tjukurpa*.

The usefulness of the terms 'Dreamtime' or 'Dreaming' is limited by the common connotation of 'dream' as a world of unreality. Many early anthropologists relegated the Dreaming stories to the realm of an imagined past time inhabited by mythic beings.[11] This position has been critiqued by Patrick Wolfe[12] who disparages the continued use of the term 'Dreamtime' because of its connotations of unreality, mystery and fantasy. However, Morphy provides a counter argument in defence of an expanded concept of the Dreamtime which has developed as anthropologists have come to appreciate the complexity of Aboriginal religion.[13] Elkin during the 1930s notably progressed understanding of the Dreaming as a 'spiritual reality' by recognising the link, via the totemic ancestors, between the mythic past to the present. He proposed the concept of the 'eternal dream-time' not as an endless succession of time-periods rather, in a philosophical sense, as an ever-present spiritual reality.[14] Eliade in 1949 recognised all religion as ontology, thus providing a framework for studying Aboriginal religion as a philosophical system that embodies abstract metaphysical concepts expressing

---

7   Spencer and Gillen 1969 [1899].
8   Gillen 1896: 161–186.
9   Elkin 1964: 210.
10   See Morphy 1996: 163–189; Austin-Broos 2010; Green 2012.
11   Radcliffe-Brown 1945: 75.
12   Wolfe 1991: 197–224.
13   Morphy 1996.
14   Elkin 1964: 210.

ideas on the nature of reality through myth, rite and symbol.[15] Stanner, in agreement with Eliade, exhorted anthropologists to respect and attempt to understand the complex ontology of the Dreaming: 'we are clearly dealing with a world-and-life view expressing a metaphysic of life which can and should be elicited'.[16]

Current linguistic study continues to develop the metalanguage terms Dreaming and Dreamtime to refer to the complex metaphysics of Aboriginal religion. Jenny Green has provided a thorough analysis of the Arandic term *Altyerre* and the related word *Alcheringa* which became glossed as 'dream-times' by Gillen in 1896.[17] While Green agrees that the translation of the Arandic terms is highly contested and problematic she does support Gillen's logic in coining the term 'dream-times' as a reasonable interpretation. Green compares the Central Australian Aboriginal languages Arandic, Walpiri and Western Desert and finds a widespread 'incidence of "dream"/"Dreaming"/"Dreamtime" polysemy in these languages'.[18] In Pitjantjatjara, for example, the verb *tjukurmananyi* refers to the act of dreaming while the noun *Tjukurpa* refers to the Dreaming or Dreamtime.

It is useful to reflect on how 'the Dreamtime' or 'the Dreaming' became associated with a past primordial era shrouded in mystery. An overview of the history of translation of Aboriginal religion as the Dreamtime suggests that the influence of Christian religious concepts was very significant. Spencer in 1905 noted the use by Hermannsburg missionaries of the term Altyerre for God and he later wrote that Hermannsburg natives who speak English refer to a man's Alchera as 'his dreaming'.[19] In his 1989 work *Encounter in Place*, the historian John Mulvaney claims that Gillen was not the first to use the term 'Dreamtime', but that precedence in its use belongs to the German missionary Carl Strehlow at Hermannsburg, in the heartland of the Western Arrernte country.[20] This early translation of Aboriginal religious concepts in Christian religious terms provides a clue as to why 'Alcheringa' has been interpreted as referring to a 'primordial time', the presupposition based on a belief in the western Biblical mythological concept of primordial time being 'in the beginning' when God created all things.

Anangu have recognised the Christian religion as the nearest philosophical equivalent in western culture to the *Tjukurpa*. A logical conceptual association as both are sacred religious systems of knowledge honouring the past acts and journeys of religious heroes whose spiritual power and significance are renewed

15 Eliade 1960.
16 Stanner 1959–63: 45.
17 Green 2012: 158–178.
18 Green 2012: 13–14.
19 Spencer and Gillen 1927: 306.
20 Mulvaney 1989.

and sustained ceremonially through song, story and ritual. Some Pitjantjatjara people refer to Christianity as 'whitefella dreaming'.[21] *Tjukurpa* is listed in the Pitjantjatjara Yankunytjatjara Dictionary as having both meanings; the lowercase *tjukurpa* refers to 'story' and 'word' or 'what someone says', while uppercase *Tjukurpa* refers to the 'Law' and 'Dreaming'.[22] Anangu commonly use the term '*Tjukurpa*' to translate the Biblical concept of 'the Word of God', as both word and Dreaming Law are *Tjukurpa*. There is a sense in both Christian and Anangu ontology that the 'word' either spoken or sung activates life, it is the creative force that brings God or *Tjukurpa* to life. Thus Rabbi Cooper convincingly argues that the Judeo-Christian concept of 'God' has no gender nor is a noun, but has the dynamic qualities of a verb.[23] Elkin experienced this active quality of *Tjukurpa* when included by some Western Desert men in the ritual performance of their *Djukur(Tjukur)* three times a day for a week. He was profoundly impressed by the active presence of the Dreaming:

> In those rituals we were 'in the Dreaming'. We were not just commemorating or re-enacting the past. Whatever happened in the mythic past was happening now.[24]

People of the Book and the Dreaming experience 'God' and *Tjukurpa* as active creation forces that continuously create all things in the 'past' or *iriti*, a long time ago, and continue to sustain all things today and into the future. In this sense '*Tjukurpa*' is an active verb, not just a noun signifying a past creative time 'the Dreamtime' or a continuing religious tradition 'the Dreaming' but *Tjukurpa* is also an active continuous creative force in all time and space.

While understanding the ontological concept of *Tjukurpa* can be expanded by comparative religious analysis, there are limitations inherent in cross-cultural conceptual translation. The Biblical concept of 'in the beginning' has been uncritically transposed into translations of Aboriginal religious concepts of time. The Pitjantjatjara language, for instance, does not have a word or phrase equivalent for the western concept of 'in the beginning'. The nearest equivalent is *iriti*, which refers to a long time ago, the time of the *Tjukurpa* creation ancestors but can also refer to the time when grandparents were alive. Cross-cultural language translation requires an awareness of one's own cultural presuppositions about reality, the western linear sequential conception of time is one such 'belief' that needs to be suspended while translating different cultural ontologies. In English translations, the Dreaming or *Tjukurpa* is commonly assumed to have existed 'in the beginning', but careful translation of Anangu

---

21 Peter Nyaningu, Pitjantjatjara Christian Minister, pers. comms, 2002.
22 Goddard 1992: 155.
23 Cooper 1997.
24 Elkin 1964: 210.

expositions of their philosophy challenges this interpretation. Nganyinytja's statement on the importance of *Tjukurpa*, at the Australian and New Zealand Association for the Advancement of Science Conference in Adelaide in 1980, presents a very different concept of sacred time:

> *Kulila, nganana tjukurtja tjunkunytja iriti ngura nganamapa winki Australiala winki tjukurtja tjunkunytja – kulila:*

> Listen to us; we were putting down the *Tjukurpa* 'Dreaming' creation law a long time ago in our many home lands, all over Australia the *Tjukurpa* creation law was laid down – Listen![25]

Nganyinytja tells us the *Tjukurpa* was laid down all over Australia *iriti*, a long time ago, and it was put there by *nganana*, we the first peoples of Australia. Anangu *Tjukurpa* does not refer to a beginning time before sentient life on earth, rather it tells us of the time when totemic beings walked the earth. The *Tjukurpa* is inhabited by the first creative beings that were both animal and human, and who purposefully created landforms, trees, food plants, water sources and fire. These beings were *tjukuritja*, of the *Tjukurpa*, and are the direct ancestors of Anangu living today. The creative ancestors were beings with extraordinary powers that were able to shift their shapes between animal, plant, rock, tree and human form, thus establishing the Anangu Law of continuous connectivity between humans and the natural environment. Anangu living on their lands today sing and dance the song sagas of the *Tjukurpa* to keep their country, the plants, animals and human beings alive.

Elders like Nganyinytja are exhorting us to 'listen and understand' the importance of the *Tjukurpa*, Aboriginal peoples' creation law laid down all over Australia. They are sharing their knowledge with the wider community through stories, song and dance, through the visual arts or rock and acrylic painting and by teaching visitors to their country to recognise the marks of the creation ancestors in the land. The following open versions of *Tjukurpa* stories provide further insights into Anangu concepts of time and history.

Intergenerational time and history

Learning to read history in the land is passed down from one generation to the next. Nganyinytja tells us the most important learning came from the *Tjukurpa* Creation Law stories told to her by her father and mother, grandfather and grandmother, uncles and aunts. Some of these were explanations of how the

---

25   Nganyinytja Ilyatjari 1983: 55; re-translated in James 2005.

world was formed, how people first got fire, why crows have black feathers and some gave instruction about the importance of respecting water sources in the desert. There were also *tjukurpa* stories with a small 't' called *ara irititja*, stories about the olden days when her grandparents were young, the coming of the first white men, the first time they saw camels or tasted white bread; the oral histories of her people.

The histories of grandparent generations are also marked in the land. Some early contact history of the Musgrave Ranges is recorded in the rock art figures of men on horses painted in ochre on the ceiling of the large overhang at Cave Hill. This human history is recorded alongside symbols of the *Kungkarangkalpa* Seven Sisters *Tjukurpa*. Outside the cave entrance, a large single rock embodies Wati Nyiru, the ancestral man who pursued the sisters across land and sky; he is intently watching the sisters inside the cave.

> *Apu palatja* (Wati Nyiru) *Kungkarangkalpa nyanganyi*:
> That stone [the Ancestor Man Nyiru] is watching the sisters.[26]

The rocks and trees embody ancestral beings of *Tjukurpa* and may also hold the spirit of deceased grandparents of the living. Anangu visiting sacred sites or waterholes in country will call out to their ancestors, their grandparents and the *Tjukurpa* spirits of place, greet them and let them know they are coming to get water or clean a site.

> *Apu ngangatja ngayuku tjamu*:
> This rock is my grandfather.
> That's a really important, sacred thing that you are climbing … [the rock].
> You shouldn't climb. It's not the proper thing.[27]

Anangu are not just talking about rocks as being 'like' people or representing them; they 'are' the person. They act towards these rocks as relatives. They respect, sing to, care for and interact with particular rocks as sentient beings in the landscape that can affect their lives. The rocks can watch, listen and get angry and shake people off their backs, as Nellie Paterson says of the Devil Dingo in Uluru, 'He shakes off tourists'.[28] Not only is *Tjukurpa* time continuously present, there is movement between the worlds of *Tjukurpa* and everyday experience, so *Tjukurpa* is a fluid concept of time and space.

---

26 Stanley Douglas, pers. comms, 1994.
27 James 2005: 57.
28 Nellie Paterson, Uluru Traditional Owner, pers. comm., 1978.

Tjukurpa and history

Wati Ngintaka, the perentie lizard who stole the grindstone, is an important *Tjukurpa* creation story that traverses the lands of the Pitjantjatjara Yankunytjatjara people. Nganyinytja tells this story where the Songline of the Ngintaka man goes through her father's country of Angatja in the Mann Ranges. The Ngintaka *Tjukurpa* contains many levels of knowledge. Some knowledge is restricted to men, while some knowledge is open to women and children, and this story is shared widely with the public through Anangu acrylic painting. It is said that the Ngintaka man journeyed from his homeland in the west at Arang'nga over 300 kilometres to the east to steal a good quality grindstone from relatives at Wallatinna. This is a creation law story about the importance of good grindstones and the grass seeds ground on them to make people's daily bread. It is interesting to reflect on how much this *Tjukurpa* may include historical information.

Mike Smith, an archaeologist who accompanied Anangu to Ngintaka sites in western APY Lands, found that the stone available for flat large millstones in the Mann and Musgrave Ranges is not the best quality for seed grinding. There is evidence that grinding stones were traded across large areas of the desert and particularly from the Anna Creek quarry to the east of Indulkana.[29] The Ngintaka ancestor could well have been travelling a trade route to obtain a good quality grindstone and been killed for stealing a special grindstone, and thus transgressing the reciprocity rules of trade. This historical dimension to the story enhances the significance of *Tjukurpa* as the repository of detailed Anangu knowledge of the physical world. It also underlines the importance of their laws of reciprocity around scarce resources like good grindstones for the production of food.

The simultaneous multi-dimensional time and space of *Tjukurpa* allows for the Ngintaka man being both a creation ancestor of *Tjukurpa* Law from ancient times and also to have been engaged in the more recent practice of trading grindstones along this east–west route. *Tjukurpa* time is essential for understanding how living elders are spoken of as incarnations of ancestors of the *Tjukurpa*. Mulkuya Ken, a traditional owner of the Ngintaka *Tjukurpa*, speaks of her father as Wati Ngintaka and says he *tjukurtja tjunkunytja*, literally he 'laid down' the Ngintaka *Tjukurpa* when he lived at Arang'nga.[30] Her father's position of authority is recognised by other senior traditional owners of Arang'nga, the highly significant site where Wati Ngintaka was eventually cornered, speared and died. This is a site in Ngintaka's home country in the Northern Territory near the tri-state border with South Australia and Western Australia in the north-western Mann Ranges.

---

29 Smith 2013: 283–284.
30 Mulykuya Ken, Ngintaka Traditional Owner, pers. comm., 2012.

Mulkuya's father had a wounded foot, the same as the Ngintaka man; he was *tjukuritja* of the *Tjukurpa*. She speaks of him as both creating the *Tjukurpa* and being created by it. That the Anangu claim *Tjukurpa* has always been there in the country is not contradicted by the present-day existence of descendants who embody this *Tjukurpa* and are responsible for keeping it alive in song, ceremony and caring for sites in country. *Tjukurpa* time is not confined to a lineal time frame. Creation time is not restricted to some past era, it continues today and there is no concept of a time in which *Tjukurpa* did not, and will not, exist.

Seasonal cyclical time in the *Kungkarangkalpa Tjukurpa*

The *Kungkarangkalpa Tjukurpa*, the Seven Sisters, is a story of young girls being pursued by an older clever man, a shape-shifter of great powers who can turn himself into ripe bush tomatoes, great big shade trees, grass seeds ready for gathering – anything to entice the young maidens into his grasp. But the older sister always discerns his disguise and warns her younger sisters to stay away. His desire thwarted, he sings them illness and the older sister starts to bleed uncontrollably, she weakens and unable to escape is raped and dies. Her sisters take her up into the sky to become what is more widely known as the Pleiades; she is the weak, faint star of the cluster. Wati Nyiru's misshapen footprint, Orion's belt, follows them forever.

The *Kungkarangkalpa* sisters' and Wati Nyiru's exploits are written in both the land and sky. Wati Nyiru becomes stone and sits next to us in country at Walingnya where he waits outside the shelter built by the *Kungkarangkalpa* that is now a cave. Inside the cave extraordinary rock art tells their *Tjukurpa* story in ochre and charcoal symbols. Wati Nyiru continues to pursue the women across the night sky; he is the red star that most of us know as Taurus and his footprint is Orion's belt. As above, so below, *Tjukurpa* creation beings walked the earth and rose into the sky – their nightly passage mirrored in the still waterholes of the desert. As they rise over the eastern rim of the horizon before dawn in September and early October the *Kungkarangkalpa* or the Pleiades star cluster heralds the spring in the southern hemisphere.

Tjukurpa as sacred time

The performance of *Inma*, traditional song and dance of the *Tjukurpa*, brings alive the presence of the creation ancestors. Ilyatjari, Nganyinytja's husband, at Angatja in 1990 said that dancing *Tjukurpa* is not *ngunti* make-believe; dancers enter the real world of *Tjukurpa*. The singers enchant the dancers and the dancing ground becomes a numinous liminal space where the *Tjukurpa* comes up out of the ground and takes over the bodies of the dancers and singers. Ilyatjari taught trainee dancers to pay attention to the significance of performing *Tjukurpa*:

> *Kulila! Nyangatja ngunti wiya! Nyangatja Tjukurpa mulapa.*

> Listen!: This is not just pretend! This true Tjukurpa! You are the Ngintaka Man vomiting up the mistletoe seeds. Pay attention![31]

Singers, performers and the audience are in sacred time and space, the re-creative continuum of *Tjukurpa* time where past, present and future are simultaneously present. This is a religious or sacred sense of time that is not entirely unusual. Comparative religious scholars like Bede Griffiths[32] identify a similar sense of time in other world religions. This would include the Buddhist sense of the 'ever present now' and the interpretations of the Christian 'God' concept as active agency creating the now.[33]

Continuously becoming time of *Tjukurpa*

Tjukurpa as ontology can avoid the reality versus myth debate. By acknowledging it as Aboriginal religion, we recognise the historical and moral charter aspects, with the premise that the physical, spiritual and moral worlds are all shaped by the *Tjukurpa*. Sacred time exists concurrently with secular time. *Tjukurpa* time existed before history was written in books; it was inscribed in the land, it is a continuous presence enlivening the land and people through song, dance and story performance and painting on bodies, rocks and canvas. *Tjukurpa* encompasses the time and space of oral and written history in a holistic ontology of the ever present now.

---

31   James 205: 318.
32   Griffiths 1994.
33   Cooper 1997.

Bibliography

Austin-Broos, Diane 2010, 'Translating Christianity: some keywords, events and sites in Western Arrernte conversion', *The Australian Journal of Anthropology* 21: 14–32.

Cooper, David A 1997, *God is a Verb: Kabbalah and the Practice of Mystical Judaism*, Riverhead Books, New York.

Downing, Jim 1988, *Ngura walytja, Country of my Spirit*, North Australian research monograph, The Australian National University, Canberra.

Eliade, Mircea 1960, *Myths, Dreams and Mysteries: The Encounter between Contemporary Faiths and Archaic Reality*, trans. by P Mairet, Harvill Press, Great Britain.

Elkin, Adolphus Peter 1964, *The Australian Aborigines*, fourth revised edition, Angus and Robertson, Sydney.

Elkin, Adolphus Peter 1977, *Aboriginal Men of High Degree*, University of Queensland Press, St Lucia.

Gale, Fay (ed.) 1983, *We Are Bosses Ourselves: The Status and Role of Aboriginal Women Today*, Australian Institute of Aboriginal Studies, Canberra.

Gillen, Frank J 1896, 'Notes on some manners and customs of the Aborigines of the McDonnell Ranges belonging to the Arunta tribe', in Baldwin Spencer (ed.), *Report on the work of the Horn Scientific Expedition to Central Australia. Part IV—Anthropology*, Dulau and Co., London, 161–186.

Goddard, Cliff (comp.) 1992, *Pitjantjatjara/Yankunytjatjara to English Dictionary*, second edition, Institute for Aboriginal Development Press, Alice Springs.

Green, Jenny 2012, 'The Altyerre story – "suffering badly by translation"', *TheAustralian Journal of Anthropology* 23(2): 158–178.

Griffiths, Bede 1994, *Universal Wisdom: A Journey through the Sacred Wisdom of the World*, Harper Collins, London.

James, Diana 2005, 'Kinship with Country: Acts of Translation in the Cross-Cultural Performance Space, a Case Study on the Anangu Pitjantjatjara Lands of Central Australia', PhD thesis, The Australian National University, Canberra.

James, Diana 2006, 'Re-sourcing the sacredness of water', in Kuntala Lahiri-Dutt (ed.), *Fluid Bonds: Views on Gender and Water*, National Institute for Environment, The Australian National University, Canberra.

Morphy, Howard 1996, 'Empiricism to metaphysics: in defence of the concept of the Dreamtime', in Tim Bonyhady and Tom Griffiths (eds), *Prehistory to Politics: John Mulvaney, the Humanities and the Public Intellectual*, Melbourne University Press, Melbourne, 163–189.

Mulvaney, Derek John 1989, *Encounters in Place*, University of Queensland Press, St Lucia.

Nganyinytja Ilyatjari 1983, 'Women and land rights: the Pitjantjatjara land claims', in Fay Gale (ed.), *We Are Bosses Ourselves: The Status and Role of Aboriginal Women Today*, Australian Institute of Aboriginal Studies, Canberra.

Radcliffe-Brown, Alfred Reginald 1945, 'Religion and society', *Journal of the Royal Anthropological Institute of Great Britain and Ireland* 75(1/2): 33–43.

Robin, Libby, Robert Heinsohn and Leo Joseph (eds), 2009, *Boom and Bust; Bird Stories for a Dry Country*, CSIRO Publishing, Melbourne.

Spencer, W Baldwin and Frank J Gillen 1969 [1899], *The Native Tribes of Central Australia*, Macmillan, London (facsimile edition, Anthropological publications, N. B. Oosterhout, The Netherlands).

Spencer, W Baldwin and Frank J Gillen 1927, *The Arunta: A Study of a Stone Age People*, MacMillan and Co., London.

Smith, Mike 2013, *The Archaeology of Australia's Deserts*, Cambridge University Press, New York.

Stanner, William Edward Hanley 1959–63, *On Aboriginal Religion*, Oceania Monograph No. 11, University of Sydney, Sydney.

Wolfe, Patrick 1991, 'On being woken up: the Dreamtime in anthropology and in Australian settler culture', *Comparative Studies in Society and History* 33: 197–224.

3. Contemporary Concepts of Time in Western Science and Philosophy

Peter J. Riggs

Time present and time past
Are both perhaps present in time future
And time future contained in time past.
If all time is eternally present
All time is unredeemable.

TS Eliot

[handwritten: DEEP TIME – ERAS DATING BACK TO THE FORMATION OF THE EARTH]

Introduction

The term 'deep time' denotes vast, extremely remote periods of (natural or other) history – distant and extensive spans of time that are almost beyond the grasp of the human mind. In western science, deep time is used to refer to eras dating back to the formation of the Earth (about 4.5 billion years ago) as indicated by empirical evidence, for example, the geological record. The geologist Stephen J Gould provides the following portrayal of deep time in his book *Time's Arrow, Time's Cycle*:

> [I]mposed by geology … 'deep time' … [is] the notion of an almost incomprehensible immensity … so outside our ordinary experience [and] so alien that we can really only comprehend it as metaphor.[1]

Disciplines other than geology have also embraced notions of deep time, as have cross-disciplinary studies.[2] Insights from cross-cultural views of time (especially Australian Indigenous perspectives) are not discussed here but are dealt with in several other chapters.

What might be thought of time itself? All conscious human beings seem to perceive time. Time provides us with the order in which events occur (their temporal order) and the order of our perceptions of the world around us. The perplexing nature of time has been more contemplated, speculated, written

[handwritten: TIME – GIVES ORDER IN WHICH EVENTS OCCUR & THE ORDER OF OUR PERCEPTIONS OF THE WORLD AROUND US]

---

1   Gould 1987: 2–3.
2   See, for example: Douglas 2010; Shryock and Smail 2011.

and debated about over the ages than virtually any other subject, with the possible exception of religion. Yet time seems more elusive than the vast majority of other metaphysical concepts. Even with the advancement of modern physics (that is, physics since the beginning of the twentieth century) we only have an elementary understanding of time. The nature of time remains both puzzling and bewildering! An oft-quoted statement by the early Christian philosopher and cleric Saint Augustine (354–430 AD) captures much of this sentiment:

> What then, is time? If no one asks me, I know. If I wish to explain it to him who asks, I know it not.[3]

The significance of knowledge about time cannot be overstated, for it goes to the core of human consciousness, perception, communication and of our desire to understand ourselves and the universe which we inhabit. Although we are better off today in respect to knowledge about time than was Saint Augustine, time is still an enigma that western philosophy and physical science have not been able to solve, despite time explicitly appearing in the mathematical expression of the fundamental laws of physics. The scientific perspective of time, however, owes much to modern physics, as observed by physicist Carlo Rovelli:

> [T]he development of theoretical physics has modified substantially the «natural» notion of time.[4]

Nevertheless, there is no consensus amongst scientifically literate philosophers or among physicists about the nature of time. Neither is there any consensus on which aspects of time are genuine features of reality. Time remains mysterious, for we lack an understanding of time at a basic physical level.

An increase in our knowledge about time would not only bring a better appreciation of the workings of the universe but also of our place as conscious beings in the cosmos. In this chapter, the principal tenets of those theories of time that have attracted and/or still retain support amongst philosophers and physicists will be summarised together with recent and potential advances. These advances may help to illuminate the deep structure of time. We will begin by discussing concepts of time in theories of modern physics and then proceed to consider time as found in contemporary western analytic philosophy.

---

3   Quoted in Fraser 1987: 35.
4   Rovelli 1995: 84.

Physical concepts of time

This section commences by acknowledging that science is an empirically based enterprise which deals only with natural phenomena. The outputs of science are physical theories and laws of nature. These laws may be thought of as general statements about causal connections between events (deterministic laws) or general statements about the probability of events (non-deterministic laws). Physics is considered to be the most mature physical science because of its quantitative methods of gathering evidence and theory development, its ability to make precise measurements, its rigorous empirical testing regime, and its criteria for eliminating theories that have failed to agree with experimental data. Only those theories in physics that meet these stringent requirements remain in contention. Time features significantly in both the conduct of physics and as a characteristic of physical theories themselves.

There are certain aspects of physics that are relevant to the scientific perspective of time. First, we must recognise that physics has shown that the common sense view of time is mistaken. The public at large clings to a notion of time that remains firmly entrenched in everyday experience. This notion requires time to be the same for everyone everywhere, regardless of their location or motion. Time is thus accepted as a physical absolute. GJ Whitrow described this attitude in his influential treatise, *The Natural Philosophy of Time*:

> [M]ost people still have the feeling that time is something that goes on of its own accord unaffected by anything else …[5]

It is known from the Special Theory of Relativity (and supported by numerous experiments to extraordinary accuracy) that time is not the same for different observers. While it seems highly counter-intuitive, there is no such thing as an absolute time.

Second, the fundamental laws of physics do not contain any terms that specify an objective present moment (the 'now') even though human consciousness is only aware of the 'now', not the past nor the future. The present moment is completely absent from the equations of physics![6]

Third, two orientations of time can be specified in physics that match with conscious experience (especially in western thought). Typically, time is graphically represented in western society by a straight line. This fits with our intuitive sense of time as being serially ordered since a straight line is obviously linear and has two orientations – extending to the left and to the right. The two

---

5 Whitrow 1980: 59.
6 Denbigh 1981: 4; Greene 2004: 131.

49

orientations of time, which we call *earlier* and *later*, correspond to left and right in the straight line representation of time.[7] Nonetheless, as explained in the previous chapter, this varies across cultures.

Fourth, the fundamental laws of physics do not distinguish between past and future.[8] All the equations of fundamental physics can be solved for either of the two orientations of time. In other words, these equations can supply results for physical phenomena that will occur (prediction) and results for physical phenomena that have already occurred (retrodiction). The technical phrase for this is that the form of the fundamental laws of physics is *time-reversal invariant*.

Fifth, a very obvious fact about the universe and time is the existence of (so-called) 'irreversible' processes. An irreversible process may be defined as a process that alters the state of a physical system such that no other (naturally occurring) process can restore the system to its original state at a later time. The coffee and milk in your cup, for example, always spontaneously mix. We never observe coffee and milk naturally staying separate nor un-mixing spontaneously, despite such events *not* being excluded by the fundamental laws of physics.[9] The term 'temporal asymmetry' is used to denote the fact that irreversible processes occur only along one orientation of time (the orientation called *later*). This need not imply anything about a structural asymmetry of time itself but merely refer to processes occurring in time.[10] At a human level, temporal asymmetry describes our experiences of having memories of the past and not of the future. We shall see that some philosophical accounts of time rule out the inverses of irreversible processes such as a broken egg reassembling itself spontaneously, regardless of these inverse processes not being forbidden by the fundamental laws of physics.

The operational definition of time

Time has always been an essential element in the study of astronomy and in navigation.[11] Aside from time in the Theories of Relativity (see below), science has tended to be pragmatic in respect to time, making use of the purely operational definition – *time is that which clocks measure*.[12] In pursuit of better means of testing physical theories, progressively more accurate technologies have been developed for the measurement of time[13] (to the current stage where time intervals

7   Reichenbach 1956: 26.
8   Denbign 1981: 5; Greene 2004: 144–145.
9   Greene 2004: 145–146.
10 Price 1996: 16.
11 Aveni 2000: 96.
12 Elton and Messel 1978: 7; Park 1980: 40.
13 Phys.org news item, 12 May 2010.

can be determined to an accuracy of 12 attoseconds[14]). Although the operational definition of time and higher accuracies of time measurement are essential for practical, observational, and experimental purposes, these operational aspects do not enlighten us about the nature of time. Further, in most of the equations of physics, time is simply a parameter (albeit one directly related to intervals measured by a clock) by which the evolution of physical systems are gauged. This parameter role also does not inform us about the nature of time.

Time in the theories of relativity

Albert Einstein publicly introduced his Special and General Theories of Relativity in the years 1905 and 1915 respectively.[15] They are two of the most empirically corroborated theories in the whole of science. Relativity has informed us more about the nature of time than any other theory in the history of science and has still more to reveal. Time plays a special role in the Theories of Relativity, over and above being just a physical parameter, as time is also an intrinsic coordinate in these theories.[16] In other words, time itself is part of what Relativity describes. Also in Relativity, one cannot hypothesise about the nature of time in total isolation from its relation to space. Time and space are *not* independent of each other, as we shall see below. This is a consequence of the speed of light in vacuum being a universal constant and thereby having the same value for all observers independent of their motion. If observers in different states of motion always find this same value then their measurements of space and time must differ. Further, Relativity requires that the speed of light in vacuum is the fastest speed for transfer of energy or the transmission of information. This 'ultimate speed limit' ensures the maintenance of causality, that is, the preservation of the temporal order of events.[17] If this limitation did not apply then circumstances could occur where cause and effect in the observable macroscopic world get reversed resulting in logical contradictions!

The Special Theory of Relativity shows that there is no absolute simultaneity between spatially distant events or with objects having different velocities.[18] Whether two or more events are simultaneous is not fixed by nature but is relative to the circumstances of different observers. This means that the present

---

14   = 0.000000000000000012 of a second.
15   Pais 1982: 239.
16   Kroes 1985: 77–82.
17   Goldberg 1984: 116.
18   Wald 1992: 14.

moment in time is relative to different observers (or in physics parlance, relative to different frames of reference) and consequently that there is *no universal* present moment, that is, my 'now' is not necessarily your 'now'.[19]

Discrepancies in time for different observers (that is, in different frames of reference) would only become obvious when the relative speed of one observer to another is more than half the speed of light in vacuum. However, even at much slower speeds, these differences are measurable. This phenomenon is called 'time dilation' and is usually depicted in a hypothetical scenario with two observers, one of whom goes off on a round trip through outer space in an advanced spacecraft at a speed close to the speed of light. On return to the Earth, the two observers compare their clocks to find the travelling clock reads much less than the stay-at-home clock (and the travelling observer is correspondingly younger than the stay-at-home one).[20] In spite of time dilation being counter to common sense, tests conducted using elementary particles on one hand, and airborne atomic clocks on the other, have experimentally verified time dilation to an amazing degree of accuracy.[21]

The General Theory of Relativity is a theory about *space-time*, which is the relativistic union of space plus time.[22] Space-time may be described as the flexible four-dimensional 'fabric' of the universe. We are all familiar (at least from primary school mathematics) of the three-dimensional geometry of space. General Relativity extends basic geometrical notions by explaining gravity in terms of the four-dimensional geometry of space-time. Gravity is a natural consequence of this four-dimensional geometry. General Relativity also shows that gravitation affects time. It turns out that time intervals between events are not only dependent on relative motion but also on the presence of a gravitational field and its intensity.[23] This leads to a gravitational version of the time dilation effect, which is also experimentally well supported.[24] The closer that a clock is to the source of a gravitational field, the shorter will be the time intervals measured by the clock. Since the time differences between different observers on the Earth are so miniscule, we would never notice them. However, they still have to be taken into account in some applications. A hand-held receiver linked to the satellite-based Global Positioning System (GPS), for example, can determine one's position on the Earth to within a few metres. The GPS incorporates corrections due to Relativity effects without which the error in any GPS navigational fix would progressively accumulate.[25]

---

19 Penrose 1989: 392.
20 Wald 1992: 24–26.
21 Greene 2004: 50.
22 Wald 1992: 34.
23 Angel 1980: 205.
24 Chou et al. 2010.
25 Pascual-Sánchez 2007: 263.

Time in quantum mechanics

Elements of Quantum Mechanics were conceived by a number of physicists in the 1920s, especially by Louis de Broglie, Albert Einstein, Erwin Schrödinger, Werner Heisenberg, Neils Bohr and Max Born.[26] It is another of the most empirically corroborated theories in the whole of science. Quantum Mechanics describes microscopic phenomena, that is, phenomena in the realm of the atom and sub-atomic (quantum) particles. Although Quantum Mechanics has a number of very bizarre consequences, it does not effectively alter the classical notion of time in depicting the states of quantum level physical systems. Quantum Mechanics describes a physical system by means of Schrödinger's Equation, which allows earlier and later states of the system to be calculated.[27] Time as it appears in Schrödinger's Equation is merely a parameter determined by something external to the physical system being studied, for example, as measured by a clock. Despite this, Quantum Mechanics may provide some important clues for an investigation of time and of the ontological status of events at the microscopic level (that is, whether microscopic events which have already occurred or events which are yet to occur can be said to be real in some sense).

A highly significant result that is inferred from Quantum Mechanics is that the universe is inherently *non-local* at the level of quantum interactions.[28] Non-locality refers to the existence of some form of action-at-a-distance, indicating that there are influences which act with speeds faster than the speed of light in vacuum. This conclusion is based on a large number of experimental results that show correlations between spatially distant quantum events. Suppose we have two quantum particles, for example, which are initially produced from a single physical process. Quantum Mechanics tells us that the physical states of these two particles will not be independent. (The technical term for this is that the particles are *entangled*). If we move one particle a large distance away and then make a measurement of a particular characteristic of the close particle, the corresponding characteristic of the distant particle changes *instantaneously*.[29]

However, it has been shown that 'quantum non-locality' effects cannot be used to send any form of *communication* faster than the speed of light in vacuum,[30] which has avoided a direct clash with Relativity. Since Relativity actually forbids causal propagation that is faster than light, the existence of

---

26   Enge et al. 1972: 161.
27   Kroes 1985: 84.
28   Riggs 2009: 104–105.
29   Rae 2004: 57.
30   Riggs 2009: 114–115.

non-local effects may eventually demand that the accepted account of relative simultaneity be modified. Indeed, quantum non-locality may turn out to have strong ramifications for our understanding of time.

Philosophical concepts of time

Philosophical theories cannot be empirically tested. The dividing zone between philosophical and scientific theories has shifted over the millennia. In ancient times, many topics which we would today consider to be science could only be the subject of philosophical debate. A classic example is the question of whether the ultimate nature of matter was atomic, as asked by the ancient Greeks. This question was settled by experiment early in the twentieth century. In recent years, a few other issues that were traditionally considered metaphysical (such as questions relating to the realist view of science) have been the subject of indirect tests through experiments on quantum mechanical systems. Whilst it is clear that physics has uncovered some characteristics of time, methods for *directly* testing theories of time have not yet been devised. While it is conceivable that experiments might be developed which would discriminate for or against a particular theory of time, it is the case that theories about the nature of time remain in the philosophical domain.

There are many philosophical questions asked in relation to time. Most frequently asked questions about the nature of time include: Does time exist? Are past and future as real as the present? Does time 'flow'? Does time have a 'direction'? The majority of philosophers are of the view that time does exist. It is just that they do not agree on what time is![31] Such questions as these assume a familiarity with the terminology used. If time does flow (in some sense) then one would expect it to be directed. In other words, the flow of time ought to 'progress' strictly in one orientation of time. The direction of time is a stronger concept than time orientation as the latter concept is neutral in regard to 'which way' in time. The graphical analogy for the direction of time is a directed straight line, that is, a line that includes an arrow which consistently *points* along only one of the orientations of time. There are a number of theories postulated in the philosophy of time, each of which provides different answers to questions about time. We shall now canvass the most popular philosophical theories of time and see what answers they offer.

---

31 Dowden 2013.

Causal theories of time

Causal Theories of Time have had much attention in the philosophy of time literature. These are members of the set of relational theories of time. In relational theories, time is postulated to be purely relative to events, that is, time does not exist in itself. Instead, events are considered fundamental and what we perceive as time is constituted by the existence of particular relations between events.[32] Relations between events or objects (in the philosophical sense) express real characteristics or connections between the events or objects, for example, for the relation of 'being taller than' to hold between two people, one of them must have a longer body length than the other.

We shall deal with the general thrust of these causal theories. They concern causal relations between events, that is, the relationships of causes to effects. It is asserted in the Causal Theories that causal relations are more basic than temporal relations, where temporal relations concern whether one event occurs before another in time.[33] If we have two events where one event causes the other event, the causal order of the events is determined by which of these events is the cause. This determination is logically independent of the temporal order of the events. Causal order is defined as the order where the event that is the cause is first, or primary, and the event that is caused (the effect) is second. Causal relations are asymmetric and transitive such that if A is a cause of B and B is a cause of C then A is a cause of C, but not vice-versa. In this view, causes in all circumstances *must* temporally precede their effects. The temporal order of events is thereby derivative from their causal order. Causal Theories of Time suffer from at least one major flaw. In all attempts to show the reduction of temporal relations to causal relations, implicit appeal has been made to temporal notions, which then undermined the whole endeavour of attempting to make this reduction.[34]

Statistical theories of time

Statistical Theories of Time are principally about the origin of the direction of time. The original Statistical Theory of Time held that our concept of time is dependent on the observed fact that physical systems when left alone will tend to become more disorganised at later times. This is quantified in terms of the entropy of a closed physical system. Entropy is a measure of disorder and

---

32 Bardon 2013: 14.
33 Sklar 1977: 319.
34 Whitrow 1980: 326; Kroes 1985: 19.

refers to the physical system as a whole rather than its individual constituents. Your home garbage has, for example, a lower entropy when stacked in your rubbish bin (less disorder) than when your neighbour's dog has spread the bin contents all over your home's front yard. Indeed, throughout our lives we see all sorts of natural processes that result in more disorder, such as biological decay and ageing.

The entropy of a closed physical system is postulated never to decrease. (In physics, this is a statement of the Second Law of Thermodynamics which, although being a law of physics, is not one of the fundamental laws referred to above.) A closed physical system, regardless of its size, is necessary in order to rigorously define entropy. However, it became clear that because the original Statistical Theory of Time dealt with the *average* variation of entropy in a closed system, it could not rule out periodic decreases in entropy,[35] and therefore is unable to unambiguously define an objective direction of time. Other attempts to define an objective time direction with respect to entropy increase have also failed.[36] This failure has undermined attempts to show that entropy-increasing activities in the human brain are responsible for generating our sensations of time (more about temporal sensations appears below).

Another Statistical Theory of Time appeared when the Noble Prize-winning physicist Richard Feynman put forward an account of the interactions of elementary particles after the discovery of anti-matter. An anti-matter particle has the same mass as the corresponding particle of ordinary matter but an opposite electric charge. An anti-electron (called a positron), for example, has a positive electric charge whereas an electron has a negative electric charge, but both have identical mass. In Feynman's account, anti-matter particles are considered to be matter particles moving 'backwards' in time (that is, along the orientation of time called *earlier*). This led to the idea that there might *not* be a unique time direction at *microscopic* scales. The familiar macroscopic time direction was then theorised to be a statistical effect due to the predominance of matter over anti-matter in the universe.

This version of the Statistical Theory of Time has some odd consequences. In particular, if our macroscopic time direction depends on there being only extremely small numbers of anti-particles, then time direction would disappear in any spatial region that contained a large amount of anti-matter! Feynman's account lacks evidence and is not taken seriously by most physicists. Consequently, this Statistical Theory of Time is not considered viable.

---

35   Whitrow 1980: 331–332; Bardon 2013: 14.
36   Price 2011: 284–285.

Realist theories of time

The realist perspective of time is that temporal relations between events are more basic than other relations and that time has an objective existence beyond mere temporal relations. There are essentially two realist theories of time. These two theories are known by several names in the literature of philosophy of time. The most commonly used names are the A-Theory (or Dynamic Time) and the B-Theory (or Block Time). The ontologies of these realist theories (that is, what they postulate to exist) are distinct and incompatible.

The A-Theory of time

The main features of the A-Theory may be listed as follows:[37]

- The primary relations between events are the tensed temporal relations of *past*; *present*; and *future*.
- The flow of time (also called passage of time or temporal becoming) by which the present moment 'moves' from past to future, entails an objective coming into being of events.
- Time has an intrinsic direction from past to future.
- Changes are only understandable in terms of tensed temporal relations.

Central to the A-Theory is the notion of an objective present moment (the 'now'), which 'moves' from past to future and is perceived as the flow of time. The present moment is a special point of time known from conscious experience that separates the closed past from the open future and is characterised by the process of temporal becoming. Temporal becoming changes the status of an event from unactualised to actualised (that is, the process by which an event comes into existence). Therefore, the past is determined and the future is undetermined. Consequently, according to the A-Theory, singular statements can be made about past events, but statements about future ones can only be general in their form.

If temporal becoming is a change in the ontological status of events from an undetermined to a determined state, then the question to be asked is determined for whom? A standard response is that an event is determined for us at this particular moment. However, by answering in this way, we merely have

---

37 Gale 1968: 77; Price 1996: 12–13; Dainton 2010: 10–12.

defined the present moment with respect to itself.[38] Such a subjective account is completely unsatisfactory. Indeed, no attempt to *objectively define* the present moment has succeeded.

In the A-Theory, the universe is intrinsically irreversible as a consequence of temporal becoming. Therefore, the observed temporal asymmetry of events arises from time's dynamic nature. The direction in which irreversible processes occur (for example, cream becoming butter) gives the direction of time.

One version of the A-Theory that has received much attention in recent years is called Presentism. This is the view that only objects and experiences in the present actually exist (where 'present' means temporally present as distinct from spatially present).[39] According to Presentism, anything that lacks the property of being present is unreal. Therefore, Presentism asserts that the past and future as such *do not exist*. Although Presentism remains popular amongst a minority of philosophers, there are robust arguments in the philosophical literature against it. In particular, the case that Presentism conflicts with the Special Theory of Relativity is well established.[40] These arguments (some invoking Relativity and others based on purely logical grounds) cast serious doubt on the truth of Presentism.

The B-Theory of Time

The main features of the B-Theory may be listed as follows:[41]

- The primary relations between events are the tenseless temporal relations of *earlier than* and *later than*.
- There is no flow of time or objective coming into being of events.
- There is no objective present moment.
- All events are equally real.
- Changes do not require tensed temporal relations.
- Temporal asymmetry is due to the boundary conditions that apply to physical processes.

In the B-Theory, what appears to be past, present or future is purely subjective and the 'now' is observer dependent. The tensed relations of the A-Theory are taken as not being objective but instead relative to particular events in much

---

38   Whitrow 1980: 349.
39   Dowden 2013.
40   See, for example, Saunders 2002; Wüthrich 2013.
41   Gale 1968: 70; Price 1996: 12–13; Dainton 2010: 10–12.

the same way as spatial tenses (for example, 'here' and 'there') are relative terms. Singular propositions about events are (tenselessly) true or false, although one might not be aware of what the truth value of a particular proposition is.

The B-Theory can accommodate the fact that the world appears to be asymmetric in time by noting that there are (*de facto*) irreversible processes which result from physical boundary conditions. Therefore, temporal asymmetry is not intrinsic to time in the B-Theory but arises from these boundary conditions. We do not see mixed coffee and milk spontaneously separate in a cup, for example, because of the boundary conditions imposed by putting these liquids into the cup (pouring one liquid into the other, limiting the space in which the liquids can spread, and so on). These conditions ensure that the probability of the coffee and milk spontaneously un-mixing is so small that it would take longer than the current age of the universe for such an event to occur.

If the B-Theory of time is correct, it would explain much about our universe and why the laws of physics take the forms they do (being time-reversal invariant). Yet, the B-Theory is not unproblematic. A major failing of the B-Theory is that it does not offer a sufficient explanation of the common feeling that there is a flow of time from the past to the future, merely ascribing this feeling to being a psychological phenomenon.[42]

Ultra deep time

If deep time dates back to the formation of the Earth, then it follows that 'ultra deep time' dates back to the origin of the universe. Precise astronomical measurements in the 1920s (and validated throughout the rest of the twentieth century) have shown that the universe is expanding, that is, the galaxies are getting further apart at later and later times.[43] Therefore, if we (theoretically) retrace the motion of the galaxies far enough back in time, then we reach a time in the history of the universe where all the galaxies would be at the same point. This was the origin of the whole universe. According to the currently accepted scientific cosmological view, the universe began with a tremendous burst of energy approximately 13.8 billion years ago, which is called the Big Bang.[44] This was *not* an 'explosion' into a pre-existing empty space, for the Big Bang constituted the creation of space and time. If this is correct, then time itself

---

42 Price 1996: 12–14.
43 Tegmark 2014: 45–46.
44 Singh 2004, chap. 5; Tegmark 2014: 44–46.

started at the Big Bang! Surprisingly perhaps, Saint Augustine eloquently and succinctly expressed the gist of this idea when he wrote 'verily the world was made *with time, not in time*'.[45]

Current astrophysical evidence indicates that the rate of the universe's expansion is actually accelerating.[46] Such acceleration has a number of serious implications, including whether the expansion provides an objective basis for temporal asymmetry, whether time will have an ending (or will continue indefinitely), and indeed, whether a physical definition of time will hold in a global sense.

There are theoretical alternatives to the standard cosmological view in which there is 'something' prior to the Big Bang (or no Big Bang at all). These alternative theories postulate either an eternally existing universe or that new, whole universes are created in a never-ending cosmic process.[47] However, the alternatives are not faring well as recent theoretical and observational findings support the proposition that the Big Bang was a physical boundary of time.[48] This physical boundary is indicated by calculations showing that the paths of objects in space-time cannot be continued indefinitely to earlier times and therefore cease (at the Big Bang).[49] The Big Bang remains the best supported theory of physical cosmology.

We should also note that the study of the very earliest moments of the universe (at a time of less than 10^{-43} of a second after the Big Bang[50]) is hampered by the problem that our current theories fail when applied to this early era.[51] In order to deal with physical systems in the most extreme conditions (such as obtained in the very early universe), we need a theory that combines General Relativity and Quantum Mechanics. This is a theoretical unification called Quantum Gravity and, despite decades of effort, is still to be achieved. The theory of Quantum Gravity is expected to provide some important insights about time, although exactly what these will be await the arrival of the theory!

There is another sense of ultra deep time which concerns the ultimate nature of time at the smallest physical scale for space, time and energy. This is known as the Planck scale. The physical constants of nature set the Planck scale at about 10^{-35} metre.[52] At this level, a principal question is whether the structure of time is discrete or continuous. There are persuasive arguments to the effect that physical space-time has a granular constitution that would only become evident

---

45 Quoted in Whitrow 1980: 33, fn. ‡ (italics added).
46 Tegmark 2014: 77.
47 Tegmark 2014: 151–152.
48 Moss et al. 2011; Grossman 2012.
49 Guth 2007: 6821–6824.
50 = 0.0000000000000000000000000000000000000000001 of a second.
51 Adler 2010: 931.
52 = 0.00000000000000000000000000000000001 of a metre.

at extremely minute distances.[53] If so, this would also imply that time is discrete and only appears to be continuous at levels much larger than the Planck scale. A discrete structure of time would have significant consequences for physical theories in general, as most assume time to be continuous at all scales.

There are also experimental results that may influence our understanding of time, which have been noticed in some kinds of sub-atomic particle interactions. These results, gained by examining data from billions of particle collisions, strongly suggest that a form of temporal anisotropy exists.[54] Temporal anisotropy is a structural difference between the two orientations of time. If temporal anisotropy does exist, it could be used to objectively and consistently distinguish between the two orientations of time. Additional experiments are needed to study the relevant particle interactions and gather more data before temporal anisotropy can be considered to have been firmly established. Clearly though, if the proposals about time possessing the properties of discreteness and anisotropy can be supported by sizeable and robust amounts of empirical evidence, then the implications for the deep structure of time are profound.

Prospects for a more complete understanding of time

Of the philosophical theories canvassed, it is the B-Theory that fits best with Relativity, which makes the B-Theory quite attractive. In this context, space-time is interpreted as being the totality of events, also called the 'Block Universe'. All events in the Block Universe have the same ontological status, that is, are equally real regardless of *when* they occur (as also postulated in the B-Theory). We also have acknowledged that the B-Theory does not properly account for the common feeling that there is a flow of time. In order to address this failure, the B-Theory needs to offer an explanation of this feeling that is comprehensible in terms of objective features of the universe. It should not be surprising then, that attempts to find improved philosophical explanations for the feeling that time flows that are consistent with the B-Theory constitute an area of ongoing philosophical research.[55]

It was also previously noted that the fundamental laws of physics do not specify an objective 'moving' present moment as implied by human consciousness. This has led some philosophers to allege that physics has not explained a basic

---

53   Greene 2004: 490–491; Adler 2010.
54   Schwarzschild 2012: 16.
55   See, for example, Riggs 2012; Prosser 2013; Deng 2013.

feature of reality and, consequently, to claim that physics is incomplete in its description of time. In order to address this claim, answers would need to be sought to the following questions:

- What is the relevant aspect that might be missing in the physical account of time?
- How could the missing aspect be discovered?
- By what mechanism would the missing aspect bring about human temporal experiences?

Finding answers to these questions and, more generally, gaining a better understanding of the nature of time may require a cross-disciplinary approach. Interestingly, the amount of research in the fields of experimental psychology and cognitive science into time perception has increased markedly over the first decade of this century.[56] Much of this research has centred on judgements about temporal intervals and how the brain might process such intervals.[57] However, the neurophysiological basis of the human experience of time is still unknown.[58] What is almost totally lacking in the cognitive experimental arena are rigorous tests into the conscious feeling of the flow of time. Such tests might prove exceedingly valuable for they may assist in discovering whether this feeling is purely mind dependent (as postulated in the B-Theory) or not.[59]

Given the rapid and in-depth development of physical science that has occurred since the early twentieth century, it is likely that further advances in physics will result in discoveries of new aspects of time. In particular, the theory of Quantum Gravity should provide novel physical insights into time. However, improving our knowledge about time might be best achieved by integrating philosophical ideas with those of physics and cognitive science. At the very least, an integrated approach should assist in identifying gaps in our understanding of time. It is an encouraging development for the study of time that philosophers and physicists are starting to engage in common dialogues on issues of mutual interest. The integration of the philosophical and the physical will also have the potential to solve some of the conceptual problems of modern physics that remain outstanding (such as quantum non-locality). The cosmologist Lee Smolin offered the following commentary about the relation of time to our understanding of the physical universe:

> [T]he extent to which we bring laws of physics inside of time is the extent to which we make them amenable to rational understanding. Time is then

---

56   Ivry and Schlerf 2008: 273; Eagleman and Pariyadath 2009: 1841.
57   See Grondin 2010, for a review.
58   Wittmann et al. 2010: 3110.
59   Some proposed tests are outlined in Riggs 2012.

the key for the aspiration to construct a theory of the whole universe …
Time is thus the most central and most difficult problem we must face as
we attempt to construct a theory of a whole universe.[60]

Research into the nature of time has an exciting future and one which holds the
potential for finding solutions to some of the most baffling questions asked in
the history of human thought.

Bibliography

Adler, Ronald J 2010, 'Six easy roads to the Planck Scale', *American Journal of Physics* 78(9): 925–932.

Angel, Roger B 1980, *Relativity: The Theory and its Philosophy*, Pergamon, Oxford.

Aveni, Anthony 2000, *Empires of Time: Calendars, Clocks and Cultures*, Tauris Parke, London.

Bardon, Adrian 2013, *A Brief History of the Philosophy of Time*, Oxford University Press, Oxford.

Chou, CW, DB Hume, T Rosenband and DJ Wineland 2010, 'Optical clocks and relativity', *Science* 329(5999): 1630–1633.

Dainton, Barry 2010, *Time and Space*, second edition, Acumen, Durham, UK.

Denbigh, Kenneth 1981, *Three Concepts of Time*, Springer, Berlin.

Deng, Natalja 2013, 'On explaining why time seem to pass', *Southern Journal of Philosophy* 51: 367–382.

Douglas, Kirsty 2010, *Pictures of Time Beneath: Science, Heritage and the Uses of the Deep Past*, CSIRO Publishing, Canberra.

Dowden, Bradley 2013, 'Time', in *The Internet Encyclopedia of Philosophy* (ISSN 2161-0002), www.iep.utm.edu.

Eagleman, David M and Vani Pariyadath 2009, 'Is subjective duration a signature of coding efficiency?', *Philosophical Transactions of the Royal Society B* 364: 1841–1851.

Elton, Lewis RB and Harry Messel 1978, *Time and Man*, Pergamon, Oxford.

---

60   Smolin 1997: 262.

Enge, Harald A, M Russell Wehr and James Austin Richards 1972, *Introduction to Atomic Physics*, Addison-Wesley, Reading, MA.

Fraser, Julius Thomas 1987, *Time, the Familiar Stranger*, Tempus Books, Redmond.

Gale, Richard M (ed.) 1968, *The Philosophy of Time: A Collection of Essays*, Macmillan, London.

Goldberg, Stanley 1984, *Understanding Relativity: Origin and Impact of a Scientific Revolution*, Clarendon Press, Oxford.

Gould, Stephen J 1987, *Time's Arrow, Time's Cycle: Myth and Metaphor in the Discovery of Geological Time*, Harvard University Press, Cambridge, MA.

Greene, Brian 2004, *The Fabric of the Cosmos: Space, Time and the Texture of Reality*, Penguin, London.

Grondin, Simon 2010, 'Timing and time perception: A review of recent behavioral and neuroscience findings and theoretical directions', *Attention, Perception, & Psychophysics* 72: 561–582.

Grossman, Lisa 2012, 'Death of the eternal cosmos', *New Scientist* (14 January 2012): 6–7.

Guth, Alan 2007, 'Eternal inflation and its implications', *Journal of Physics A* 40: 6811–6826.

Ivry, Richard B and John E Schlerf 2008, 'Dedicated and intrinsic models of time perception', *Trends in Cognitive Sciences* 12: 273–280.

Kroes, Peter 1985, *Time: Its Structure and Role in Physical Theories*, Reidel, Dordrecht.

Moss, Adam, Douglas Scott and James P Zibin 2011, 'No evidence for anomalously low variance circles on the sky', *Journal of Cosmology and Astroparticle Physics* 4: 1–7.

Pais, Abraham 1982, *Subtle is the Lord...: The Science and the Life of Albert Einstein*, Oxford University Press, Oxford.

Park, David 1980, *The Image of Eternity: Roots of Time in the Physical World*, University of Massachusetts Press, Amherst, MA.

Pascual-Sánchez, J-Fernando 2007, 'Introducing relativity in global navigation satellite systems', *Annalen der Physik* 16: 258–273.

Penrose, Roger 1989, *The Emperor's New Mind: Concerning Computers, Minds, and the Laws of Physics*, Vintage Press, London.

Phys.org News 12 May 2010, '12 attoseconds is the world record for shortest controllable time', Phys.org (online), phys.org/news192909576.html.

Price, Huw 1996, *Time's Arrow and Archimedes' Point: New Directions for the Physics of Time*, Oxford University Press, Oxford.

Price, Huw 2011, 'The flow of time', in Craig Callender (ed.), *The Oxford Handbook of Philosophy of Time*, Oxford University Press, Oxford.

Prosser, Simon 2013, 'Passage and perception', *Noûs* 47: 69–84.

Rae, Alastair IM 2004, *Quantum Mechanics: Illusion or Reality?*, second edition, Cambridge University Press, Cambridge.

Reichenbach, Hans 1956, *The Direction of Time* (ed. Maria Reichenbach), University of California Press, Berkeley and Los Angeles.

Riggs, Peter J 2009, *Quantum Causality: Conceptual Issues in the Causal Theory of Quantum Mechanics*, Springer, Dordrecht.

Riggs, Peter J 2012, 'What do we feel when we "feel" time "passing"?', *Journal of Consciousness Exploration & Research* 3: 1064–1073.

Rovelli, Carlo 1995, 'Analysis of the distinct meanings of the notion of «Time», in different physical theories', *Il Nuovo Cimento B* 110: 81–93.

Saunders, Simon 2002, 'How relativity contradicts presentism', in Craig Callender (ed.), *Time, Reality and Experience*, Cambridge University Press, Cambridge, 277–292.

Schwarzschild, Bertram M 2012, 'Time-reversal asymmetry in particle physics has finally been clearly seen', *Physics Today* 65(11): 16–18.

Shryock, Andrew and Daniel Lord Smail 2011, *Deep History: The Architecture of Past and Present*, University of California Press, Los Angeles.

Singh, Simon 2004, *Big Bang: The Most Important Scientific Discovery of All Time and Why You Need To Know About It*, Fourth Estate, London.

Sklar, Lawrence 1977, *Space, Time and Spacetime*, University of California Press, Berkeley and Los Angeles.

Smolin, Lee 1997, *Life of the Cosmos*, Phoenix, London.

Tegmark, Max 2014, *Our Mathematical Universe*, Knopf, New York.

Wald, Robert M 1992, *Space, Time, and Gravity*, second edition, Chicago University Press, Chicago.

Wittmann, Marc, Alan N Simmons, Jennifer L Arona and Martin P Paulus 2010, 'Accumulation of neural activity in the posterior insula encodes the passage of time', *Neuropsychologia* 48(10): 3110–3120.

Whitrow, Gerald J 1980, *The Natural Philosophy of Time*, second edition, Clarendon Press, Oxford.

Wüthrich, Christian 2013, 'The fate of presentism in modern physics', in Roberto Ciunti, Kristie Miller and Giuliano Torrengo (eds), *New Papers on the Present: Focus on Presentism*, Philosophia Verlag, Munich, 91–131.

4. The Mutability of Time and Space as a Means of Healing History in an Australian Aboriginal Community[1]

Rob Paton

The poet Seamus Heaney in his famous work *Bogland*[2] speaks to the connection of the Irish people to their land:

> Every layer they strip
> Seems camped on before.
> The bogholes might be Atlantic seepage
> The wet centre is bottomless

He imagines Ireland's peat bogs to be a timeless, bottomless land that has forever been camped on. For Heaney, these bogs are as deep and mysterious as the ancient Irish whose archaeological relics are uncovered by modern-day peat miners who strip away the layers. Of course, we know Ireland's peat bogs are neither timeless nor bottomless. Scientists have shown that they are relatively recent landscape features. But we also know Heaney's imagined bogland is poetic country. In this country, time and space are allowed to be used and changed to tell us a story about people and their profound attachment to their homeland. But most of us live in different countries from poets. In the academy, or at least in the historic disciplines in which many of us operate, we are not as flexible as poets with time or space. Most of us perceive time as linear, moving from the past to the present in a straight line, with events occurring in a roughly ordered fashion relative to one another in time and space. This suits most of us. It is how we lead our lives and how we structure our stories about the past.[3] But for scholars engaged with Aboriginal histories, the architecture of linear history, while sometimes a useful tool, is perhaps just as deeply imaginary as Seamus Heaney's poetic country.

1   Thanks to the Mudburra and Jingili people who worked with me over a 30-year period. I acknowledge their generosity in giving me permissions to share their culture and insights with others. I am particularly indebted to my good friend Nuggett Collins Japarta and his family. I would also like to thank my supervisor Professor Ann McGrath, who encouraged me to write this paper and gave freely of her time and knowledge. Denis Byrne and Maria Nugent read drafts of the paper, and I thank them both for their insightful comments. The content of the paper is entirely my own, except where otherwise acknowledged.
2   Heaney 1969.
3   Price 1997.

We readily accept that our colleagues from other academic disciplines see time and space operating very differently to the conventional linear model. Western cosmologists, for example, see space and time as a continuum called 'space-time' that can be warped and changed.[4] It should not come as a surprise then that some other cultures, those of Aboriginal Australians, also recognise time and space in ways very different to the linear model. When dealing with space, historians and archaeologists like Read,[5] Harrison,[6] and Byrne and Nugent[7] have in the past decade or so made strong cases for other human geographies, recognising that Aboriginal space exists alongside European geographies in urban and rural environments.

Cross-cultural perceptions of time, however, have received a somewhat confused treatment in the literature. In the context of Aboriginal Australia, when we come to consider how time operates, we are usually drawn to concepts of the Dreamtime. While acknowledging the 'timelessness' of the Dreamtime, scholars have nevertheless attempted to historicise it, likening the Dreamtime to a kind of quasi-religious Aboriginal history.[8] This treatment is analogous in some senses to the plethora of attempts to rigorously historicise the Bible. While such attempts have been met with varying success, in its crudest form we have seen Bishop Ussher, in 1648, dating the beginning of the world to Sunday, 23 October 4004 BC, primarily by analysing the ages of individuals and the reigns of kings in the Bible.[9] I would argue that by too closely linking the Dreamtime to Aboriginal history, we are perhaps also in danger of contriving fables that occasionally, and for the most part serendipitously, triangulate to factual data. This is not to deny the significance of the Dreamtime within Aboriginal societies. Nor does it downplay the debates around the nature, role and efficacy of the Dreamtime for researchers.[10] Rather, my argument is that by considering the role of more secular concepts of Aboriginal time, newer perceptions can emerge similar to the human geographies of Aboriginal space that we now acknowledge as part of the Australian landscape.

How time and space are imagined by Aboriginal people is as sophisticated as it is varied. My intention here is simply to look at a case study from the Top End of the Northern Territory, showing how one group imagine their time and space. Through a detailed example, I will show how the gravity of one very hurtful

---

4   Hawking and Mlodinow 2011.
5   Read 2000.
6   Harrison 2004.
7   Byrne and Nugent 2004.
8   This topic is covered very well in David 2002.
9   Barr 1984–85.
10 See, for example, Wolfe 1991.

event involving several deaths was perceived by the Aboriginal community, and how they came to resolve it by engaging the inherent mutability of secular time and space in order to rewrite the past.

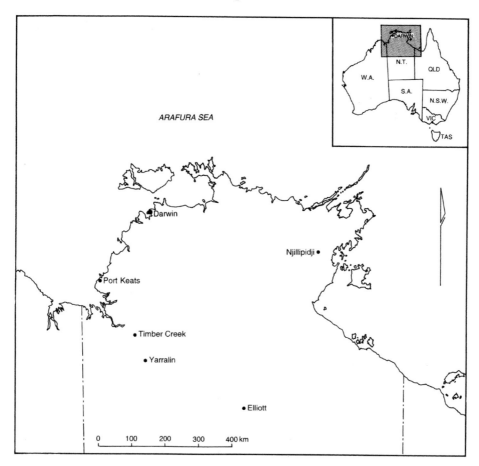

Figure 4.1: Map of northern Australia showing places mentioned in the text.

Source: Robert Paton Collection.

The event I look at occurred near Elliott, a small settlement of several hundred, mostly Aboriginal, people in the central Northern Territory (Figure 4.1). In the summer of 1985–86, a small party of people left Elliott to hunt on the vast Newcastle Waters cattle station. They headed about 50 kilometres north-west into harsh, inhospitable country mostly devoid of any standing water. Led by highly experienced bushmen and women, the party had planned to hunt and camp and then return home after a day or so. But when nothing was heard from them after a few days, concerns began to be raised. However, it was still assumed at this point that these experienced people could handle most situations.

Their family and friends at the small Aboriginal community at Elliott, which they had left days earlier, had no idea about the life and death drama unfolding some 50 kilometres away.

By the time search parties were sent out a short time later, all of the group were dead, and had been for some time. The police report details a sad account of the small family car in which they were travelling breaking down on an isolated farm track. In the extreme heat, members of the party had apparently sought water at a nearby artesian bore. They could not have known that the water at the bore contained high levels of bacteria. The more water they drank, the sicker and more dehydrated they became. The vicious combination of 40 degree heat, thirst and sickness eventually overcame the group. Their bodies were found at various distances from the bore. It was surmised that as the weaker members of the group died close to the bore, the stronger individuals, realising that the water was making them sicker attempted to walk out for help. By then it was too late. In their fragile state, and probably suffering from delirium, they walked in different directions until eventually they simply fell and died.[11]

The effects of heat and scavenging animals on the bodies was particularly distressing for the local Aboriginal Police Trackers who first came across the tragic scene. Stories about what the Trackers had found and reports from relatives who formally identified the bodies swept through the community. Rumours abounded about what had caused the deaths. People said that witnesses had seen bullet holes on the bodies, and that the authorities were falsely reporting these as the effects of heat and animals. Suspicions about who had killed the family began to circulate and there was a widely held belief that something 'unnatural' had happened.[12]

I arrived in the community a few months after the deaths to undertake some archaeological research. I had been working with this community for a number of years and I was shocked to see how the tragic and perceived unnatural manner of these deaths had left the community in the grip of a moribund lassitude, well beyond the ordinary grieving experience. The normally close-knit community began to fracture, with some families moving away to nearby settlements and other people isolating themselves from important communal responsibilities. As a result, nearby communities began to see the settlement at Elliott as 'diseased'. This diseased state was also seen to be uncontained and spreading. Strings of mythological creation sites and stories that connected Elliott to the surrounding communities were said to have become infected. These sites and

---

11 See taped interview (Longreach Winnun 24 June 1986, 16:32 to 18:45) at deepeninghistories.anu.edu.au/ sites/pelican-dreaming/ and *NT News* January to March 1985 *passim*.
12 See taped interview (Longreach Winnun 24 June 1986, 16:32 to 18:45), deepeninghistories.anu.edu.au/ sites/pelican-dreaming/.

the stories attached to them form an important part of what Aboriginal people refer to as 'Dreaming histories' or creation myths. All relationships between people, and between people and the land, are intimately tied in some way to these Dreaming histories. They form part of the fabric of the cosmos. So this was an extremely serious situation.

As the months passed, community elders attempted to cope with this great sorrow by managing the space of their settlement. They abandoned the houses where the deceased had lived. Most of the personal possessions of the deceased were destroyed and their names were not referred to directly. These sorts of customs that deal with living space are well documented in Aboriginal communities and are generically known as part of 'sorry business'.[13] They are usually maintained for a year or so, or in some northern communities until the monsoonal rains arrive to wash away the sorrow. But for the Aboriginal community at Elliott, management of their living space seemed to have limited impact on the great sorrow. The community remained in the grip of grief. Those remaining at the settlement hardly ventured outside of their homes; there was talk of cancelling important initiation ceremonies planned for later that same year.

For most of us who have dealt with terrible grief like this, we are comforted by the knowledge that time will heal. We recognise that linear time distances us from hurtful events. In this sense, the cliché that 'time heals' often has some efficacy. But as I have hinted, not all cultures, or scholars, imagine time in this way.

For many Australian Aboriginal communities, linear time is perceived to have a depth of only a generation or two. This linear time exists along with what I call 'temporal wave time'. In temporal wave time all events exist alongside each other on a flat temporal plain, like the face of a wave that moves forward, capturing all history as it progresses. People certainly also see time as working in other ways – linear, and in categories like 'cattle time' or 'rain time'. But the main way of perceiving time is as this flat, wave-like structure. Others[14] have commented on this view of time, referring to instances where relatively modern events enter this wave of progressing time and become incorporated into it – the Cigarette Dreaming, the Toyota Dreaming and the Captain Cook Dreaming.[15] As the names imply, scholars have tended to lump these events together with Dreamtime creation myths because the two exist on the flat temporal plain alongside one another. But events on the flat temporal plain are not all the same. They do not all have the same gravity, nor are they all associated with religious creation events. Day-to-day secular events are compartmentalised (in the sense of being

13 www.indigenousaustralia.info/culture/mourning-ceremonies.html.
14 Rose 1992.
15 See, for example, Rose 1984; Hokari 2011: 254–260.

discrete), as are creation stories, though any event may link to another through song, myth or physical tracks. This linkage is reported most often for Dreamtime creation myths (such as along Songlines). But day-to-day secular events may also affect other events across the temporal wave, depending on their gravity.

It is for this reason that very hurtful and tragic events like the deaths described earlier can attain a constancy in these communities, and a gravity that disrupts other events on the temporal wave. And this is what was happening in Elliott. The severity of the hurt caused by the multiple deaths was too overwhelming to be dealt with by actions like the abandonment of houses and the destruction of dead people's property. No temporal distance was being created between the deaths and the immediate lives of people. Moreover, the magnitude of the events surrounding the deaths was eclipsing everything else on the flat temporal plain. And this was unlikely to resolve itself as the wave of time moved forward, meaning the event remained unresolved and ever-present.

It is important to understand that the hurtful event was not just confined to the temporal dimension. It also affected places across the landscape, much further afield than the domestic spaces that were abandoned or destroyed to help remove the pain as part of 'sorry business'. This is because both time and space are indelibly locked together in the temporal wave through Dreaming history stories. These stories about the creation of the cosmos exist, like all things, on the flat temporal wave, constantly and immediately. The stories can also be influenced (and sometimes consumed) by other large events that may appear suddenly on the temporal wave. The crucial connection of these Dreaming history stories to places in the landscape was made clear in a conversation I participated in and recorded at a site called *Kankiritja*. The conversation explains some of the general unrestricted Dreaming stories associated with the site and the much wider landscape. These Dreaming stories, as I have discussed elsewhere,[16] help explain the creation of large geological outcrops of quartzite that form the backbone of one of the main ranges around Elliott. Within these outcrops are massive stone quarry sites, where for many centuries people manufactured large stone knives. The names of the two men talking are Nuggett Collins Japarta (NC) and Abby Thomas Jungala (AT). The taped conversation that relates unrestricted information was recorded in 1985.[17] It has been edited slightly to remove some irrelevant material and to help clarify points.

---

16   Paton 1994.
17   For a full account of this conversation on video see deepeninghistories.anu.edu.au/sites/pelican-dreaming/index.php?action=video.

AT: Pelican you call him. We call him *wallambee*.

NC: That's where they been comin' here [pointing around to the quartzite outcrops]. Land on this place. That why they call *Kankiritja* [means pelican landing place].

AT: *Kankiritja* this one now. That's his knife [pointing to a blade]. Pelican been have this. Cut anything or kill someone. And he used to have that spear, that mouth he got now, that pelican [showing how two blades, one on top of the other, makes the shape of a pelican's beak].

NC: That's the one pelican Dreaming, this one [points to a blade]. Pelican been come in, land here. Well this is the stone he made.

AT: He made him for knife. We call him *giru* [local name for the *leilira* blade].

NC: Three names; *giru, jabiri, marubu* [different languages]. This one now. Pelican been land here. Oh, big mob. Million. That why the hill over there. That why the big hill right there, round and round. All this, all the way along. Some over there where we went this morning. This way. Keep going thataway and some big hill there now. This a pelican Dreaming. That's why he been come in. Make Dreaming stone.

AT: Yeah. Some all through. And that [fire for burning stone] come down from that way [pointing north-west]. That's them two sparrowhawk. Sparrowhawk sing out *kiri kiri kiri kiri kiri kiri kiri*. He sing out like that. That's the one been made it. From our country … They [the pelican] been bringing this [the blades] and that people [the two sparrowhawks] used to been using the fire sticks. They been bad eh? Some two been comin' along, they had him here. They been gone give it that fire stick on to them here … Ah that good man. That's what we gotta do now, all do.

The linking of important Dreaming history stories that exist on the temporal wave to places in the landscape is well illustrated by the two Aboriginal men in the recording. But how can such stories be influenced by significant, though apparently unrelated, hurtful events like the deaths? One way of conceptualising this is to imagine the Dreaming stories to be like a bright star casting light onto the landscape, illuminating its features. Then imagine a body of immense gravity, like a black hole, suddenly appearing near the star, capturing its light, and in the process warping both time and space and distorting reality. Such a destructive event, if left unresolved, would clearly continue to play havoc with the cosmos, far beyond its own borders.

When it became clear after several months that the hurt caused by the deaths would not resolve, people began to discuss how they might heal the community by breaking the link between these very sad historic events and their own immediate lives. A decision was made about six months or so after the deaths to engage an elegant mechanism called *winnun* to help heal the temporal wave.[18] *Winnun* in its most basic manifestation involves trade of material objects. However, it is much more than this. *Winnun* is best understood as it was described to me; as being like blood circulating in a body. Carried within the blood are all of the things necessary to keep an organism alive and healthy. In this sense, the objects traded in *winnun* are not in themselves as important as what they carry. These objects are embedded with special meanings that are exchanged with the objects as a way of rewriting community memories and healing the past.

In this instance, the *winnun* ceremony involved an exchange of boomerangs made in Elliott for items from the Aboriginal settlement at Yarralin, 325 kilometres to the north-west. From Yarralin the exchange was to be continued through to Port Keats a further 275 kilometres away (see Figure 4.1). The idea behind the *winnun* exchange was to help heal the community through initiating an event which would demonstrate to others that the stigma associated with the deaths had been overcome. The exchange was initiated through a series of telegrams and telephone calls. Arrangements were made for some bamboo spears to be flown by light aircraft from Port Keats to Yarralin via a small settlement near Yarralin called Timber Creek.

It was decided after negotiations that certain boomerangs with attached Dreaming stories would be traded from Elliott in exchange for the spears. The people at Yarralin had arranged for some of the boomerangs to be flown to Port Keats after the exchange had taken place at Yarralin.

The whole process of this *winnun* cycle took between two and three months to complete, and I was fortunate enough to be living with the community for this time, working with people to collect the wood for the boomerangs.

The wood was gathered over several weeks by men, women and children. The type of wood used for boomerang manufacture grows abundantly throughout the area. However, trips were never made to the nearest or most accessible sources of timber. Furthermore, even though the areas visited on the first trips contained ample wood to make return visits attractive, such visits were never seriously considered. The rationale behind this strategy seems to contain two elements. Firstly, people went to trees or places that were connected to Dreaming stories and that were said to have been 'diseased', or infected,

18   McGrath 2014.

by the deaths. Each boomerang, as it was made, was said to absorb elements of this diseased Dreaming story. For this reason, people said it was important that each boomerang be called a particular name and be kept separate from all the others. A second, and equally important reason for making an apparently simple procurement task more complicated, was the extended time it allowed for discussion between the people collecting the wood. Each trip involved many hours of talk about the forthcoming exchange and the healing this would bring back to the community.

Thirty boomerangs were made and covered in a red ochre which had been quarried to the south and traded to Elliott in a related but separate *winnun* exchange. The bundles were tied together; three bundles of seven and one of nine. The bundles were then driven about 300 kilometres to Yarralin, an Aboriginal settlement on the Victoria River. Shortly after, 20 to 30 local men arrived for discussions. A car then arrived carrying a bundle of 17 bamboo spears that were exchanged for the bundles of boomerangs. Some more discussion occurred and a bolt of red cloth was added to the spears as payment for the boomerangs. Both the cloth and the spears were then loaded onto our truck and within 10 minutes we departed.

Figure 4.2: Nuggett Collins Japarta making boomerangs for the *winnun* exchange, circa June 1986.

Source: Robert Paton Collection.

Figure 4.3: The bundles of ochred boomerangs ready for exchange, circa June 1986.

Source: Robert Paton Collection.

On return to Elliott, the spears and the cloth were divided amongst the men and women who had made the boomerangs or collected the wood. Shortly after, these items were deliberately destroyed or sold to European tourists, effectively removing them from the community. Similarly, the boomerangs that I was able to trace at the other end of the *winnun* trade cycle were also deliberately destroyed. To further illustrate this point, one of the men from Elliott was given a Kung Fu video cassette as part of another exchange (the exchange further to the south to obtain red ochre to apply to the boomerangs).[19] This occurred despite the fact that nobody at Elliott had a video cassette player. This point was discussed during the exchange, but in the end was not considered to be important. The cassette was left out in the sun and then later thrown in the sand and presumably destroyed, having served no utilitarian function at all.

19 For a fuller discussion of this trade and exchange cycle see Paton 1994.

Figure 4.4: The *winnun* exchange taking place at Yarralin Aboriginal community, circa July 1986. One of the bundles of boomerangs is in the foreground and the bamboo spears are tied to the roof of the truck.
Source: Robert Paton Collection.

The destruction of the *winnun* goods had an almost immediate effect on the community. People moved back to the settlement and the community began to rapidly heal from the hurt the deaths had brought. The clearest manifestation of this was the resumption of men's and women's initiation ceremonies that had been suspended after the deaths almost nine months before. People were also able to speak about those events with a tone of quiet resolution. The accusations of blame for the deaths had been completely resolved and the gravity of the incident was palpably dissipated, albeit still ever-present. It seems that the *winnun* trade items, although inanimate objects, were infused with the gravity of the deaths and then were deliberately discarded as a means to rewrite history and heal a great hurt.

Though poignant, this example of reshaping the past through the *winnun* cycle is, I suggest, not an isolated or exceptional case. Management of events on the flat temporal wave occurs constantly, both at a local level and much further afield. Moreover, it appears that *winnun* is very old. It can be traced in the deep prehistoric archaeological record, where for thousands of years people's memories took the shape of healing objects that were reshaped to rewrite the past. My research[20] has shown that large stone knives called *leilira* blades once formed the backbone of a *winnun* system that covered most of the Top End of Australia, stretching from the Arafura Sea south to Alice Springs, and from western Queensland to the Kimberley Ranges in Western Australia.[21] These *leilira* blades were manufactured in their millions at massive stone quarries.[22] They were elaborately named, bundled and traded over vast distances, often for morphologically identical blades. Once exchanged, they were then deliberately destroyed. I have argued elsewhere that the material signature of the *winnun* network is widespread across Australia, sometimes comprising up to a quarter of the artefacts found at archaeological sites.[23]

20 Paton 1994. See also Thomson 1949; Jones and White 1988.
21 Paton 2013, deepeninghistories.anu.edu.au/sites/pelican-dreaming/.
22 For example, at one *leilira* blade quarry near Katherine there are approximately 45 million stone artefacts. Eleven per cent of these (nearly 5 million) are estimated to be *leilira* blades. Several similar quarries have been recorded by me near Elliott. See Paton 1995.
23 Paton 1994.

Conclusion

To conclude, I would like to return to Seamus Heaney's poem *Bogland*.[24] Like the Aboriginal people whose story I have told here, Heaney sees both the infinity and immediacy of time in the landscape, and in objects from the past. He expresses this when he writes about the bogs being the receptacle of memory, conserving and linking the deep past and present.

> Butter sunk under
> More than a hundred years
> Was recovered salty and white

He also sees the bog as being 'kind', melting away to reveal its secrets.

> The ground itself is kind, black butter
> Melting and opening under foot

I hinted, at the beginning of this chapter, that perhaps those who research Aboriginal Australia should reflect upon how poets like Heaney imagine the past. Scholars have certainly done so in the area of human geography, where Aboriginal landscapes have been resolved into focus even in the heart of Australia's major cities. But conventional temporal discourse continues to remain largely driven by the academic disciplines, particularly archaeology, which seems the most conservative. I do not think we in the academy are any more 'right' about our view of time than Aboriginal people about theirs, other than that it makes writing linear chronologies of the past easier.[25] It might suit historians dealing with the modern period.[26] But for those of us who research the deep past, particularly that past as experienced and understood by Indigenous people, a fuller discussion of the discourse seems useful. I am reminded of a story by Denis Byrne[27] who, like me, when working as an archaeologist was often confronted by Aboriginal people who had an appreciation of our archaeological view of the past, yet could not understand why archaeologists did not reciprocate. Denis's story shifted my own view of this temporal discourse enough for me to write this chapter. It also made me understand some of the consequences that might flow from these discussions. For example, when museums return objects to Aboriginal communities, perhaps they should consider if these objects (although chronologically old in linear time) are part of a *winnun* cycle and have agency beyond their material value. By originally giving them to collectors, were these objects being disposed of?

---

24 Heaney 1969.
25 Rosenberg and Grafton 2010.
26 Shryock and Smail 2011.
27 Byrne 2013.

Returning them could potentially reignite the hurt embedded in the object, regardless of its age in linear time. Similarly, heritage managers, charged with attributing significance to Aboriginal sites and objects, do so via legislation that focuses on slices of linear time. They usually attribute greater significance to those sites and objects that have been scientifically calibrated to be older. Germane as this may be to archaeologists, it often has little meaning for many Aboriginal people who do not see the past as consisting of scientific material, locked statically in deep linear time.

When I began this research some three decades ago, my focus was on the economic and social 'chain of connection'[28] along Aboriginal trade routes, through slices of linear time – and this continues to be the way these trade systems are portrayed in recent archaeological publications.[29] But it was the obvious intimacy that people had with objects from the deep past that in the end shaped my own thinking.[30] The deep past began to collapse into the present, revealing an abiding temporal chain of connection that was more important than any material objects in themselves.

Bibliography

Barr, James 1984–85, 'Why the world was created in 4004 BC: Archbishop Ussher and Biblical chronology', *Bulletin of the John Rylands University Library of Manchester* 67: 575–608.

Byrne, Denis 2007, *Surface Collection: Archaeological Travels in Southeast Asia*, Altamira Press, New York.

Byrne, Denis 2013, 'Looking for difference in the Aboriginal contemporary past', in Rodney Harrison, Paul Graves-Brown and Angela Piccini (eds), *Oxford Handbook of the Archaeology of the Contemporary Past*, Oxford University Press, Oxford.

Byrne, Denis and Maria Nugent 2004, *Mapping Attachment: A Spatial Approach to Aboriginal Post-contact Heritage*, Department of Environment and Conservation NSW, Sydney.

David, Bruno 2002, *Landscapes, Rock-art and the Dreaming: An Archaeology of Preunderstanding*, Leicester University Press, London.

---

28   Mulvaney 1975: 72–94.
29   Smith 2013.
30   For a discussion of the intimacy of the past for modern people, see Byrne 2007.

Harrison, Rodney 2004, *Shared Landscapes: Archaeologies of Attachment and the Pastoral Industry in New South Wales*, Department of Environment and Conservation NSW and the University of New South Wales Press, Sydney.

Hawking, Stephen and Leonard Mlodinow 2011, *A Briefer History of Time*, Transworld Publisher, United Kingdom.

Heaney, Seamus 1969, *Door into the Dark*, Faber Paperbacks, London.

Hokari, Minoru 2011, *Gurindji Journey*, University of New South Wales Press, Sydney.

Jones, Rhys and Neville White 1988, 'Point blank: stone tool manufacture at the Ngilipitji quarry, Arnhem Land, 1981', in, Betty Meehan and Rhys Jones (eds), *Archaeology with Ethnography: An Australian Perspective*, Department of Prehistory, Research School of Pacific Studies, The Australian National University, Canberra.

McGrath, Ann 2014, 'Is history good medicine', *Journal of Australian Studies* 38(4): 396–414.

Mulvaney, D John 1975, '"The chain of connection": the material evidence', in Nicolas Peterson (ed.), *Tribes and Boundaries in Australia*, Australian Institute of Aboriginal Studies, Canberra: 72–94.

Paton, Rob 1994, 'Speaking through stones: a study from northern Australia', *World Archaeology* 26(2): 172–184.

Paton, Rob 1995, *Mt Todd Mining Project, Mitigation Phase of the Aboriginal Archaeology: report on the salvage of Site MT17*. A report to Zapapan NL, Sydney.

Paton, Rob 2013, 'Pelican Dreaming', deepeninghistories.anu.edu.au/sites/pelican-dreaming/.

Price, Huw 1997, *Time's Arrow and Archimedes' Point: New Directions for the Physics of Time*, Oxford University Press, New York.

Read, Peter 2000, *Belonging: Australians, Place and Aboriginal Ownership*, Cambridge University Press, Cambridge.

Rose, Debra 1984, 'The saga of Captain Cook: morality in Aboriginal and European law', *Australian Aboriginal Studies* 2: 24–39.

Rose, Debra 1992, *Dingo Makes Us Human: Life and Land in an Australian Aboriginal Culture*, Cambridge University Press, Melbourne.

Rosenberg, Daniel and Anthony Grafton 2010, *Cartographies of Time*, Princeton Architectural Press, New York.

Shryock, Andrew and Daniel Smail (eds) 2011, *Deep History: The Architecture of Past and Present*, University of California Press, Berkeley.

Smith, Mike 2013, *The Archaeology of Australian Deserts,* Cambridge University Press, Cambridge.

Thomson, Donald F 1949, *Economic Structure and the Ceremonial Exchange Cycle in Arnhem Land*, Macmillan, Melbourne.

Wolfe, Patrick 1991, 'On being woken up: the Dreamtime in anthropology and in Australian settler culture', *Comparative Studies in Society and History* 33: 197–224.

5. Arnhem Land to Adelaide

Deep histories in Aboriginal women's storytelling
and historical practice, 'irruptions of Dreaming'
across contemporary Australia

Karen Hughes

In conducting historical research with Aboriginal women and their families between 1984 and 2007, I became aware of how contemporary manifestations of deep time, as an 'irruption of Dreaming',[1] frequently coursed through their life narratives and storytelling practice. Evidence for this phenomenon is from elders from the Roper River (Ngukurr) region of south-east Arnhem Land, Northern Territory, and from Ngarrindjeri elders of the Coorong and Lower Murray Lakes of south-eastern South Australia who were residing in suburban Adelaide. These were women from widely divergent backgrounds but with a similar way of understanding, structuring and speaking about the past or its lived-ramifications in the present. Permission to reproduce and discuss these stories here has been granted from the women's families, with whom I have ongoing research collaborations and working relationships.

I respectfully borrow the term 'irruptions of Dreaming' from Basil Sansom's influential essay in which he considers how the appearance of Dreamings in outwardly colonised spaces unsettle and challenge assumed paradigms of historical understanding and causality. 'Dreamings,' he contends, 'irrupt into contemporary histories and act in ways that have political significance, contesting whitefella paradigms and re-asserting the world-view of the original Australians.'[2]

It is important to clarify that 'irruptions' are only viewed as such for 'whitefellas'. For Indigenous people, as the chapters of Diana James and Martin Porr also discuss, they are manifestations of an ever-present reality, an underlying structure that shapes, interprets and continuously creates the world.

A number of Northern Territory elders influenced Sansom's thinking on this matter. Foremost among them was Ngukurr elder Dennis Daniels, who gifted this analytical concept to Samson as he embarked on his first fieldwork venture in Aboriginal Australia.[3] Daniels shared with him a causality story about

---

1   Sansom 2001: 1.
2   Sansom 2001.
3   Sansom 2001: 18–20.

Cyclone Tracy, the cyclone that destroyed much of Darwin in 1974, attributing this to a clash between ontologies and the intervention of a clever man and clever woman taking the form of two whirly winds or twisters that clashed and then came together, amplifying their power.

On my second visit to Ngukurr in 1984, it was Dennis Daniels who drew my attention to the palpable presence of Dreaming forces underscoring a recent cross-cultural history from the inter-war years that I was researching for the documentary *Pitjiri: The Snake That Will Not Sink*.[4] At that time, I was accompanied by an elderly Ruth Heathcock, a South Australian nurse and non-Indigenous woman who lived at Roper Bar in the 1930s. Ruth Heathcock was renowned in the community for her covert medical care of leprosy patients on Country at the strong behest of local Roper River women in defiance of Northern Territory public health policy, and for her utmost respect for Aboriginal Law.[5]

A senior *djungaiyi* for the Yabudurawa ceremony at Roper River, Daniels was tall and impressive, with a deep baritone voice.[6] In the cross-cultural setting of our meeting, he consciously deployed story as an educative tool. He elaborated on the intricate, webbed connections between the foundational travels of Nguru, the ancestral Catfish-hero in Creative times, and a 1937 trip Ruth Heathcock made in the company of local women and elders (including Daniels' grandfather) to the sacred place of Burrunju (also known as Ruined City). This is in the Ngandi Arnhem Land stone country, where leprosy sufferers were hiding at the time, being cared for intermittently by their families. Daniels expertly wove these events – millennia apart – into a singular narrative which spectacularly collapsed time. It harnessed the forces of the Dreaming in the present moment, while simultaneously rendering the recent historical past part of the Dreaming. This temporal juncture was enlivened through kin relationships across human, animal and land forms. It included classificatory-kin such as Ruth Heathcock, who had been incorporated into the Roper River kinship system through her close relationships with the women working with her.[7] Daniels' rich recount grounded recent history into a broader epistemological context that gave apprehension to the ways in which 'historical' events cohabit the present, the recent past and the deeper history of the Dreaming concurrently. Moreover, as he emphasised how Ruth and the women's travels had lately become incorporated into contemporary performance of the ceremony-business associated with Burrunju, Daniel's telling of this story fused the secular and sacred worlds.[8]

---

4 Hughes 1986.
5 Hughes 1986, 2005, 2013b.
6 See Elkin 1972.
7 See Rose 1998: 262–264, for a description of what she calls 'species intersubjectivity', and Bell 2002: 18–36, for an expanded understanding of how classificatory kin relations work. See Hughes 2005: 89–96, and Hughes 2013a, for a detailed account of the kin relations between Ruth and the Roper River women.
8 For a fuller account on this see Hughes 2005: 94.

Daniel's rendition offered a philosophical frame for understanding the stories held by the women *djungaiyi* and traditional owners with whom I was about to work over the coming months. We travelled to Burrunju in order to retrace part of this history in Country, and explicitly to 'wake me up' to the history and to 'get the history straight'.

Working with Ngarrindjeri women more than a decade later, in the heavily colonised regions south of Adelaide, it became clear that their stories followed a similar pattern and pedagogy to those of the Ngukurr elders who had a greater access to land.

The Dreaming, '1958' and a moment of now – Dinah Garadji (1921–2006)

The first story is from Dinah Garadji (neé Joshua), a Warndarrang-Marra-Yugul elder born in 1921, a published author, successful artist, cultural custodian and church deacon, who divided her time between the larger hub of Ngukurr and her family's homeland Boomerang Lagoon, Malambuybuy, 50 kilometres to the north.[9] I met Dinah Garadji en route to Burrunju in 1984. With us was her cousin, the Warndarrang elder Rosalind Munur, who was soon to become my classificatory-mother and greatest teacher, and Dawson Daniels, a younger brother to Dennis, employed by the Department of Aboriginal Affairs to maintain infrastructure and services to the numerous Roper River outstations. Members of the Joshua family – Dinah, along with her sister Eva Rogers, and her brother Andrew Joshua – invited us to camp at Boomerang Lagoon overnight. They had recently established an outstation on their specific Country[10] where they had erected a number of hand-built living shelters, a neat bough-shaded schoolhouse used daily by the children, and a sturdy cattle-mustering yard.

Old Joshua, their father, was one of the people who had negotiated the establishment of the Roper River Mission on his country in 1908 as a response to the 'killing times' in the Roper River region.[11] He also worked as one of the key guides and translators for the anthropologist Donald Thomson in south-east Arnhem Land during the 1930s and early 1940s.[12] In 1948, Old Joshua was thought to have leprosy and was taken to the Channel Island leprosarium where he died in the 1950s. A month before my arrival in June 1984, the Joshua family

---

9   Garadji 1982.
10   Here I use the Aboriginal English term 'Country' which encompasses home, clan estate, and the powerful complex of spiritual, animate and inanimate forces that bind people and place.
11   Harris 1998: 9–12.
12   Thomson 1983: 30–42.

had participated in a two-week long ceremony to see their father's spirit safely on to 'the next world', as Eva Rogers put it. It had taken them 12 years of protracted negotiations to secure the safe return of his remains from Channel Island, some 30 years after his death.

That evening over supper, Dinah began to explain to me how Boomerang Lagoon/Malambuybuy, the lily-filled lagoon in front of our camp, was created by the ancestral-giant, Ngarkaran. This was the place where Ngarkaran hurled his boomerang when on his celebrated journey to Burrunju to the very first *business for that place,* shaping the features of the landscape as he travelled during the creative period of the Dreaming.[13] I wondered how big Ngarkaran was – and for comparison, I was mentally invoking the Cyclops from Homer's *Odyssey.*

Dinah paused, thinking deeply before responding. 'I don't know,' she said, 'but when he died in 1958, it took four men to carry his boomerang. It took a long while for his body to decompose. Some people carried his body to a cave near the coast,' she explained, 'and they said his spine was this wide.' Dinah stretched her arms two metres or so apart.[14]

Recalibrating time

Stars filled the night sky, almost touching one another as I listened to a story of events that had shaped the land where we sat. Dinah's answer came as a powerful inaugural history lesson, pointing me, as Dennis Daniels' story had earlier, to a remarkably different sense of temporality and indeed of time-space continuum, and subsequently to a more monumental sense of history that confounds and indeed shatters all notions of western historiography. It was not only *munangna* (white people) like Ruth Heathcock who became enveloped in stories told as part of *business* originating in the Creative period, but ancestral beings, millennia old, crossed over into modern times, traversing the post-war world into which I was born.

What became starkly apparent was that 'historical stories', including on occasion those in which white people played a significant role, are not separate from but rather part of the big ceremonial stories, belonging to a temporality far deeper and more intricate than I had hitherto imagined, in which locale and kinship – not only human but interspecies kinship – superseded, or perhaps indeed swallowed or enveloped, ordinary time. Creation accounts, for example, fuse spatial and temporal realms, and render present lived-experiences

---

13 See Capell 1960.
14 Dinah Garadji, pers. comm., 1984.

coexistent with the Creative past.[15] As anthropologist WEH Stanner eloquently noted: 'Dreamings populate an everywhen – all the instants of being, whether completed or to come.'[16]

Figure 5.1: *Devil Devil*, **Djambu Burra Burra (1937–2005), 2001.**
Source: Synthetic polymer on canvas, collection of the Australian Institute of Aboriginal and Torres Strait Islander Studies, reproduced with kind permission of the family of Djambu Burra Burra, AIATSIS and the Ngukurr Art Centre.

15   Westphalen 2011: 13–14.
16   Stanner 2009 [1966] quoted in Sansom 2001: 2.

The Catfish sisters – Rosalind Munur's story (1931–2005)

Leaving Boomerang Lagoon, continuing towards Burrunju in the company of Rosalind Munur, a *djungaiyi* for Burrunju, and Dawson Daniels (whose country of Wiyakibu connects to Burrunju along the Catfish Dreaming track), I was further instructed in multiple ways how such richly complex understandings of temporality played out in the landscape and through the family histories of those belonging to it. We drove along rough bush tracks, very often through Country where there was no road at all, yet where the bush navigators were sure of their directions. Burrunju in the stone country of central Arnhem Land is an important place for *Gunabibbi business*. It is a spectacular labyrinth of spiralling sandstone tors covering more than four square kilometres, where a number of big Dreaming stories, including that of the giant Ngarkaran, intersect and meet.[17] Each of the sandstone tors embody a Catfish ancestor.[18] Sam Thompson, the senior *djungayi* for Burrunju at that time confirmed that these were extraordinarily ancient rocks, dating to a time before dinosaurs and other mega-fauna walked this Country.[19] As we approached Burrunju through sparse savannah country, Rosalind asked Dawson to stop the vehicle. 'See those rocks over there,' she said, drawing my attention to three large rounded sandstone tors that guard the entrance into Burrunju, 'they are my mother and my two aunties, their names are Ngangigee, Dulban and Mungranjyajua – they are all Catfish.'

Ngangigee is Cara Thompson, Rosalind's mother, a Warndarrang woman born in the 1910s, a *minininggi*, (traditional owner) for Burrunju, and one of the group of women who worked closely with Ruth Heathcock in the 1930s, escorting her to Burrunju in 1937.[20] Cara also worked as an assistant nurse on the Roper River Mission. She died there suddenly in the late 1950s. Dulban, Cara's sister, country-woman and fellow *minininggi*, is the late Hannah Dulban, also Warndarrang, and wife of the notable Alawa land rights activist and medical officer Phillip Roberts.[21] Hannah Roberts died under tragic circumstances in Katherine in the early 1970s, the result of a violent assault from a non-Indigenous man.[22] Mungranjyajua, the third sister and fellow *minininggi*, I assumed also to have passed away sometime during the mid-twentieth century.

---

17 See Capell 1960.
18 Rosalind Munur, pers. comm., September 1984.
19 Sam Thompson, pers. comm., September 1984.
20 Hughes 2005: 89–96.
21 See National Museum of Australia, 'Phillip Roberts', *Collaborating for Indigenous Rights*, indigenousrights.net.au/person.asp?pID=1019; Lockwood 1962: 108–117.
22 Philip Bush, pers. comm., November 2013.

Figure 5.2: Warndarrang elder Rosalind Munur points to the three Catfish tors that guard the entrance to Burrunju, 1984. Also in the photograph is Ngukurr elder Dawson Daniels.

Source: From the documentary *Pitjiri, the snake that will not sink*, directed by the author.

Figure 5.3: Warndarrang elder *Ngangigee*, Cara Thompson, late 1930s.

Source: Collection of Ruth Heathcock, from the film *Pitjiri, the Snake that will not sink*, directed by Karen Hughes, with permission from Cara Thompson's family.

Two decades later, in 2004, I was at Ngukurr, again working under Rosalind Munur's expert guidance, pursuing a project that more deeply traced the biographical trajectories of the Roper River women essential to Ruth Heathcock's covert work with leprosy. Rosalind this time insisted we travel to Mainoru (Bulman) in central Arnhem Land to speak with one of her aunties, Ruth Cook, who I was informed held an important part of this story. [23] Holding a story infers a custodianship, an authority to speak, as well as at times a right to bestow that authority on others. [24] To my astonishment, Ruth Cook, a Warndarrang-speaking woman aged in her 80s, was Mungranjyajua, the third and still living Catfish sister who protected Burrunju's entrance. As a child of 15, she had also travelled on the 1937 trip with Ruth Heathcock. As I continued to work over many years on varied aspects of this history, I came to realise how these ancient Catfish rocks are not only a vital part of an enormously important ceremonial cycle and matrix of Dreamings, but that they also embody very specific recently departed women ancestors and close living-kin born into the Catfish Dreaming, as in the case of Mungranjyajua, Ruth Cook (1922–2009), who took her European name from the nurse Ruth Heathcock (1901–1995).

'The information visible in the landscape', as anthropologist Fred Myers has shown, is not 'sufficient in itself to illuminate the underlying reality'. [25] The immanence of the three sisters that Rosalind identified in a totemic landscape – vitalised with knowledge, kin and Dreaming – points to a vastly deeper and broader essence of personhood than is conceived within present academic understanding across fields of history and biography, or even in much of the literature on totemic relationships. It calls for, as historian Minoru Hokari has persuasively argued, an indigenisation of approaches to history and a cross-culturalisation of the discipline itself. This is yet to be taken up in the academy at large. [26] Notably, the agency and embodiment of Rosalind's women-kin as sentinels of the Dreaming is an undeniable material, as well as a conceptual element, of personal and family biography that moves through time from its beginnings millennia ago, and resides infinitely in place. The responsibility of these women ancestors as protectors of a matrix of Dreamings in this highly sacred-restricted landscape illuminates, too, the significance of women's crucial role in upholding Law. [27] Further, this can be seen to deepen an entwined history and biography of people and place. Crucially, the Aboriginal concept of relationality [28] embraces not only people, country, totems and other living things, but also encompasses the multiple dimension of time. [29]

---

23 Hughes 2005: 89–98.
24 For amplification of this see Hughes 2013a.
25 Myers in Sansom 2001: 2.
26 Hokari 2011.
27 See Bauman and Bell 1982; Bell 2002.
28 See Moreton-Robinson 2000; Arbon 2007.
29 Victoria Grieves, pers. comm., 2007.

Figure 5.4: Warndarrang elder Ruth Cook, Mungranjyajua, Katherine, Northern Territory, 2006.

Source: Photograph by Karen Hughes, collection of the author.

Rupturing and the colonised world, purposeful ghosts – Aunty Hilda Wilson's story (1911–2007)

The third story arose from a conversation in 2002 with Aunty Hilda Wilson, the revered Ngarrindjeri elder and storyteller, who was an accomplished community historian and genealogist. It took place in the Adelaide home she shared with her youngest son's family.[30] The Ngarrindjeri are a South Australian Aboriginal nation, comprising several peoples with a common language, whose land and waters (*yarluwar-ruwe*) take in the River Murray, Lakes Alexandrina and Albert, the vast Coorong wetlands, and the Southern Ocean coast. While Ngarrindjeri bore the harsh brunt of first wave invasion in the South Australian colony in 1836 (and indeed in the unruly decades that preceded formal colonisation), as a nation they have managed to survive, and today flourish, nurturing strong cultural connections to their land and waters, and to one another.

---

30 Aunty Hilda Wilson also has Barngarla and Wirrungu ancestry through her father Wilfred Varcoe's lineage. Olive Rankine, her mother, was Ngarrindjeri. Aunty Hilda was born and raised on Ngarrindjeri country at Raukkan.

During the early onslaught of Ngarrindjeri dispossession, when people were left near-starving and decimated from introduced diseases, Hilda's third generation great-grandfather Pulame (c1808–1888), the *rupuli* (the elected leader of the Ngarrindjeri *Tendi*, or parliament), decisively steered his people through the traumatic changes, eventually negotiating a middle-path after the Point McLeay Mission was established at Lake Alexandrina on Ngarrindjeri country in 1859.[31] Pulame's granddaughter, the accomplished, independent-thinking Ellen Sumner or *Tumpoweri* (1842–1925), played an influential educative role during Hilda's youth. Like other Ngarrindjeri women in her lineage, Ellen Sumner was skilled in *putari* practice (female doctor) and midwifery culture (teaching her 'what to do and what not to do'), on which Hilda herself drew throughout her long life.[32] It is these explicit knowledges, passed along through the 'information superhighways' of genealogies such as Aunty Hilda's, and vested in Ngarrindjeri Law, that inform her interpretation and storytelling practice here.

One late winter morning, Aunty Hilda Wilson, together with her countrywomen, Aunty Daisy Rankine and Aunty Daisy's sister, Aunty Emily Webster, and I were recording stories around Hilda's kitchen table.[33] And although I have called this a story, this is really about what happened between stories in a quiet moment when we broke for lunch. Aunty Hilda was reading *The Advertiser*[34] when a real estate feature caught her attention. The article concerned a nineteenth-century commercial property for sale in Milang, a historic town founded in the 1850s on the Lake Alexandrina foreshore near the River Murray mouth, in Aunty Hilda's ancestral country. Her grandfather, William Rankine, was born at Milang in 1866, in the country of his grandmother, Kunjawarra, daughter of Pulame.[35] The property, a former general store built in 1850, was close to the old ceremonial ground, now the site of a caravan park, where each of the women's grandmothers (Grandmother Ellen Sumner and Grandmother Pinkie Mack) had participated in big ceremonial gatherings at the beginning of the twentieth century, and also very near the site outside the Milang hotel where the noted Aboriginal cricketer Harry Hewitt was killed by another Ngarrindjeri man in a fight in 1907.[36] Following Hewitt's death, Ngarrindjeri, observing Law, ritually avoided the site. Although now a predominately settler town, Milang takes its name from the Ngarrindjeri word *milangk*, 'place of sorcery'.

---

31 Hughes 2013c; Jenkin 1979.
32 Hilda Wilson, pers. comm., 2002; Hughes 2013c.
33 See Hughes 2009.
34 Adelaide's daily newspaper.
35 Kartinyeri and Anderson 2007: 91, 97.
36 Hewitt, a Boandik man, was married to Mary Unaipon, sister of David Unaipon. The Unaipons and Hilda Wilson's family are both descended from Pulame.

Aunty Hilda began to read aloud a passage from the article. It referred to the presence of a ghost, on which the women's attention sharply focused. 'They should *know*!' Hilda proclaimed with an uncharacteristic sternness, ignoring my presence and speaking principally to the other elders. Her tone signalled the significance of the information as important *business*. 'That means they *aren't meant to be there*,' she concluded firmly.

Aunty Daisy and Aunty Emily paid close attention to Aunty Hilda's pronouncement, nodding in solemn agreement. A particularly important aspect of such reflection comes from the knowledge gained through one's *miwi* during this process. *Miwi* for Ngarrindjeri is 'the inner spirit', which is one's sixth sense, and through which important knowledge is gained or verified.[37]

I later discovered, during fieldwork at Milang, that the property that Aunty Hilda referred to subsequently sold, but that the ensuing commercial venture failed, with illness and divorce simultaneously affecting its new owners within an exceptionally short period. The building itself remained vacant for a long while afterward in what we are reminded was, is and, for Ngarrindjeri, will continue to be (among many other things), a powerful place of sorcery, energised and governed by Dreaming Laws of the Kaldowinyeri (and the lineages connected to these), through which deep time can be experienced as an active force in interactive continuum with the present. Exerting care over country, Aunty Hilda, as the senior-most elder with a direct lineage to this part of Lake Alexandrina, brought a different sense of time, relationality and analysis of the elements that shaped history and behaviour there.[38]

This collision at the border of differing worldviews reveals how a Law that is violated or disregarded, knowingly or not, can result in formerly healthy places transforming into sickness country, even in places that, like Milang, have been perceived as 'settled' for a century and a half. The imposition of alternate ways of being and understanding arising from the recent European settlement appears as a thin veneer over the enduring Ngarrindjeri world. Sansom notes that when Dreamings intervene in the everyday, the 'message proceeds from a concealed and "inside" place of essential verities into the "outside" space of contingencies and surface appearances that are inherently deceptive'.[39] Here, the manifestation of the ghost marks the outward appearance of the property as 'inherently deceptive', alerting to the probability of danger and unfinished business that needs to be appropriately addressed.[40]

---

37 See Bell 1998: 218–225; Hughes and Trevorrow 2014: 178–180.
38 For an insightful analysis of haunted places in Australia across cultural boundaries see Read 2003.
39 Sansom 2001: 2.
40 Gelder and Jacobs 1999: 179–199.

Hilda Wilson's distinctive reading of this sign of significance in her country throws into sharp relief the ways in which, in places that appear outwardly colonised, Indigenous readings of place and time actively co-exist with what westerners might conceive therein as 'past' and 'present'. It reinforces understanding of the multiple ways in which – through an 'irruption of Dreaming' – deep time punctures the present across the Australian continent. Hilda Wilson's story, too, serves to emphasise the governance system of elders, through the potency and continuity of cultural practice.

Conversations with George – Aunty Inez Jean Birt (1911–2005)

The fourth and final story is from Aunty (Inez) Jean Birt (née Rankine) who, like Aunty Hilda, is descended from Pulame, the Ngarrindjeri *rupulle,* and his granddaughter, the Ngarrindjeri matriarch, Ellen Sumner. Jean is the daughter of Ellen Sumner's son George Rankine (1875–1957) and his non-Aboriginal wife Eva Mugg, who enjoyed a happy and successful inter-cultural marriage, despite the Mugg family's opposition.[41] Jean was born in Adelaide in 1911, the same year as Aunty Hilda, and raised outside Country in the Adelaide seaside suburb of Glenelg. Yet her story is just as firmly rooted in her traditional (Ngarrindjeri) homelands as those of the previous women. When I met Jean in 2002 she was living in an aged-care facility in Adelaide. She described herself emphatically as being 'from the Lake'.[42] She was also privy to many of Lake Alexandrina's stories of *ngatjis* (totems, or to use Hilda Wilson's translation, *close relations*), traditional basket-weaving, the mid-nineteenth and early twentieth-century Ngarrindjeri camps at Milangk and the 'little people' that her father spoke of. These stories had been passed orally through her paternal lineage, especially from the grandmother she shares with Hilda Wilson, her father's mother Tumpoweri (Ellen Sumner), despite Jean being raised in Adelaide.

Because of her direct embodied connection with her family's colonial and pre-colonial past, meeting Aunty Jean Birt gave me a feeling of time-travelling. I had the privilege of travelling to Lake Alexandrina with Jean when she was 91. When we stopped near the Milang jetty, where her father was born in 1875 and where her grandmother traded fish with the white townsfolk, Aunty Jean got out of the car and confidently walked to the water's edge on her frame. She knew this was where wurlies once stretched along the foreshore and is the site of the old ceremonial ground. She turned to face the Lake, calling up the Country. There

41   Jenkin 1979: 207–209, 229, 257–258; Jean Birt, pers. comm., 2002.
42   Jean Birt, pers. comm., 2002.

she began to directly address her father as if he were physically present, calling out his name at the place he was born a century and a quarter earlier. She was using her voice as an instrument to 'open up' Country and usher in the Dreaming (Kaldowinyeri). This was a conversation across time and generations, but back in place. For Ngarrindjeri the word for body is *ruwar* and for land, *ruwi*; land is the plural of body.[43] This is reflective of this indivisible relationship that we saw also expressed in Rosalind Munur's account of the Catfish sisters.

Such a speech-event addressed to a close family member no longer living is consistent with practices of ritualised mourning and caring for Country practised by older Ngarrindjeri women and men, as well as those with whom I worked at Ngukurr. The ancestors are evoked as a mark of respect and safety. Jean Birt's potent evocation demonstrates the power of being on Country and connecting across time to those who belong to it. Her father is literally *in* the land and landscape. Through this infoldment of her presence on Country, and observing correct behaviour, she is able to fuse with him at that moment. It is interesting to note that the place this conversation occurred at is less than 150 metres from the haunted property that had independently captured Hilda Wilson's attention at around the same time. Hilda's concern and Aunty Jean's speech act are both practices that keep the visible as well as the unseen dimensions of country healthy.

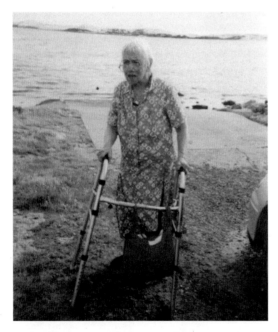

Figure 5.5: Ngarrindjeri elder Aunty Inez Jean Birt, the Coorong, South Australia, 2002.

Source: Photograph by Karen Hughes, collection of the author.

---

43   Bell 1998: 262–265.

From this brief story fragment, it is possible to chart how knowledges from the Lake travel *with* the body, and by implication how aspects of Country travel with people who are born of and belong to it. As the Ngarrindjeri historian Doreen Kartinyeri affirms, it is 'our lineage that takes us back to our land'.[44] In this way the importance of genealogies can be understood as metonymic of a process of narrative circulation across time, giving access to deep historical knowledge that is activated by being on country and through *miwi*.

Connective threads

In all these elders' stories, a deep sense of history is conferred through the mechanisms of Law, which disrupts, and calls into question, the concept of linear time and its relationship to spatiality. Sociologist Anthony Giddens defines 'time-space distanciation' (the severing of time from space) as *the* enabling feature of modernity, underpinning the construction of 'the west' and its notions of progress and rationale for colonial domination over 'others'.[45] Moreover, this temporality is reflected in linear approaches to history and narrative, which effectively erase the presence of the past from space, and from what might be termed 'place-making'.

The women demonstrate that the linear temporality of colonial displacement, assumed to be achieved from the policies that removed Indigenous people from their country as well as often from their kin, is in fact occluded by the living presence of elders and their knowledge. Country and people are interchangeable and indivisible, and the Dreaming is party to this relationship. 'The Dreaming inheres in all things and partakes of all times.'[46]

Genealogies: Superhighways of deep histories and deep time

One important way in which narrative sequences travel in all of these women's stories is through the connective spaces of genealogies, expressed in the reflexive relationship between body and country. This nexus is fundamental to Ngarrindjeri as well as to most other Indigenous Australian people's formulations

---

44   Kartinyeri in Bell 1998: 232.
45   Giddens 1990.
46   Stanner 2009 [1966], cited in Sansom 2001: 2.

of identity.[47] Thus genealogies provide highly complex renderings of land, culture and narrative disclosed via memory through the medium of the bodies and voices of the ancestors.

The active persistence of deep time, as embodied in the women's storytelling practices and as a charged underlying force outside colonial systems, is a potent dimension and expression of Aboriginal sovereignty and is purposely used in this way. A combination of carefully chosen dramatic moments and reflexive engagement stitches together teller, listener and narrative, amplifying the lessons of events from the past into the present, widening their sphere of influence. The stories served an educative function as a conduit of complex understanding between cultures, and exhibit an authoritative quality of skilful performance. Deep histories are thus radically decolonising. Used together with spatiality as a dispossessing agent, they resist temporality.

Conclusion: Rethinking historiography

In such diverse places as Adelaide and its regions and remote places within Arnhem Land, individual storytellers purposely deploy representations of deep time as a pedagogy that serves a range of explicit cultural and political purposes. They work to 'undo the prevalent misconception that Aboriginal belief was posited on the notion of a finished universe fashioned by creator Powers who retired into inaction once the age of primary genesis was done'.[48] They are stories that affirm an ontological sovereignty and governance in that they reassert a deeper history in which the Dreaming reshapes worlds ruptured by colonial intrusion and defined by narrow notions of linear time.

I am always astounded by the way it is possible to touch the deep past in the present, and it is this that has largely inspired me as a historian of Aboriginal history and the contact zone. For Indigenous people, they signal the continuum of an ever-present reality which affirms another way of being in contemporary Australia that pulses in parallel with the 'colonised' world. In this way, performative moments such as these assert a continuity of Aboriginal sovereignty and governance.

---

47 Bell 1998: 263. Knowledge of country can be thought of as inscribed on the body, and is expressed or transferred in the connective spaces that link the relationships of a person's genealogy. Despite perhaps multiple dispossessions, aspects of 'country' are still able to travel with the body, with people.
48 Sansom 2001: 2.

Bibliography

Arbon, Veronica 2007, 'Thirnda ngurkarnda ityrnda: Ontologies in Indigenous Tertiary Education', PhD thesis, Deakin University, Victoria.

Bauman, Toni and Diane Bell 1982, *Cox River (Alawa-Ngandji) Land Claim: Women's Interests*, Northern Land Council, Darwin.

Bell, Diane 1998, *Ngarrindjeri Wurruwarrin*, Spinifex, Melbourne.

Bell, Diane 2002, *Daughters of the Dreaming*, Spinifex, Melbourne.

Capell, Arthur 1960, 'The Wandarang and other tribal myths of the Yabuduruwa ritual', *Oceania* 30: 206–224.

Collins, Patricia Hill 1991, 'Learning from the outsider within: the sociological significance of black feminist thought', *Social Problems* 33(6): 14–32.

Elkin, Adolphus Peter 1972, *Two Rituals in South and Central Arnhem Land*, Oceania Monograph 19, Sydney.

Garadji, Dinah 1982, *Nakaran, the Giant*, Bamyili Press, Barunga.

Gelder, Ken and Jane M Jacobs 1996, 'The postcolonial ghost story', *Journal of the Association for the Study of Australian Literature*, 110–120.

Ken Gelder and Jane Jacobs 1999, 'The postcolonial ghost story', in Peter Buse and Andrew Stott (eds), *Ghosts: Deconstruction, Psychoanalysis, History*, St Martin's Press Inc, New York, 179–199.

Giddens, Anthony 1990, *The Consequences of Modernity*, John Wiley & Sons, Cambridge.

Harris, John 1998, *We Wish We'd Done More: Ninety Years of CMS and Aboriginal Issues in North Australia*, Openbook, Adelaide.

Hokari, Minoru 2011, *Gurindji Journey: A Japanese Historian in the Outback*, University of New South Wales Press, Sydney.

Hughes, Karen 1986, *Pitjiri: The Snake That Will Not Sink*, Ronin Films, Canberra, DVD re-release 2008.

Hughes, Karen 2005, 'Same bodies, different skin: Ruth Heathcock', in Anna Cole, Victoria Haskins and Fiona Paisley (eds), *Uncommon Ground: White Women in Aboriginal History*, Aboriginal Studies Press, Canberra, 83–106.

Hughes, Karen 2009, 'My Grandmother on the Other Side of the Lake', PhD thesis, Department of History and Department of Australian Studies, Flinders University.

Hughes, Karen 2010, 'Fluid waters: cultural exchange in the land of the Ngarrindjeri, a poetics and a politics', *Le Simplegadi* 8(8): 24–35.

Hughes, Karen 2012, 'Microhistories and things that matter: opening spaces of possibility', *Australian Feminist Studies* 27(73): 269–278.

Hughes, Karen 2013a, 'Becoming Rosalind's Daughter: Reflections on intercultural kinship and embodied histories', in Vicki Grieves (ed.), *Indigenous Marriage, Family and Kinship in Australia, Aotearoa New Zealand and the Pacific: the Persistence of Life and Hope in Colonial and Neo-Colonial Context*. Special Issue of *Journal of the European Association for Studies of Australia* 4(1): 76–91.

Hughes, Karen 2013b, '"I'd grown up as a child amongst natives": Ruth Heathcock', *Outskirts: Feminisms along the Edge* 28, www.outskirts.arts.uwa.edu.au/volumes/volume-28/karen-hughes (accessed 10 April 2015).

Hughes, Karen 2013c, 'Resilience, agency and resistance in the storytelling practice of Aunty Hilda Wilson (1911–2007), Ngarrindjeri Aboriginal elder', *Media-Culture Journal* 16(5), journal.media-culture.org.au/index.php/mcjournal/article/viewArticle/714 (accessed 12 January 2014).

Hughes, Karen and Ellen Trevorrow 2014, 'It's that reflection: photography as recuperative practice, a Ngarrindjeri perspective', in Jane Lydon (ed.), *Calling the Shots: Aboriginal Photographies*, Aboriginal Studies Press, Canberra, 175–204.

Jenkin, Graham 1979, *Conquest of the Ngarringjeri*, Rigby, Adelaide.

Kartinyeri, Doreen and Sue Anderson 2007, *My Ngarrindjeri Calling*, Wakefield, Adelaide.

Kearney, Amanda Joanne 2009, *Before the Old People and Still Today: An Ehtnoarchaeology of Yanyuwa Places and Narratives of Engagement*, Australian Scholarly Publishing, North Melbourne, Victoria.

Lockwood, Douglas 1962, *I the Aboriginal*, Rigby, Adelaide.

Moreton-Robinson, Aileen 2000, *Talkin' Up to the White Woman*, University of Queensland Press, St Lucia.

National Museum of Australia, 'Phillip Roberts', *Collaborating for Indigenous Rights,* indigenousrights.net.au/people/pagination/phillip_roberts (accessed 10 April 2015).

Read, Peter 2003, *Haunted Earth*, NewSouth Publishing, Sydney.

Rose, Debra 1998, 'Consciousness and responsibility in an Australian Aboriginal religion', in William Howell Edwards (ed.), *Traditional Aboriginal Society*, Macmillan, Sydney, 257–269.

Sansom, Basil 2001, 'Irruptions of the dreamings in post-colonial Australia', *Oceania* 72(1): 1–28.

Stanner, William Edward Hanley 2009 [1966], 'The Dreaming', in *The Dreaming and Other Essays*, Black Inc, Melbourne, 59–73.

Thomson, Donald 1983, *Donald Thomson in Arnhem Land*, O'Neil, South Yarra.

Westphalen, Linda 2011, *An Anthropological and Literary Study of Two Aboriginal Women's Life Histories: The Impacts of Enforced Child Removal and Policies of Assimilation*, Edwin Mellen Press, New York.

6. Categories of 'Old' and 'New' in Western Arnhem Land Bark Painting

Luke Taylor

Introduction

This chapter compares two instances of development in the market for bark painting in western Arnhem Land at the towns of Oenpelli (Kunbarlanya) and Maningrida, east of Kakadu National Park in the Northern Territory. The intention is to compare the impacts of the agency of art collectors with that of the artists on the developing market for bark paintings, including a consideration of the entanglements of art creation and its respective intellectual frames in intercultural circumstances. In particular, I examine the effects of western categories used to define the bark paintings and how this in turn shapes the translation of their meaning in different periods. In addition, western curatorial perspectives of the art have influenced the expectations of the market and thus the trajectory of market development in each locale.

Theoretical conversations of the western art world often play out with little regard for the non-western artist's perspective. Western concepts of 'fine art' obscure the fact that non-western artists have a strong understanding of the historical circumstances of their art production, of what the works mean in the context of their ever-increasing engagements with the market, while possessing local theories of aesthetic value. Art history and anthropology as western disciplines of thought are now required to be reflective of their own categories, and to acknowledge the existence of a multiplicity of alternate histories of arts in the world context.

Spencer at Oenpelli

Baldwin Spencer travelled to Oenpelli in 1912 and his collection of bark paintings, made with the help of Paddy Cahill, brought this art to world prominence.[1] Spencer worked with Kakadu-speaking artists and with a group called the Kulunglutji from further east, who are most likely to have been

---

1   Spencer 1914, 1928. See also Mulvaney 1985, 2004.

Kunwinjku-speaking people. After Spencer was in touch with them, they moved to settle in Oenpelli. A Professor of Biology at Melbourne University and Honorary Director of the National Museum of Victoria,[2] Spencer was supported by the Commonwealth Government to conduct fieldwork in the Northern Territory as Special Commissioner and Chief Protector of Aborigines and to report on their needs. To this end, he conducted fact-finding visits across the Northern Territory as well as extended visits to a number of communities to conduct ethnographic fieldwork and make collections of material culture. At the time of his visit, Oenpelli was a pastoral enterprise run by Paddy Cahill, whose relationships with local groups greatly facilitated Spencer's research. Spencer collected around 50 bark paintings at Oenpelli in 1912. Cahill worked as intermediary, sending another 110 artworks to Melbourne between 1912 and 1920. The bark paintings, along with a major collection of magnificent basketry, ceremonial objects and personal adornment, were eventually donated to the National Museum of Victoria.

Trained in England in social evolutionary theory, Spencer was a key field researcher in Australia who worked closely with mentors in England who assisted in the rapid publication of his work.[3] Social theorists such as EB Tylor and James George Fraser praised his work, undertaken in association with local compatriot, the postmaster, Frank Gillen. Spencer and Gillen's publication *The Native Tribes of Central Australia* was facilitated by Fraser and found an eager world audience.

In the social evolutionary models promulgated by these researchers, there were three stages to the ascent of man: 'savagery' to 'barbarism' to 'civilisation' (an intentional echo of the 'stone age', 'bronze age', 'iron age' stages of Europe discussed in the chapter by Harry Allen). In this schema, Australian Aborigines were at the lowest rung. The view was that by conducting field research in Australia, researchers were effectively 'stepping back in time' to research the origins of Europeans. Such theorists of human development considered Aborigines to be bereft of religion and viewed their material culture as only fractionally distinct from unworked natural materials.

Through his research in central Australia, Spencer developed a particular theory that Aborigines were people possessed of magic in a pre-religious state.[4] He concluded that the elaborate ceremonies that he witnessed in central Australia were directed at the magical increase of food animals. Similarly, when Spencer encountered the spectacular rock art and bark painting of the

---

2   By proclamation of the *Museums Act 1983* (Vic), the National Museum of Victoria and the Industrial and Technological Museum of Victoria (later known as the Science Museum of Victoria) were amalgamated to form what is currently known as Museum Victoria.

3   Mulvaney 1981: 62.

4   Mulvaney 1981: 62.

Oenpelli region, he interpreted them as an expression of this concern for food.[5] For example, he understood the x-ray detailing of the pictures as related to the hunter's knowledge of food cuts that are good to eat (see Figure 6.1).

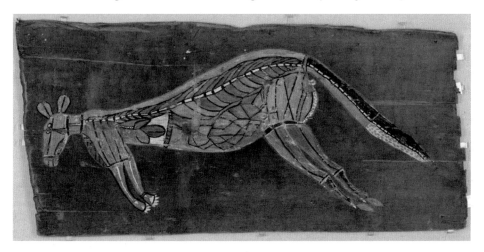

Figure 6.1: A kangaroo painted in x-ray style, Gaagudju people, western Arnhem Land, 1994.
Source: Paddy Cahill Collection, reproduced courtesy Museum Victoria (x19917).

He interpreted the major Muraian (Mardayin) and Ober (Wubarr) ceremonies that he witnessed as primarily ensuring the supply of food species through magical means.[6]

In his 1914 publication *The Native Tribes of the Northern Territory*, there is very little information about the process Spencer used to collect the bark paintings. Rather, the rock art of Oenpelli is introduced in the chapter entitled 'decorative art', despite the fact that the chapter text refers to the stories for bark paintings without explanation of their connection to the rock art.[7] One might speculate that publication of the details of his collecting activity were not included in his work as they would have undermined the momentousness of his publication as a revelation of the most 'primitive' art in the world – supposedly untouched by the western world. Yet, Spencer provides illustrations and an interpretation for 15 bark paintings in this publication, concluding that these works represent the 'highest artistic level' among Australian Aboriginals.[8]

---

5   Spencer 1928: 810.
6   Spencer 1914: 187–188.
7   Spencer 1914: 432–433.
8   Spencer 1914: 439.

In respect to the barks, Spencer's focus was their link backwards in time to the Stone Age tradition of rock art. In this scheme, there is no need to document names of artists. Historian and curator Philip Jones has speculated that this is because Spencer saw the paintings as reiterative, the product of a timeless tradition.[9] As Spencer was looking beyond the present to the past, his material culture collection was meant to be an exemplar of traditional life prior to the cultural loss or contamination that resulted from the cultural contact associated with settlement. He believed that the Kakadu were destined for inevitable cultural decline as the result of colonisation, and explicitly stated this was his reason for collecting some of the most sacred artefacts that the Kakadu possessed.[10] Ethnographer James Clifford has identified this point in respect to the 'primitive art' market that was developing at the same time in America and Europe. As tribal life was considered to be doomed in the face of contact with a superior modernism, researchers and western collectors positioned themselves as the experts who could identify and redeem the value of 'uncontaminated' pieces.[11] The unfortunate irony is that non-western groups were damned by the fact of their very engagement with this market, since making works for sale within the market economy implied a break from 'tradition' and thus a contamination.

In a later publication, *Wanderings in Wild Australia* (1928), Spencer is more revealing of his methods of collecting the bark paintings, and was able to publish an additional two illustrations. He noted that he first saw the art in the bark shelters at Oenpelli and he collected a number by cutting down these shelters.[12] Later he asked three of the best artists to produce works for him on portable pieces of bark of any subject they chose. He originally paid tobacco and later cash for these commissioned works.

In this publication, Spencer was more forthcoming about his personal response to the work and comments about its aesthetic excellence. He noted that his views echoed the considerations of the artist's group:

> To-day I found a native who, apparently, had nothing better to do than sit quietly in camp, evidently enjoying himself, drawing a fish on a piece of stringy-bark about two feet long and a foot broad. His painting materials were white pipe clay and two shades of red ochre, the lighter made by mixing white pipe clay with the pure ochre, and a primitive but quite effective paint brush, made out of a short stick, six or eight inches long, frayed out with his teeth and then pressed out so as to form a little disc,

---

9   Jones 2011: 32.
10 Spencer 1914: 227; Spencer 1928: 839.
11 Clifford 1988: 189–214.
12 Spencer 1928: 792–794.

shaped like a minute, old-fashioned, chimney sweep's brush. This was most effective and he held it just like a civilised artist sometimes holds his brush or pencil, with the handle between the thumb, then crossing the palm and out below the little finger, so all four finger tips rested on it, or sometimes it passed out of the hand above the little finger. Held in this way he did line work, often very fine and regular, with very much the same freedom and precision as a Japanese or Chinese artist doing his more beautiful wash-work with his brush.[13]

Statements about the marvellous facility of the artists, the beauty of the work, and comparisons between local people's artistic judgement and Spencer's own are peppered throughout this publication, suggesting an interest in aesthetic universals. Yet, he concludes that the works were ultimately 'crude'.[14]

Although Spencer's own field records sowed the seeds for the demise of evolutionism, the historian John Mulvaney records that Spencer held to his theories of social evolution to the day he died.[15] The publications fuelled a fascination for this 'primitive art', and subsequent collectors were keen to obtain collections on the Spencer model. Even in the 1960s, researchers such as Mountford and Kupka were describing their similar collections as documenting the 'dawn' of art. At the same time, as Mulvaney notes, Spencer's theories of magical totemism were drawn into interpretations of European Palaeolithic cave art.[16] In writing about Spencer's theories and the impact of World War One on his scholarship, anthropologist Howard Morphy suggests that Spencer's ideas regarding a universal aesthetic, if developed, would have critiqued hierarchical views of Aboriginal art. Nonetheless, Spencer did not develop this critique in his lifetime.[17] It was left to others, such as Franz Boas in America in 1927, to develop the models of 'cultural relativism' that broke down the evolutionary scheme.[18]

. The continued existence of this collection in Museum Victoria makes it possible to analyse these works to shed light on the agency of the artists. Spencer records that, through the assistance of Cahill, the Kakadu with whom he worked were keen to assist his research and in particular to promulgate the importance of their culture and beliefs.[19] On this basis, in 1912, he was able to access secret Mardayin ceremonies and negotiated the purchase of sacred carved wooden sculptures from these ceremonies, among many other items of material culture.

---

13 Spencer 1928: 792–793.
14 Spencer 1928: 809.
15 Mulvaney 1981: 62.
16 Mountford 1956; May 2010: 104; Kupka 1965; Mulvaney 1981: 62.
17 Morphy 2013: 167.
18 Morphy 2008: 178.
19 Spencer 1928: 839.

Spencer was also told the ancestral precedent for these ceremonies and the key stories of creation concerning Imberombera, Wuraka, Numereji, and Jeru Ober, along with their creation journeys. When reviewing the full list of paintings held at Museum Victoria collected before 1920, a number of these very important subjects feature in the paintings, suggesting a systematic response by the artists over the 1912–1920 period to Spencer's research.

The leader of the Wubarr, Nadulmi, or *Macropus Bernardus*, and of the Kunabibi, the Rainbow Serpent, Ngalyod, feature in the paintings. Turkey, brolga and yam are all mentioned as Mardayin ceremonial beings. Murnubbarr, or Magpie Goose, is a local Dreaming at Oenpelli and, while Spencer did not record the names of the artists in relation to each work, we know that one named artist that he commissioned, Nipper Kumutun, was the local landowner.[20]

Anthropologist Ronald Berndt recorded the desire of Aboriginal people in central Arnhem Land to share knowledge about ceremonial matters as a means of transforming their relationship with white administrators.[21] Where non-Aboriginal people have an interest, their induction to the meaning and value of ceremonial matters is an important avenue to the appreciation of the religious fabric of Aboriginal life. Writers such as Howard Morphy, Jenny Deger and Franca Tamisari in the Arnhem Land context have elaborated this argument, revealing how Aboriginal people are politically motivated and strategic in the way they bring whites to an understanding of their religious values.[22] Participation in the aesthetic experience of ceremony, and associated arts, binds non-Aboriginal people into a sacred contract and appreciation of the power that emanates from ancestral places and artefacts. Similarly, artists say that, beyond the generation of cash income, they participate in the market as a way of teaching audiences about the importance of their culture.[23] The beauty of the works, the aesthetic power of the works, make it possible to influence successive generations of Australians by virtue of their acquisition and use. The beautiful and important subjects in Spencer's barks, combined with his recording of the ceremonies in which these ancestors are venerated, allows us to see the artists' attempt to educate at least two influential white men, Spencer and Cahill, on topics of great import.

X-ray detailing is common in these works, and so too is a variant where the internal decoration is more highly stylised and geometric (see Figure 6.2).

20 May 2010: 170.
21 Berndt 1962.
22 Morphy 1983; Deger 2006; Tamisari 2005.
23 Taylor 1996, 2008.

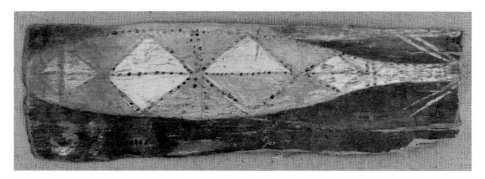

Figure 6.2: A yam painted with diamond patterns, Oenpelli, western Arnhem Land, 1994.

Source: Paddy Cahill Collection, reproduced courtesy Museum Victoria (x26345).

Spencer might well have commented on the similarity of such designs to paintings used in the Mardayin ceremony, and indeed to be found on the objects he collected from that ceremony, but he did not. His focus upon the magical involvement of art in the food quest obscured his understanding of other levels of meaning.[24]

One bark in Spencer's collection that he did not publish represents a buffalo (see Figure 6.3).

Figure 6.3: A buffalo painted in x-ray style, Gaagudju people, western Arnhem Land, 1994.

Source: Paddy Cahill Collection, reproduced courtesy Museum Victoria (x20034).

24　Taylor 1996.

The buffalo was hugely important in the Aboriginal and settler economy of this region at the turn of the nineteenth century. Cahill had originally come to the area as a buffalo shooter, and many local Aboriginal people worked in hunting, processing and the selling of hides and buffalo meat, all of which were extremely important in the kin-based economy. Similarly, there is a lively record of contact history represented in the rock art that Spencer does not mention. Presumably, the publication of such evidence of contact history would have contaminated the 'primitive' status of the artists and the glimpse of the 'Stone Age' that he aims to provide in the collection. Spencer was looking past these historical people to imagine their past, and further, the primeval European past.

Yet, to this day, the barks reveal an infectious enthusiasm for present-day subjects, with brilliant patterning and complex compositions often quite unlike the rock painting genres. Rather than a baseline of traditional Aboriginal practice before contact, it is more appropriate to interpret these works as revealing excitement at the prospect of intercultural communication in a new mode of interaction. Thousands of tourists now travel to Kakadu in part to see the art that Spencer identified. Unfortunately, the unproductive trope of this art being a window to the Stone Age recurs in the region to this day.

Post-modernism at Maningrida?

The second example I wish to address is the reception of the bark paintings of John Mawurndjul, a Kuninjku-speaking artist from the Maningrida region, who rose to critical acclaim in the 1980s. Mawurndjul now has an established international reputation as a 'contemporary' artist. Increasing use of the term contemporary is explicitly intended to counter the primitive/modern binary that attached to the appreciation of Aboriginal art as 'primitive fine art' in Australia's galleries and museums until the early 1980s. Ian McClean has examined the history behind the introduction of the term and noted that Aboriginal activism was central in its insertion into Australian art marketing.[25] While the term was originally used to refer to central desert artists working in acrylic paint on canvas, it required specific activism from individuals based in Arnhem Land to ensure that bark painters using ochres and tree bark were included in the contemporary category.

McLean shows that discussions about whether the term contemporary artist could be used in respect to Aboriginal and Torres Strait Islander artists were intense in the early years of the 1980s.[26] Curator Bernice Murphy's inclusion

25 McLean 2011.
26 McLean 2011: 50–55.

in 1981 of large Papunya canvases in the *Perspecta 81* exhibition at the Art Gallery of New South Wales prompted strong reactions, particularly from post-modernists who argued that this represented a return to incorporation of Aboriginal art in Australian exhibitions as an exotic primitivism. Arguments against the inclusion of Aboriginal art on this basis ran particularly in the *Art and Text* magazine.[27] Authors such as Imants Tillers argued against the proclaimed links between Aboriginal and other Australian contemporary art on the basis of very thin conceptions of shared interest in abstraction and connections to land.[28] In post-modernist theory, a key wellspring of art is the appropriation of imagery that circulates through time and across the globe by means of mass media. This was considered just as true for Aboriginal artists living in settler society, who must now be acknowledged as having moved beyond their 'tradition'. It was no longer possible to have Aboriginal art displayed as a separate, and somehow more authentic, Australian art. Anthropologists were accused of promoting Aboriginal art on the basis of essentialisms that belied the intercultural circumstance of contemporary Aboriginal life.[29]

However, with greater understanding of the creativity involved in Aboriginal artists modifying ceremonial imagery in order to develop art for the market, the position of some post-modern theorists began to soften.[30] Some theorised that Aboriginal arts shared something of the irony and conceptualism of other contemporary western artists, especially given their erasure of traditional sacred symbolism deemed too secret for public consumption.[31] Eric Michaels who had worked with Warlpiri artists suggested that the use of new materials and motifs represented sophisticated appropriations by Aboriginal artists from the ubiquitous media of western art.[32] Thus central desert art, which so obviously borrowed the new media of acrylic paint on canvas, and was being exploited by artists in ways that diverged from ceremonial forms, was eventually elevated to contemporary status. These new forms were interpreted as representing a post-modern rupture with tradition. In the lead up to the Australian Bicentenary of British settlement in 1988, central desert acrylics were increasingly included in major surveys of Aboriginal and Australian contemporary art, as well as travelling international exhibitions, with commercial success secured from this point.[33]

---

27 McLean 2011: 51.
28 Tillers 1982.
29 Michaels 1994.
30 McLean 2011: 52–53.
31 McLean 2011: 52; Tillers 1983.
32 Michaels 1989: 29.
33 Myers 2002.

At Maningrida, there was a strong belief that bark painters should not be left out of the contemporary art market simply because of the materials used in the construction of the works. While not using canvas and acrylic paint, many bark painters worked at painting full time and were keen to access exhibitions in fine art locales. They insisted that their art was at least as good as other Australian artists. Local arts advisers promoted the inventiveness of such painters.

From the early 1980s at Maningrida, the arts advisers Djon Mundine and Diane Moon were very keen that John Mawurndjul received recognition for his extraordinary works. Significantly, Mundine advised the Art Gallery of New South Wales on an exhibition of bark paintings in 1981, the same year that Murphy included desert works in the *Perspecta* exhibition.[34] Mundine later became a 'curator at large' for that organisation. Diane Moon, Mundine's partner, became the arts adviser at Maningrida in 1985.[35] Both advisers had close relations with Maningrida, Ramingining and Milingimbi-based artists, and with commercial galleries and curators at the Art Gallery of New South Wales, the National Gallery of Australia and the Museum of Contemporary Art Australia newly established in Sydney. All these institutions began collecting Mawurndjul's art in the latter half of the 1980s. Mawurndjul was able to travel to the opening of the new National Gallery of Australia in 1983 and to visit the major collections held in their stores.[36] Later a 1988 work 'Nawarramulmul, shooting star spirit' by Mawurndjul from the collection of the Museum of Contemporary Art Australia was chosen for the Aratjara exhibition catalogue, which was specifically designed to introduce the contemporary nature of Aboriginal art in Europe in 1993.[37] Moon and Mawurndjul travelled to visit the European venues of this exhibition and visited a number of other major European cities to view their collections.

By 2000, Mawurndjul was included in the program of the Sydney Biennale and met with other artists from around the world, including Yoko Ono. He made public statements about the equivalence of his art with Ono's.[38] In 2003, Mawurndjul won the Clemenger Contemporary Art prize in Melbourne (see Figure 6.4). This was an award that included both Aboriginal and other Australian artists. Mawurndjul looked back on that award and his other successes as evidence that Aboriginal art and non-Aboriginal art were now considered 'level'.[39]

---

34 Mundine 2001.
35 Altman 2004: 179–181.
36 Altman 2005; Taylor 2005, 2008.
37 Luthi 1993.
38 Perkins 2003: 58–59.
39 Mawurndjul 2005: 137.

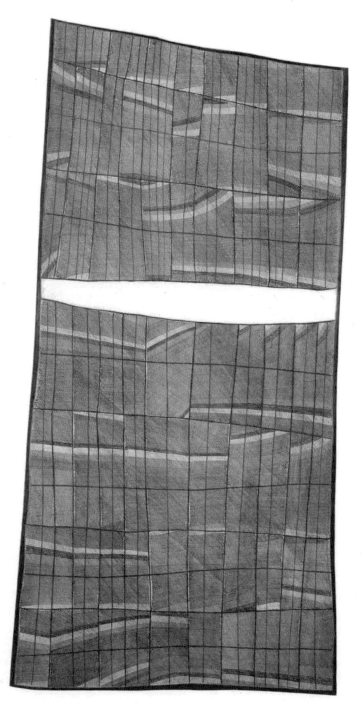

Figure 6.4: John Mawurndjul *Mardayin at Kudjarnngal*, 2003.

Source: © John Mawurndjul/Licensed by Viscopy, 2013.

In earlier years, Mawurndjul's inclusion in the contemporary art arena was based upon application of a formalist aesthetic rather than strong understanding of his trajectory as a Kuninjku artist. Morphy has noted that the entry of Aboriginal art into the fine art realm of Australian art galleries has, to a large extent, been theorised on the basis of a putative 'disinterested aesthetic' that emphasised a response to 'pure' form as against a more culturally informed aesthetic.[40] Mawurndjul's bark paintings in the 1980s were highly inventive, with figurative forms. Ultimately, he settled for painting more geometric works that he said derived from the Mardayin ceremony. In these latter works, in like manner to the desert artists, part of Mawurndjul's experimentation derives from trying to find a means of producing works for the market that avoid the release of sacred ceremonial designs.[41] Mawurndjul spoke readily of this experimentation, which could be too easily interpreted as a desire to create a rupture with notions of 'tradition'. Galleries received Mawurndjul's art as a contemporary and individual production, not purely as culturally or communally framed. Rather than attempting to understand his cultural background – which transformed interpretation into anthropology – his work was treated as 'contemporary fine art' and as such the pure visual experimentation and energy of his work was discerned and his individualistic genius subsequently lauded.

Nonetheless, the themes of figure transformation and use of geometric designs that Mawurndjul explores have a long history in western Arnhem Land, and indeed can be discerned in works collected by Spencer 100 years ago.

Reflecting upon his art practice, Mawurndjul explained:

> When I was a teenager I saw Yirawala and other old people [deceased artists]. I am familiar with their work and learned from them. I have put their knowledge and images in my mind. I also know their paintings on rock too, like the ones by my uncle [Peter Marralwanga] who also taught me to paint rarrk. We have a lot of bim [rock art] in my country. I often visit these places. Later on in my life, when I have been travelling I saw their paintings in museums; paintings from artists like Midjawmidjaw, Yirawala and Paddy Compass. I have placed this knowledge into my head. They only used solid patterns of colours and lines of black, yellow and red. We young people [new generation] have changed to using rarrk. White, yellow, red, black, that's what we use in the crosshatching.[42]

---

40   Morphy 2008.
41   Taylor 2008.
42   Mawurndjul 2005: 25.

This is not an ironic commentary on being rootless in a post-modern world. Rather, Mawurndjul speaks of his connection to the past and the changes to art that he engineers in the present. In fact, he is speaking to his own local art history and beyond this, to his understanding of the original ancestral creativity which made his world. He touches on his own innovative role only within this broader context.

The risk in using the term 'contemporary' in the post-modern theoretical sense is that tradition is forgotten in a focus upon the new. What becomes blinkered from view is the explicit link with the historical and ancestral past and with core spiritual ideas regarding Kuninjku attachments to country. The focus on innovation, the influence or borrowing from external sources, on individualism, and the formal qualities of the paintings, divorces Mawurndjul's art from its grounding in his belief in the primacy of the ancestral realm.

We need to understand how Mawurndjul himself learnt to paint and his knowledge of the art of his kin. Indeed he can now access the works of earlier generations of Kuninjku in institutions throughout the world. In turn, it is important to understand Mawurndjul's own role in respect to others that he now teaches – his wife Kaye Lindjuwanga, sons and daughters, and many others of his extended family.

There is a strong local understanding of the trajectory of Kuninjku art that should inform broader world appreciation. This was the intention behind the <<rarrk>> retrospective exhibition of Mawurndjul's art held at the Tinguely Museum of Contemporary Art in Basel in 2005.[43] The European curator who initiated the concept, Bernhard Luthi, was concerned with developing an exhibition that would stimulate thinking about the issue of world arts in a locale where barriers between ethnographic arts and western fine arts were still firmly set.[44] The exhibition comprised a retrospective of Mawurndjul's work, film screenings, a major publication and a two-day curatorial symposium. Luthi explained that he was inspired by seeing Mawurndjul's 1988 work 'Nawarramulmul, shooting star spirit' displayed next to that of a Jean Tinguely sculpture in Sydney's Museum of Contemporary Art collection catalogue. It was vitally important that the exhibition was held in this contemporary art gallery and not the ethnographic museum in the same city. To date, no major Australian gallery has attempted a similar exercise with Mawurndjul's work. Demonstrating the contemporary aspects of bark painting is a relatively more complex exercise in respect to Australian audiences that currently focus upon central Australian Aboriginal artists' experiments in colour and form in the acrylic medium. Bark painters are burdened by shallow perceptions linking the

43   Kaufmann 2005: 22.
44   Kaufmann 2005: 22.

contemporary with the use of new materials, whilst new uses of old materials and the more subtle intricacies of development within local art histories do not yet register strongly within art institutions and among the broader public.

This art would be more usefully considered contemporary in the sense that there are a multitude of developments around the world that are running in parallel that may or may not contribute to some notion of a western avant garde. Morphy has written on the need to acknowledge the multiplicity of local artistic trajectories and not to simply assimilate various examples into the category of 'fine art' as institutionally defined.[45] Local art histories are required to be contextualised appropriately in time and space. This requires anthropologists to address the issue of form and style of the art in terms of both the artist's intention regarding aesthetic effect and the production of meaning. In order to produce more nuanced histories that address local conceptions, art historians will be required to conduct fieldwork with the artists, as well as work with collections and personnel in galleries.

Conclusion

The examples in this chapter demonstrate the effects of theoretical frames in the reception of Aboriginal art and how the activity of the artists has ultimately subverted those frames. Ideas regarding the importance of bark painting as primitive art persisted in academia into the 1960s, and these ideas live on in the marketing and audience reaction to such paintings to this day. In Oenpelli, an expression of this was the introduction of pre-prepared paper backgrounds as a new medium for works in 1990. This was expected to stimulate art production that more closely resembled rock painting.[46] In an interesting response, senior artists used the medium to produce highly elaborate figurative depictions of ceremonial scenes that are more detailed than anything in the later phases of the rock art. In Maningrida, on the other hand, there are strong views expressed by the market and by the artists that geometric art is more important than figurative work. In response to such views, Kuninjku artists rarely produce bark paintings other than in the 'mardayin' style instituted by Mawurndjul.

In part, this situation has been created by the Australian market interest in more abstract work based on aesthetic responses to the formal properties. However, for Kuninjku, such abstract works are considered to have power deriving from the ancestral realm, and there has been a long history of artists working to gain audience acceptance of these more culturally important forms. Through growing

---

45   Morphy 2008.
46   Taylor 2000: 109–118.

political awareness, Kuninjku artists consider that the most appropriate way of engaging with the broader world is to reveal such elements of the ancestral realm, in particular the way that ancestral powers are invested in the land.

These two communities are adjacent in Arnhem Land and the artists share extensive cultural continuities. Yet, the history of the development of the art appears divergent. The examples provide a snapshot of how interactions between the artists and researchers and collectors in each locale has been somewhat different, contributing to the stylistic distinctions between the works that are now produced. As the cross-cultural intellectual engagements involved are place and time-specific, investigating their detail provides an explanation for the differing heritage of each community. What emerges from the detail is the creative excitement of the artists for the opportunities provided by marketing this work and their inventiveness in the way they negotiate the intercultural relations involved.

Bibliography

Altman, Jon 2004, 'Brokering Kuninjku art: artists, institutions and the market', in Hetti Perkins (ed.), *Crossing Country: The Alchemy of Western Arnhem Land Art*, Art Gallery of New South Wales, Sydney, 173–187.

Altman, Jon 2005, 'From Mumeka to Basel: John Mawurndjul's artistic odyssey', in Christian Kaufmann (ed.), <<*rarrk*>> *John Mawurndjul Journey Through Time in Northern Australia*, Museum Tinguely, Basel, 30–41.

Berndt, Ronald M 1962, *An Adjustment Movement in Arnhem Land*, Mouton, Paris.

Clifford, James 1988, *The Predicament of Culture: Twentieth-century Ethnography, Literature and Art*, Harvard University Press, Cambridge, MA.

Deger, Jenny 2006, *Shimmering Screens: Making Media in an Aboriginal Community*, University of Minnesota Press, Minneapolis.

Jones, Philip 2011, 'The art of contact: encountering an Aboriginal aesthetic from the eighteenth to the twentieth centuries', in Jaynie Anderson (ed.), *The Cambridge Companion to Australian Art*, Cambridge University Press, Port Melbourne, 22–37.

Kaufmann, Christian (ed.) 2005, <<*rarrk*>> *John Mawurndjul Journey Through Time in Northern Australia*, Museum Tinguely, Basel.

Kupka, Karel 1965, *Dawn of Art: Painting and Sculpture of Australian Aborigines*, The Viking Fund, New York.

Luthi, Bernhard (ed.) 1993, *Aratjara: Art of the First Australians*, DuMont, Koln.

McLean, Ian 2011, *How Aborigines Invented the Idea of Contemporary Art*, Institute of Modern Art, Brisbane.

Mawurndjul, John 2005, 'I never stop thinking about my rarrk', in Christian Kaufmann (ed.), <<rarrk>> *John Mawurndjul Journey Through Time in Northern Australia*, Museum Tinguely, Basel, 25–29.

May, Sally K 2010, *Collecting Cultures*, Altamira Press, Lanham.

Michaels, Eric 1989, 'Postmodernism, appropriation and Western Desert acrylics', in Sue Cramer (ed.), *Postmodernism: A Consideration of the Appropriation of Aboriginal Imagery*, Institute of Modern Art, Brisbane.

Michaels, Eric 1994, 'Bad Aboriginal art', in Eric Michaels (ed.), *Bad Aboriginal Art: Tradition, Media, and Technological Horizons*, Allen and Unwin, St Leonards, New South Wales, 143–163.

Morphy, Howard 1983, '"Now you understand" – an analysis of the way Yolngu have used sacred knowledge to retain their autonomy', in Nicolas Peterson and Marcia Langton (eds), *Aborigines, Land and Land Rights*, Australian Institute of Aboriginal Studies, Canberra, 110–133.

Morphy, Howard 2008, *Becoming Art: Exploring Cross-Cultural Categories*, University of New South Wales Press, Sydney.

Morphy, Howard 2013, 'Spencer at Oenpelli', in Michelle Hetherington (ed.), *Glorious Days Australia 1913*, National Museum of Australia Press, Canberra, 159–168.

Mountford, Charles P 1956, *Art, Myth and Symbolism: Records of the American-Australian Expedition to Arnhem Land, 1948,* Vol. 1, Melbourne University Press, Melbourne.

Mulvaney, D John 1981, 'Gum leaves on the Golden Bough: Australia's palaeolithic survivals discovered', in John D Evans, Barry Cunliffe and Colin Renfrew (eds), *Antiquity and Man: Essays in Honour of Glyn Daniel,* Thames and Hudson, London, 52–64.

Mulvaney, D John 1985, *'So Much That Is New' Baldwin Spencer, 1860-1929, A Biography*, Melbourne University Press, Carlton.

Mulvaney, D John 2004, *Paddy Cahill of Oenpelli*, Aboriginal Studies Press, Canberra.

Mundine, Djon (ed.) 2001, *The Native Born: Objects and Representations From Ramingining, Arnhem Land*, Museum of Contemporary Art, Sydney.

Myers, Fred 2002, *Painting Culture: The Making of An Aboriginal High Art*, Duke University Press, Durham, NC.

Perkins, Hetti 2003, 'Parallel universe, other worlds', in Nikos Papastergiadis (ed.), *Complex Entanglements: Art, Globalisation and Cultural Difference*, Rivers ORAM Press, London, 58–59.

Spencer, Baldwin 1914, *The Native Tribes of the Northern Territory*, Macmillan, London.

Spencer, Baldwin 1928, *Wanderings in Wild Australia*, Macmillan, London.

Tamisari, Franca 2005, 'The responsibility of performance: the interweaving of politics and aesthetics in intercultural contexts', *Visual Anthropology Review* 21: 47–62.

Taylor, Luke 1996, *Seeing the Inside: Bark Painting in Western Arnhem Land*, Clarendon Press, Oxford.

Taylor, Luke 2000, 'Rock art as inspiration in western Arnhem Land', in Sylvia Kleinert and Margo Neale (eds), *The Oxford Companion to Aboriginal Art and Culture*, Oxford University Press, Melbourne, 109–118.

Taylor, Luke 2005, 'John Mawurndjul "I've got a different idea"', in Christian Kaufmann (ed.), <<rarrk>>*John Mawurndjul Journey Through Time in Northern Australia*, Museum Tinguely, Basel, 42–49.

Taylor, Luke 2008, '"They may say tourist, may say truly painting": aesthetic evaluation and meaning of bark paintings in western Arnhem Land', *Journal of the Royal Anthropological Institute* (NS) 14(4): 865–885.

Tillers, Imants 1982, 'Locality fails', *Art and Text* 6: 51–60.

Tillers, Imants 1983, 'Fear of texture', *Art and Text* 10: 8–18.

7. Dispossession is a Legitimate Experience

Peter Read

This is a legitimate Aboriginal experience to be dispossessed, to be lately impacted, to be pale-skinned, these are legitimate things.
— Shane Smithers[1]

Darug people, that is, the Aboriginal clans of Sydney's west, claim that they are entitled to the privileges and responsibilities that derive from their clear heritage of Aboriginal descent. They assert that they have always been so entitled, the more so since they formed themselves into two corporations. These are the Darug Custodians Aboriginal Corporation, and the Darug Tribal Elders.[2] Since becoming incorporated in 1997, the two Darug groups meet regularly for social functions, offer Welcomes to Country, produce books and maintain a vigorous cultural centre.[3] They cannot, however, form another Local Aboriginal Land Council because, under the terms of the *Aboriginal Land Rights Act 1983* (NSW), only one Land Council is allowed to represent each area.

Yet their claims to recognition were, and continue to be, opposed by other Aboriginal bodies already constituted under the *Aboriginal Land Rights Act*. One of these challengers is the existing Darug Local Aboriginal Land Council (LALC), formed soon after the Act, but which, significantly, had changed its name from the Darug to the Deerubbin LALC in 1996. The newly renamed Deerubbin Land Council asserted its right under the Act to represent all Aboriginal people living in the area, irrespective of their place of origin. In 2012, its website claimed to support 'genuine assertions and respectful recognition of traditional ownership (and formal recognition of native title) wherever they occur'. Then followed the caveat:

---

1   Shane Smithers, 'The history of the west', [video interview, historyofaboriginalsydney.edu.au (henceforth HOAS)].
2   Kohen's meeting served as a catalyst that promoted Darug families to seek formal recognition. Many families had already accelerated interest in their own family history in the previous decade. See Gordon Workman, 'We've been invaded twice', [video interview, HOAS].
3   For example, Tobin 2002. A remarkable book produced from the Dharawal Sydney region, is *D'harawal Climate and Resources* (Bodkin and Robertson 2013).

> Deerubbin LALC [Local Aboriginal Land Council] is skeptical, however, that there are Aboriginal people alive who credibly lay claim to traditional ownership of the area.[4]

Such an assertion may seem surprising, since it was in Darug country that Governor Macquarie established the first Aboriginal school, the Native Institution, in 1814. It was in Darug country that he awarded the first Land Grant, supposedly in perpetuity, to a Darug man (Colbee) and to a woman (his sister Maria). The Darug were granted one of New South Wales' earliest reserves, to be shared with Darkinjung people, and established by the Aborigines Protection Board at Sackville Reach on the Hawkesbury River in 1889.[5]

The position of Darug people was trenchantly put by the Gai-Mariagal scholar Dennis Foley in his article, 'What has Native Title done to the Urban Koori in New South Wales who is also a Traditional Custodian?'[6] He wrote that:

> [LALCs] were often [formed] without any involvement or consent from local Aboriginal people who were direct descendants of the traditional people of the lands in question. Guringah [a northern Sydney coastal] people generally were still recovering from wearing the brunt of nearly 180 years of physical and psychological trauma (dating from the establishment of Sydney town adjacent to our lands in 1788 through to the 1967 referendum which removed discriminatory clauses from the Australian constitution). These traumas included firstly dispossession of our land, enforced segregation and discrimination, and then assimilation and the denial of our culture. Guringah people were not fully conversant with the new opportunities that the Act bestowed upon them, nor savvy enough about the workings of the new legal system. There was a lag in the granting of these opportunities and in local resolution as to how to respond to them. Another group of Indigenous people however stepped into the vacuum and took advantage of this significant historical event. We Guringah custodians could not believe other Aboriginal people could act against us to both deny our existence and then steal our traditional lands from under us. But they did and history will show that the medium to allow this was the LRA. [*Aboriginal Land Rights Act 1983* (NSW) As Amended].[7]

---

4   Deerubbin Local Aboriginal Land Council, www.deerubbin.org.au/Final-CLBP-290609.pdf (accessed 5 October 2013).
5   Brook 1999.
6   Foley 2007.
7   Foley 2007: 168.

One response to Foley's assertion of denial and theft was made by a researcher for the Federal Court who, assessing evidence for a 2004 Darug Land Claim under the Act, found 'little to suggest on-going *traditional* values and practices, other than a strong sense of kinship bolstered by a practical reliance upon each others' support'.[8] A second response was made by the Indigenous scholar Suzanne Ingram in her article 'Sleight of Hand: Aboriginality and the Education Pathway'.[9] Here she argued that the Darug Sydney custodians were 'noticeably absent throughout' the 'highly active and visible period of the Aboriginal movement' of the 1920s and 1930s. They 'have no actual Indigenous reference point'. Seized with a desire to 'belong' analogous to the much discussed European Australian spiritual quest in the 1980s and 1990s, she claimed that the Darug had no strong sense of culture or togetherness comparable to that of the La Perouse community.[10] This was an argument similar to the contentious dismissal by Justice Olney on the Native Title claim of the Yorta Yorta people of Victoria. The tide of history, he wrote in the late 1990s,

> has washed away any real acknowledgment of their traditional laws and any real observance of their traditional customs. The foundation of the claim to native title in relation to the land previously occupied by those ancestors having disappeared, the native-title rights and interests previously enjoyed are not capable of revival. This conclusion effectively resolves the application for a determination of Native Title.[11]

Several scholars have noted what they see in Olney as an unwarranted privileging of the written word over the oral.[12] Given that so much of the Darug's claim to custodianship is based on oral evidence, it seems pertinent to present a little of it here. It is not the point of this article to argue one side or the other of what seems to be less an Aboriginal *historical* argument but rather one deeply entangled in the contemporary politics of self-representation. Rather I propose to embrace the historian's task, which is to contextualise and explain the social context of any period under discussion, upon which basis non-specialists may then form their own judgements. Needless to say, the European colonisers' persecution of Aboriginal people was not directed at the Darug alone. I do not seek here to represent the historical context of only those who, like the Darug, demand recognition as Sydney's Indigenous custodians. Aboriginal people from the bush who came to the inner city were treated as harshly if they bore obvious Aboriginal features. The Redfern race riots of the 1970s, in which of course some Sydney traditional custodians also took part, revealed that police brutality and

---

8   Ward 2001: 7; Quoted by Ingram 2008: 14; See *Gale v Minister for Land and Water Conservation (NSW)* [2004] FCA 374 (31 March 2004), Madgwick J.
9   Ingram 2008.
10   Ingram 2008: 8.
11   *Yorta Yorta Aboriginal Community v Victoria* [1998] FCA 1606 (18 December 1998), Olney J., at [129].
12   Furphy 2013: 192.

injustice, encouraged by the state government, could be worse again than the casual but bitter hurts endured daily at Parramatta or the Hawkesbury half a century earlier.

In presenting the context in which this cultural loss occurred, I shall advance very many instances, drawn from research by the team producing the website historyofaboriginalsydney.edu.au, that will outline some of the reasons why Aboriginal people in Sydney had very good reason not necessarily to extinguish their identity, but to take it 'underground'. Indigenous descent sometimes became a secret shared only by the immediate family or Aboriginal neighbours.[13]

While it is true that Darug people had little part in the confrontations with state authority in the 1920s and 1930s, there were good reasons for their not having been in a position to do so. Much of the traditional teaching has been lost. Like most southern Australian languages, the Darug language has also been effectively lost (though possibly capable of revival). Many formal or collective cultural practices, such as renewal or initiation ceremonies, ceased many years ago, though some have been re-enacted. Creation stories generally lack precise geographical detail. These positions are not much disputed. Tracy Howie, President of the 2010 Guringai Tribal Elders, expressed her despair at the planned attempted obliteration of her people:

> That's another difficulty with Native Title in New South Wales. We were the hardest hit. They came in and they either killed us, or they bred it out of us or they disease-riddened us. And all of our culture, all of our language, was outlawed. It became illegal ... so how can we therefore prove native title, when, had our ancestors done that, we wouldn't be alive today? Native Title law contradicts itself ... When people say 'stolen generations', and not taking anything away from the people who were removed from their families, but it goes deeper than just the removal of a person, of a body, but it was the removal of our culture, our song, the removal of our dance our language, everything, it was all stolen. Not just the children. Everything.[14]

To map the historical context, we need some signposts to Sydney's urban history. First, like other parts of Australia, Sydney Aboriginal people have occupied every point on that spectrum of self-identification that has changed from one generation to the next. Today, one can first recognise a category of those who denied their identity for so long that it is now quite forgotten and cannot be revived. Others know of their part-Indigenous descent but have no intention of exploring or revealing it. There are those who recently discovered a concealed identity and embraced it. There are those who are still reticent about an openly

---

13   Dennis Foley, 'From Redfern to Chester Hill', historyofaboriginalsydney.edu.au [website HOAS]
14   Tracy Howie, 'It's not easy claiming Native Title in NSW', [video interview, HOAS].

declared identity, but whose children openly and proudly do so. There are Sydney people, including many Darug, who have for two centuries lived as Aborigines, known their genealogy, and openly and fiercely associated with each other.

Video available online: press.anu.edu.au/titles/aboriginal-history-monographs/long-history-deep-time/.

Richard Green, 'My family history'
Source: historyofaboriginalsydney.edu.au.

Secondly, working class areas like Balmain, Glebe and Brooklyn were areas of great ethnic diversity in which Aboriginality, or any other ethnicity, simply was not thought to be important. Many older people testify to this: the Dharawal (south-eastern coastal) woman Margaret Slowgrove, growing up in Botany in the 1940s, knew of her descent, but an identity as one belonging to any ethnicity in particular was irrelevant in a dockside community that included Malays, Maori, Chinese, South Sea Islanders and Filipinos. But the new western suburbs after World War Two were much more homogeneous. Confessing one's Aboriginal inheritance invited trouble. It was here in the west that Aborigines formed a secret army of knowledge holders. The Gai-Mariagal (Camaraigal people, northern Sydney coastal) man Dennis Foley spent some of his teenage years in Fairfield, western Sydney, in the 1960s. As he drove around the suburb in 2010 he could identify house after house once occupied by Aboriginal families – as many, in fact, as made up a typical reserve! Few of his neighbours knew their clans or language names. If they did bear any noticeably Aboriginal features, not many openly identified; but identity remained strong among the secret sharers.

Video available online: press.anu.edu.au/titles/aboriginal-history-monographs/long-history-deep-time/.

Dennis Foley, 'From Redfern to Chester Hill'
Source: historyofaboriginalsydney.edu.au.

The government station at La Perouse, as Ingram suggested, presented a telling contrast. That reserve, while mainly composed today of people with links to the south coast, has always contained a mix of different peoples dating from its establishment in 1883 as a holding-paddock for people removed from other areas of Sydney like Circular Quay. On the station, they were subjected to a book full of punitive rules, presided over by a manager, regulating entry and egress, card playing, drinking, tidiness and general submission to White authority. The effect, ironically, was to drive people together psychologically. Disparate though they were, the manager's strictures acted to forge a common identity not of families or clans, but of 'Aborigines'. To observe the shift towards a group identity in process, consider this exchange reported by the manager of another large government reserve, Warangesda, in Wiradjuri country.

There was another bother with MRS SWIFT today. She openly accuses FANNY HELAND of being enceinte [pregnant] & told the girls in the Dorm they ought all to laugh at her & while she was at the washtub yesterday called her a sulky looking pig. FANNY came & told manager this AM & when she spoke to MRS SWIFT she said it was all false, that she did not use any such expression. The manager asked her if she had ever said of NANCY MURRAY that she was a Chinese looking thing. Which she indignantly denied but Buckley said he heard her use the expression and FANNY HELAND says she heard her call NANCY a yellow Chinaman. And called the manager a hypocrite and that all the whites were a lot of hypocrites. After the bother MRS SWIFT poked her tongue at Fanny and made faces at her. NANCY MURRAY says she said to the girls in the Dorm she would put the people against the manager, & as far as the manager has been able to find out has not done so.[15]

The extract shows the ready potential for a quarrel to escalate into an 'us against them' mentality that served to reinforce identity through a consciousness of difference. Thus the imposition of salaried managers and punitive regulations on reserves like La Perouse served only to heighten resentment of the Whites through a strong and developing collective identity. Other Sydney Aboriginal people were ironically, in this sense, not to have had such punitive unity imposed on them. It was only as individuals and families that they endured, for more than two centuries, the daily insults, challenges and punishments for openly asserting their Indigenous heritage. Even if they wanted to, La Perouse residents could never carry their descent underground.

Lastly, identities are often plural. Children who formed themselves into gangs were often Aboriginal *and* Irish, Aboriginal *and* Catholic, or from a particular street, family or sports team. Siblings formed gangs to fight other gangs; it was only after their teens that they realised 'we were seen as an Aboriginal gang, but to us, we were just family'.[16]

Living together brought trouble

Managed reserves were created by government; after 1883, by the NSW Aborigines Protection (later Welfare) Board. There was only one such reserve in Sydney – La Perouse, holding few residents, compared to the newcomers gathering in inner city suburbs after 1900. Like the Darug in Sydney's west,

15 Warangesda Manager's Mission Diary, 7 June 1894, typescript in National Library of Australia; quoted in Read 2000: 55.
16 Peter Radoll, 'My uncles gave me complete freedom', [video interview, HOAS]; McGrath, 2010.

they rented houses; those who could not built humpies in Yarra Bay or Glebe. In the west, those who could not or did not rent often gathered in Town Camps. People who could not rent, or chose to live with their own mob, took residence in such camps, often sited near water. Such was 'Blacktown Road', an empty paddock near Freeman's Reach, Hawkesbury River, occupied till about 1910.[17]

The biggest town camps shared by Darug people included Sackville, established as an unmanaged reserve in 1889, and Plumpton, close to the old Blacktown Institution site, on land owned by the Darug identity William Locke. Locke allowed his farming block to be used from about 1903 as an area for his relatives' cottages and humpies, a base for Aboriginal Inland Mission activities, and a Welfare Board ration distribution point.[18] But living together in poverty was unhealthy; in Plumpton in 1908, two children died of influenza after heavy rains.

More sinisterly, town camps invited the pernicious attention of welfare authorities. At least six children were removed to private homes or the United Aborigines Mission Home at Bomaderry before 1910.[19] Threatened and persecuted, the people began to leave. The tin mission church closed in 1910. To re-signify what everyone already knew to be the dangerously impermanent nature of town camps, the remaining members of William Locke's family, and others, were finally evicted from the site in 1920. Where were they to go? Many chose the other large town camp familiar to them, at this time mainly occupied by Gundangara (south-western Sydney) families, just outside Katoomba, called the Gully. Until about 1905, Katoomba had seemed to be a safe town for Aborigines; but as the refugee population of the Gully grew, so in proportion grew hostile Welfare interference. Seven children of the Stubbings family were removed in that year.[20]

By 1958, no less than 27 Aboriginal children had been removed from the Gully. Threats of child removal could be almost as deadly as separation itself. Even in the late 1950s, the Stubbings family was told that if the family did not leave the Gully, the children would be taken. Colin Locke's parents, also ordered by the Katoomba Shire Council to leave the Gully, settled legally in the water catchment area of Blackheath with several related Darug families. 'If the white government car comes,' his mother told him, 'grab your brothers, run into the bush, and don't stop running.'[21] Nor, like Plumpton, was the Gully secure even for adults. Tolerated for decades by the Whites for the labour force the Aborigines provided at the tourist hotels, hospital, sawmills and abattoirs,

---

17   Julie Janson and Shane Smithers, 'The people of Blacktown Road', [video interview, HOAS].
18   Johnson 2007: 148–149.
19   One of these children was Ruby Hilda Castles; see 'Laraine Sullivan', in Sobott 2013: 156. Laraine is Mary Castles' daughter.
20   Johnson 2007: 148, 212.
21   Colin Locke, 'Catchment Kids', [video interview, HOAS].

all the dozens of Gully residents were evicted in the years between 1955 and 1957 to make way for a racetrack. Some were forced into trucks and left by the roadside in north Katoomba. Five years later, the racetrack had failed, a costly and ill-advised bungle. Today the former residents have renewed the site as an Aboriginal Declared Place.

Choosing to live away from other Aboriginal people brought new problems, while retaining most of the old. In about 1960, at the age of 15, Diane O'Brien was thrown out of her Granville house by her adopting father after she was raped and made pregnant. To protect her baby from removal, she took refuge in an abandoned car in the Granville tip. Here she lived for several weeks until the welfare authorities caught up with her and informed Diane that to keep her child she must marry the rapist. She consented.

Video available online: press.anu.edu.au/titles/aboriginal-history-monographs/long-history-deep-time/.

Diane O'Brien, 'Adopted, Raped and Pregnant'
Source: historyofaboriginalsydney.edu.au.

Dennis Foley recalls two older cousins in the same school as he in Chester Hill, western Sydney. One afternoon in the 1950s, the police struck, the children were seized and have never been seen by their extended family again. Was he aware of the possibility of his own removal? 'No, you never thought it would happen to you.' But in the end he was scooped up too. Nearly two years passed before he was able to return.[22] Removed in about 1952 with his siblings from their tent, concealed on a creek near Berowra, Robert Kitchener reflected after years spent in institutions, 'White was right. That's what they wanted. They wanted us to have another identity.'[23]

Nor did choosing or being forced to move from a town camp by any means guarantee family security. Colin Locke's family had gone from the Blackheath catchment by 1969. In the same decade, Janny Ely and Judy Chester, two Wiradjuri-born youngsters were living in Salt Pan Creek, Georges River. 'Pepper-potted' (that is, allotted a house surrounded by non-Aboriginal neighbours) in a Housing Commission cottage in Green Valley, they discovered that some other residents of the street had taken up a petition to get rid of the newcomers (the petition failed). Ely was forced to hide below the windows of the Green Valley home when the Welfare Officer was out looking for her.[24]

---

22 Dennis Foley, 'Children Removed from Chester Hill Primary School', [video interview, HOAS].
23 Robert Kitchener, 'What amazes me is that anyone can lock you up on the grounds of your culture', [video interview, HOAS].
24 Judy Chester and Janny Ely, 'Get those blacks out of Green Valley', 'High School and the Welfare', [video interviews, HOAS].

Don't be conspicuous

Learning language was difficult and invited trouble. Frances Bodkin recalls speaking Dharawal at home only when the blinds were drawn at night.[25] Carol Cooper believes that her parents at Katoomba were ordered never to lock their doors so that the police could enter at any time to check if English was being spoken.[26] June McGrath, who in 2012 was the President of Link Up Aboriginal Corporation, grew up in Bexley. All her life, she was put down by her sisters for 'daring' to identify as Aboriginal.[27] As a child in Brisbane, Pat Eatock was ordered to play on the other side of the divided school playground after her father, of obviously Aboriginal descent, came to visit the school. Twenty-five years later, living in a Housing Commission house in Mt Pritchard, near Liverpool, she casually revealed her Indigenous descent to her neighbour, who promptly told her to leave the house, refusing permission for her own son to continue to play with Eatock's.[28] Karen Maber, of Dharawal descent, worked in her primary school in Kogarah just hard enough to keep herself in the middle of the class roll, and sat as far out of sight as possible, at the back. 'I really loved school. But I didn't want to come first in anything. Too much attention … I would rather not do well or I'd have to go up to get a certificate.' She kept her Aboriginality to herself until the class, watching a documentary, accused the filmed Aborigines of cruelty. Upset, she confided her identity to her teacher. 'Don't worry dear,' was the reply, 'Nobody will know.' Karen carries the hurt to this day.[29] Peter Radoll received a hard time from both teachers and other boys at Colyton High School after he received his first Aboriginal Studies Grant cheque in the 1980s.[30] His mother, at length acquiring loan funds from the western Sydney Foundation for Aboriginal Affairs to buy a house, entered the Bank of New South Wales at St Mary's to transfer the purchase funds to her account, only to find the manager refused to allow the procedure – she could not be Aboriginal, he declared, she was not dark enough.[31] Carol Cooper and John Mulvay both received much hostility from their teachers in Katoomba; this was worsened, Mulvay reflected, by his family's noticeable poverty.[32] For 150 years, in north coastal Sydney, the Guringai children of Matora, first wife to Macquarie's friend Bungaree, lived in and around Marra Marra Creek. In 1910, six closely related families lived in Shuttle Bay, at the mouth of the creek. Surrounded by people of many ethnicities they lived as all the others – in fishing, water services and

---

25 Frances Bodkin, 'I was told we spoke Spanish', [video interview, HOAS].
26 Johnson 2007: 121.
27 June McGrath, 'I'm so proud', [video interview, HOAS].
28 Pat Eatock, 'We never spoke again', [video interview, HOAS].
29 Karen Maber, 'Memories of Kogarah Primary School I', [video interview, HOAS].
30 Peter Radoll, 'It was here that I realised I was different', [video interview, HOAS].
31 Peter Radoll, 'The downside of owning an Aboriginal house', [video interview, HOAS].
32 John Mulvay, 'School was pretty horrific', [video interview, HOAS].

local labour. In a waterside area of very diverse ethnic heritage, Aboriginality didn't seem to matter much; except to the police. These families too kept their identity to themselves; any overt display of Aboriginality would have promptly caused the health authorities to find a reason to move them on. Dennis Foley's uncles, he recalled, could fish all day with a rod or line in the Terrigal lagoon. But as fast as an Indigenous fishing spear appeared, so did someone to prevent its use or to move the fishermen on. The historian of the Gully, Dianne Johnson, observed the maxim that has guided Aboriginal people in all of Sydney, and much of Australia: 'The need for most of them to blend in, accompanied by their reluctance to put themselves forward unduly, is still paramount. These are survival skills instilled in them with childhood.'[33]

Aboriginality is shameful

Pam Young has worked proudly for many Aboriginal organisations. But as a child she describes herself as a 'little shame job'.

> [She] used to walk under the water drains to the city and go and get the groceries at Woolworths and Waltons, always walking, come back, go under the water drains and walk to my [adopted] parents' place. It was safer for me to do that because I was so ashamed of my colour and my identity.[34]

Today it takes equal courage to admit one's descent, especially if that descent has been obscured by older family members. Not everyone in a family may choose to identify, even within the same generation. Chris Tobin's mother discovered late in her life that some of those that she had been raised to think of as friends, were actually cousins. Tobin, now in his 30s, revealed how much determination it still takes to declare oneself an Aborigine.

> It's a matter of keeping quiet so your kids don't get taken, we were told the reason why we were so dark was that we were Spanish. [We were told] [w]e've got Aboriginal blood, but we're not Aboriginals. Aboriginal people were smelly, untrustworthy, unclean kind of people, that there was Spanish in the family, and there's members of the family [now] who do not want to know that. It's a lot like how people treat you as well. People need to be encouraged, and I get that people don't put their hand up to say they're Aboriginal, I really do, gosh, who wants an argument. You can tell [people] you're Macedonian, you tell them you're Croatian

---

33   Johnson 2007: 151.
34   Pamela Young, 'No more a little shame job', [video interview, HOAS].

or whatever, no one's going to give you an argument, but gosh you tell someone you're Aboriginal: 'No you're not!' Jesus – all right, well. So I certainly think the generation before us, they don't want to have that argument with their friends thank you very much, so they just keep quiet. I love that today in our world … that you can proudly be an Aboriginal person, the Darug community's very accepting, that's a huge step I think.[35]

Several odd results have flowed from maintaining a surreptitious identity. Clearly, it can be kept underground for so long that finally everyone forgets it was ever there. Today's Darug sometimes challenge the identity of others, 'Oh, we never heard of her when I was a kid', unaware that these unrelated families may have adopted the same survival practices as themselves in taking their Indigenous descent underground. And today, in circumstances less difficult (as far as recognition by non-Aboriginal people is concerned) an almost forgotten identity can be rediscovered, and embraced. Bob Waterer, another descendant of Matora Bungaree, and now in his mid-80s, explained that the few hints he received as child of his Aboriginal descent he had been quite willing to discountenance.[36] Only after his sister's death did documents, coinciding with the publication of a book of Hawkesbury River history, reveal to him his Guringai descent. All his life he had lived comfortably as a non-Aboriginal. But now, openly declaring his new-found identity, he was surprised and gratified to be greeted warmly both by well-intentioned Whites, and even by members of the non-local Aboriginal community who had seen themselves as caretaker-custodians until the actual Guringai could recover, or declare themselves.[37] What, perhaps Waterer could not understand because he had never experienced life as a declared Aborigine, were the everyday insults and necessary concealments that he had escaped all his life. No doubt his mother had very well understood the consequences of open identification, even if Waterer himself did not.

The costs of concealment have been heavy for many. Shane Smithers, descended from the Blacktown Road mob, insists on the historical circumstances of the loss of cultural practices:

Not so in the west [of Sydney], where disease and fighting very quickly decimated the communities … This is a legitimate Aboriginal experience to be dispossessed, to be lately impacted, to be pale-skinned, these are legitimate things. Doesn't make me less Aboriginal than anybody else.

---

35 Chris Tobin, 'It takes a lot of courage to identify', [video interview, HOAS].
36 Bob Waterer, 'I wasn't very interested in it in my younger days', [video interview, HOAS].
37 Susan Moylan-Coombs, 'I feel very connected to this country', [video interview, HOAS].

> It robs me of my identity because I don't have that same richness of culture that you find in the [Northern] Territory … The language has been lost, I don't know any Darug words.[38]

Smithers' cousin Julie Janson, having been certain of but unable to pinpoint her Darug descent, at length tracked her family's town camp to the same Blacktown Road town camp. Her father, probably for mixed motives, chose to deny this (rather obvious) descent. After finally confirming, through research, what she had suspected all her life, Janson related her story to a class she was teaching. The next time she entered the classroom she heard a voice at the back of the room stage-whispering 'boong … boong … boong'. She reflected:

> Ah, that's what my father and my family's secret saved me from putting up with. Unlike Aboriginal people who all their lives had suffered and been discriminated against, I grew up thinking I could do anything in the world, and I was anybody, go to university, get a great result, get a couple of degrees, become a writer, anything I wanted, because no one was putting me down. And I realised that in a way that this was a kind of a gift. But it's so hard that that racism stopped my dad and my grandmother from being able to acknowledge their Darug roots from being able to acknowledge that they were Aboriginal.[39]

Living as an Aborigine was never a picnic at St Marys, or Parramatta, or Windsor. It has never been easy declaring and living an urban identity, then or now. It went hard on everybody. Yet perhaps it was worse for the self-styled traditional custodians of the wider Sydney region who, like Colin Workman, maintain:

> We were the only nation to have been invaded twice … First by Cook when he got here, second by the Indigenous people of the rest of Australia.[40]

Bibliography

History of Aboriginal Sydney

Bodkin, Frances, 'I was told we spoke Spanish' [video interview, historyofaboriginalsydney.edu.au].

Chester, Judy and Janny Ely, 'Get those blacks out of Green Valley', 'High School and the Welfare', [video interviews, historyofaboriginalsydney.edu.au].

---

38 Shane Smithers, 'The history of the west', [video interview, HOAS].
39 Julie Janson, 'My father's secret', [video interview, HOAS].
40 Colin Workman, 'We were invaded twice', [video interview, HOAS].

Eatock, Pat, 'We never spoke again', [video interview, historyofaboriginalsydney. edu.au].

Foley, Dennis, 'From Redfern to Chester Hill', [video interview, historyofaboriginalsydney.edu.au].

Foley, Dennis, 'Children Removed from Chester Hill Primary School', [video interview, historyofaboriginalsydney.edu.au].

Howie, Tracy, 'It's not easy claiming Native Title in NSW', [video interview, historyofaboriginalsydney.edu.au].

Janson, Julie, 'My father's secret', [video interview, historyofaboriginalsydney. edu.au].

Janson, Julie and Shane Smithers, 'The people of Blacktown Road', [video interview, historyofaboriginalsydney.edu.au].

Kitchener, Robert, 'What amazes me is that anyone can lock you up on the grounds of your culture', [video interview, historyofaboriginalsydney.edu.au].

Locke, Colin, 'Catchment Kids', [video interview, historyofaboriginalsydney. edu.au].

Maber, Karen, 'Memories of Kogarah Primary School' [video interview, historyofaboriginalsydney.edu.au].

McGrath, June, 'I'm so proud', [video interview, historyofaboriginalsydney. edu.au].

Moylan-Coombs, Susan, 'I feel very connected to this country', [video interview, historyofaboriginalsydney.edu.au].

Mulvay, John, 'School was pretty horrific', [video interview, historyofaboriginalsydney.edu.au].

O'Brien, Diane, 'Adopted, Raped and Pregnant', [video interview, historyofaboriginalsydney.edu.au].

Radoll, Peter, 'My uncles gave me complete freedom', [video interview, historyofaboriginalsydney.edu.au].

Smithers, Shane, 'The history of the west', [video interview, historyofaboriginalsydney.edu.au]

Waterer, Bob, 'I wasn't very interested in it in my younger days', [video interview, historyofaboriginalsydney.edu.au].

Workman, Gordon, 'We've been invaded twice', [video interview, historyofaboriginalsydney.edu.au].

Young, Pamela, 'No more a little shame job', [video interview, historyofaboriginalsydney.edu.au].

Other sources

Bodkin, Frances (compiler) and Lorraine Robertson (illustrator) 2013, *D'harawal Climate and Resources*, Envirobooks, Sussex Inlet.

Brook, Jack 1999, *Shut out from the World: The Sackville Aborigines Reserve and Mission, 1989–1946*, Deerubbin Press, Seven Hills.

Foley, Dennis 2007, 'What has Native Title done to the urban Koori in New South Wales who is also a Traditional Custodian', in Benjamin R Smith and Frances Murphy (eds), *The Social Effects of Native Title Recognition, Translation, Coexistence*, Centre for Aboriginal Economic Policy Research Monograph No. 27, ANU E Press, Canberra, 166–179.

Furphy, Samuel 2013, *Edward M. Curr and the Tide of History*, Aboriginal History Monograph 26, ANU E Press, Canberra.

Ingram, S 2008, 'Sleight of Hand: Aboriginality and the Education Pathway', paper delivered to World Indigenous Peoples Conference on Education, Melbourne.

Johnson, Diane 2007, *Sacred Waters: The Story of the Blue Mountains Gully Traditional Owners*, Halstead, Sydney.

McGrath, Ann, 2010, 'Shamrock Aborigines: the Irish, the Aboriginal Australians and their children', *Aboriginal History*: 34: 55–84.

Members of the Aboriginal Community 1987, *La Perouse: The Place, the People and the Sea*, Aboriginal Studies Press, Canberra.

Read, Peter 2000, 'Freedom and control on the southern institutions, New South Wales, 1879–1909', in Peter Read (ed.), *Settlement: A History of Australian Indigenous Housing*, Aboriginal Studies Press, Canberra.

Sobott, Gaele (ed.) 2013, *Young Days: Bankstown Elders Oral History Project*, BYDS, Bankstown.

Tobin, Colin 2002, *The Dharug Story, An Aboriginal History of Western Sydney from 1788*, fifth edition, Chris Tobin, Glenbrook, New South Wales.

Ward, A 2001, 'Gale for Darug Native Title Claim in Western Sydney', Report to the Federal Court of Australia: New South Wales District Registry.

8. Lingering Inheritance

'We were brought up with this … stuff'

Julia Torpey Hurst

My doctoral research focused on developing a spatial approach to oral history storytelling to create a biographical landscape history scattered across locations in the Blue Mountains, Western Sydney and areas of coastal Sydney, as directed by the Aboriginal storytellers. Together, our aim has been to illuminate the subtleties of attachment to place that inform Aboriginal identity – the contemporary and historical, political, environmental, and artistic representations and connections to, and in, place. In our project, 'place' refers to a chosen locality significant to the storyteller's history. It has become a metaphor or signifier, a catalyst to connect, add to, or withdraw from, dominant historical narratives of Aboriginal Sydney as storytellers choose to locate and to frame their own history and ways of being/belonging.

Following these ideas, this chapter will focus on these stories: the 'intangible' ones, the unreal, the peripheral knowledge and feelings for place which many people are developing, or asserting. People's way of telling and knowing, when talking about their relationship to place and history in urban locations, challenges their previous erosion as Aboriginal people who continue to have place connections.

This chapter draws upon research around the production of an enhanced ebook, *At the Heart of It…Place Stories Across Darug and Gundungurra Lands,* which is linked with a larger Australian Research Council-funded project at The Australian National University called 'Deepening Histories of Place: Exploring Indigenous Landscapes of National and International Significance'. The stories in this chapter have been reproduced with the permission of the storytellers.

With the assistance of Aboriginal people living in Western Sydney and the Blue Mountains, we visited places of personal significance – talking and listening. We have often come across a voice, a wind, a shadow and a lingering feeling of the land … or something. What is it that we are experiencing? A warning? A welcoming? A testing?

As I began to invite people to talk with me, to record and film their history in place, I was given a list from a local Aboriginal community organisation of people who might 'be the best to talk to' to inform my research. I was warned not to talk with people who were described as being 'off with the fairies'. This direction implied, purposefully or not, that such people's ways of being were not a good representation of the Aboriginal people, or the Aboriginal history of the area, often identified as 'Darug'. Such people's history does not fit within the conventional practices of academic history[1] and they are not a 'good' representation of 'us' (referring to the community who in this case at the preliminary stage of my research project was the representative organisation) as urban Aboriginal people or of who and what 'we' think our Aboriginality should be.

Within this project, the personal and spiritual narratives of the storytellers have been recorded and honoured to create a larger historical narrative about the places 'in between' more dominant narratives of Aboriginal history in Western Sydney; the important personal places that inform a person's history, identity and connectivity to the people around them and the landscape they frequent. As Aboriginal philosopher Mary Graham has commented, 'The two most important kinds of relationship in life are, firstly, those between land and people, and, secondly, those amongst people themselves, the second always being contingent upon the first'.[2]

To complete my oral history research, I have worked with a 'storywork methodology' as defined by Jo-ann Archibald, a Sto:lo woman of the Lower Fraser River of British Columbia. Archibald explains:

> the words *story* and *work* together signal the importance and seriousness of undertaking … [the] work of making meaning through stories, whether they are traditional or lived experience stories. Seven principles comprise storywork: respect, responsibility, reverence, reciprocity, wholism, interrelatedness and synergy.[3]

Positioning my research within a storywork methodology is important as the research seeks to honour the traditional, cultural and ecological knowledge each storyteller shares in our conversations, and to also bring together and to bind the historical and the contemporary stories that inform their identity and the process of being able to 'tell'; that these personal histories and experiences in place are valid irrespective of *known* traditional stories or established place-based narratives. This process of storytelling is informed by the relationship between the listener and the storyteller and, most importantly for this project, the 'relationships among the self'.[4] Many of the storytellers who agreed to work

---

1   Hokari explains that a conventional practice of history which is based on time-oriented chronology, teleology and historicity is only one mode of exploring the past. See Hokari 2000: 1.
2   Graham 1999.
3   Archibald 2008b: x.
4   Archibald 2008a: 373.

with me have had to look inwards to find the courage to talk, to be filmed, and to be open to their own insecurities about their history and to heal from the criticism their stories have historically incurred from family members, friends and their own community.

This project has occurred against a wider landscape that has been re-inscribed, erased and over-written;[5] a product of colonialism and the 'recalling and forgetting, selecting and erasing [of] memories'.[6] A postcolonial discourse of power has emerged as a result of this forgetting, erasing and selecting within and between Aboriginal community groups, government and corporate institutions and even within families.

As George Morgan has explained in his book *Unsettled Places: Aboriginal People in Urbanisation in New South Wales,* it was not until the late 1940s that some academic researchers began to notice Aboriginal people living in cities and towns.[7] When they were eventually noticed, Morgan explains, 'there was almost a universal perception among researchers, that those living in cities had experienced "cultural loss" and were in a state of stalled transition between tradition and modernity'.[8] Similarly, urban Aboriginal people were seen as 'stubbornly adhering to remembered cultural remnants, supplemented with the folklore of persecution'.[9] Marcia Langton has commented that previous researchers have framed urban Aboriginal people's lifestyle negatively against assimilationist assumptions and ideals and the 'culture of poverty' theory to 'explain away the tragic living conditions of Aboriginal people which has resulted from their dispossession'.[10] Failing to perceive the insider's view – how Black people themselves perceive and understand their conditions[11] – it appeared that the movement of Aboriginal people from their original homelands and their survival in urban areas resulted in the loss of attachment to land, as if the original people of Sydney had moved somewhere.[12]

As such, conclusions regarding 'who and/or what is/was a particular kind' of Aboriginal group are derived from often patchy historical evidence and ethnographic interpretations.[13] The Darug language group whose landscape includes Western Sydney and the site of Sydney itself, was originally recorded by surveyor and anthropologist RH Mathews in the 1890s. As well as being affiliated through kinship ties and trade, and while acknowledging differences

---

5   Ashcroft et al. 1995, cited in Taylor 2000.
6   Healy 1997: 5, cited in Taylor 2000: 29.
7   Morgan 2006: 55.
8   Morgan 2006: 56.
9   See Rowley 1972: 17, cited in Langton 1981: 17.
10 Langton 1981: 18.
11 Langton 1981: 16.
12 Morgan 2006: 56.
13 Everett 2006: 63.

in vocabularies, RH Mathews considered the Darug people to have grammatical affinities with the Gundungurra people of the Blue Mountains, and with language groups that covered the 'Hawkesbury River and Cape Howe, extending inland till met by the great Wirajuri [sic] nation.'[14] Jim Kohen has also suggested a contested landscape of 'Darug Country', including the Blue Mountains in the west that stretched to the Pacific Ocean in the east, the Hawkesbury River in the north and Appin in the south.[15] Archaeological evidence suggests the Darug and Gundungurra were connected prior to European disruption, sharing an inter-tribal ceremonial ground in the Linden area of the Blue Mountains.[16] What is widely considered by the Aboriginal people I have worked with to be 'Right History' (tested, truthful, academic) versus 'Wrong History' (experiential and unverifiable experiences and knowledge) continues to be tested in Western Sydney and the Blue Mountains as the people I have been working with negotiate and renegotiate their place against a narrative of dispossession,[17] academic boundaries, emerging research, geographical landscape and changing cultural contexts. Historical, anthropological and archaeological academic re-writings of land and people are therefore powerful and often damaging tools; seeking the 'truth' through varied lenses and for often competing purposes, they can contradict or disregard beliefs held through Aboriginal oral history, family genealogy, family history, claims to Country and experiential events that cannot be easily explained.

Ideas of being, of what is the right way or the wrong way, the truthful way or the 'pretend' way to *be* an urban Aboriginal person in Western Sydney and the Blue Mountains are consciously and publicly debated. Kristina Everett has stated in her research on what she describes as a newly imagined Darug community, 'it is primarily the assumption that there is an on-going, continuous *genetic* link between living Darug descendants and the pre-contact Aboriginal people that contemporary Darug descendant identity claims are founded'.[18] Following what Marcia Langton has described as the 'insidious ideology of tribal and de-tribalised Aborigines',[19] Everett positions the Darug people in a historically colonial, administrative, assimilationist anthropological frame; that to be an urban Aboriginal person is to have lost the basis for any legitimate claims to be Aboriginal. This argument denies the lived experience of urban Aboriginal people as they have negotiated and survived colonisation and dispossession.

14 Mathews 1902: 49, cited in Everett 2006.
15 Kohen 1993: 9.
16 Kelleher 2009: 100.
17 In her thesis Kristina Everett creates a narrative of early dispossession of culture and country claiming that urban Aboriginal people who now claim traditional ownerships are invariably culturally bereft and sometimes even physically extinct. See Everett 2006: 71.
18 Everett 2006: 64.
19 Langton 1981, cited in Carlson 2011: 35.

To be an Aboriginal person today then is to meet the official criteria[20] of the Australian government's three-point identification system endorsed since the 1980s. This system is often used as a framework to provide a means of 'formal' confirmation of ancestry and Aboriginal identity and 'belonging'. It is also used to identify 'access' to Aboriginal identified services.[21]

> An Aboriginal or Torres Strait Islander is a person of Aboriginal or Torres Strait Islander descent who identifies as an Aboriginal or Torres Strait Islander and is accepted as such by the community in which he [or she] lives.[22]

This criterion maintains an assumed locality of belonging and way of being, and a presumed shared historical experience of Aboriginal people that denies a person's unique history and identity that often includes change and movement, disconnection and reconnection with family, community and country.

Bronwyn Carlson has commented, 'individuals find and express their Aboriginal identities in a range of ways',[23] via their employment, education, friendships and family, even choosing for example whether or not to publicly signal their Aboriginal heritage.

Many of the Aboriginal people I invited to share their stories have declined to be involved, concerned they might have been singled out to speak on behalf of the many – the representatives of a type of belonging, connection, or community. They were anxious about being called upon for this reason, despite my assurances that this was not what I was seeking.

I realised 'history making' is not for everyone. Some people just *don't*. They don't want to be filmed; they don't want to be identified. 'How did you get my number?' I have heard numerous times down the telephone line, fear and mistrust wavering in their voice. They *don't get* what this project is about, they don't get what connection with place might be, they don't have *it*, haven't experienced *it* and don't buy into *it*. They don't know why I would seek to talk with them.

I noticed during this process of invitation, and the establishment of relationships throughout my research, that there was a fear of community humiliation, which I think serves to further Aboriginal and non-Aboriginal people's disconnection from valid and real urban Aboriginal histories and experiences that are occurring on the ground at this time. Many of these experiences remain unknown to wider

---

20 Carlson 2011: 12.
21 Carlson 2011.
22 Department of Aboriginal Affairs 1981, cited in Gardiner-Garden 2000: 2.
23 Carlson 2011: 18.

audiences, and thus perhaps strange and individual. Storytellers sometimes knowingly conveyed to me sensitive information during their oral history interview, criticising their friends, family and community organisation, and their own ideas and imaginings of belonging. The storytellers forged degrees of guarded trust and intimacy with me to confide, complain, explain and justify their ways of 'being' against others around them, comparing themselves and their knowledge of place, history, community and 'connection' against those people. Pausing mid-sentence, they would often reflect upon a thoughtless throw-away line that nevertheless was extremely valuable to my process of history making and place making because these unguarded comments consciously, or not, informed a wider network of relationships and connections across place, and provided a glimpse into the social fabric of the community I was working with. Directed by the storyteller, I was warned not to share these illuminating comments publicly in our final videos, our 'makings of history', with anyone else: 'edit that out!'; 'don't say I said that!'; 'that bit's confidential!'; 'no one else knows!' These comments and moments of self-reflection ironically framed the storyteller with a point of valuable cultural difference – perhaps even notoriety – in which they revealed to me the foundations of their 'making', yet refused to allow me to share this with anyone else. During the process of making history in our private oral history interviews, information was at first shared openly, only to be reworked as the storytellers censored their own representations of themselves and their history for public consumption. To tell with a fear of repercussion from the community or not at all, to make public or to keep secret an experience, a belief, a way of doing or being. These decisions maintained a balance of power within the Aboriginal communities I was working with during our process of history making by managing and denying access to knowledge to myself and a wider audience.

The places we have visited in the Blue Mountains and Western Sydney are therefore representative of living histories; a diverse 'social-scape' crossing country that could conventionally be described as urban, but includes world heritage, national park, private property and mining lands. My journey has taken me to wastelands of discarded memory and second-hand goods, to family homes of 50 years, and to places in between: where a 'place's past speaks into our present',[24] revealing itself as a ghostly presence, dreamtime event or supernatural occurrence to the Aboriginal people I have talked with, those 'who see, listen and feel history'.[25]

---

24 Thrush 2011: 58.
25 Hokari 2000: 2.

The strange and the familiar have manifested themselves in the landscape we have chosen to visit together. Perhaps validating our identity and connection to place as Aboriginal people of Sydney, unsettled histories and memories are experienced by some as non-conventional understanding or communication with country that is signalling to us as we walk – a knowing, emotional landscape that recognises the history of the people who are visiting; providing them with an access point to deep time as they carry with them their contemporary Aboriginal identity and worldview.

'This is why we are here, I was told to bring you here,'[26] she said.

It became clear to me that over the past 30 years, the Darug people have been experimenting, discussing and living various ideas about how to 'be' Aboriginal.[27] They have begun to talk about who they are, to educate the public about their history and they are actively choosing how they are *being*. For example, Aboriginal people who identify with the Darug community have formed two separate groups. Both groups practise a different form of identity making. To cement (support) their claim of Aboriginality, the Darug Tribal Aboriginal Corporation seeks information and support by engaging with scholarly practices. Conversely, the Darug Custodian Aboriginal Corporation has developed a more cultural form of expression and behaviour to inform their identity.[28] These claims of an Aboriginal identity are, however, often 'black-washed' from the historical landscape[29] by land councils and other Aboriginal people who belong to different language groups. As Leanne Tobin has commented, 'we have *real* dealings with the Land Councils here, they don't recognise us as Darug people, they *refuse* to recognise us'.[30]

Video available online: press.anu.edu.au/titles/aboriginal-history-monographs/long-history-deep-time/.

Leanne Tobin, 'Don't Deny Me My Heritage'
Source: Oral history interview by Julie Torpey.

In its most recent reincarnation, in October 2012, the Darug peoples' identity was called into question yet again by the Deerubbin Local Aboriginal Land Council and the Metropolitan Local Aboriginal Land Council. Both of these councils are located within the boundaries of Darug land. Local newspapers and Sydney's *Daily Telegraph* reported accusations of 'ethnic fraud' and 'having no legitimate claim to being the descendants of Blacktown's Aborigines'.[31]

---

26 Dianne Ussher, oral history interview by Julia Torpey, 8 August 2012, 'Billabong'.
27 Everett 2009: 53.
28 Everett 2009: 53.
29 Foley 2007: 172.
30 Leanne Tobin, oral history interview by Julia Torpey, 3 April 2012, Springwood.
31 McClennan 2012.

Consequently, Blacktown City Council suspended its Indigenous policy at the time, excluding specific reference to the Darug people as traditional owners of the land.[32] Peter Read explains this situation further in his chapter, 'Dispossession is a Legitimate Experience'.

Threatening and unknown, the apparent 'newcomers' are routinely questioned about who they are and what constitutes their history. Branded as liars, as not being Aboriginal at all,[33] they have been told that 'the Darug do not exist' by members of the Deerubbin and Metropolitan Land Councils and other Aboriginal people in New South Wales. The Darug are not easily placed, they look Aboriginal, they live in the city where little Aboriginal heritage is visible and their culture is thought to have vanished.

The people I have been speaking with as part of my research, and the Deepening Histories of Place project, have often been walking across the land silently, between the loud voices and larger shadows and, for many, their history and identity has been unspoken, has tried to be forgotten, or does not fit nicely into what is imagined to be Australian Aboriginal history; it is on the periphery and vague. One Darug women commented to me 'talking about history, caused a lot of drama for the Older Ones, they didn't want to acknowledge it, because of that time'.[34]

Continuing their existence, transforming and surviving via an ongoing dialogue with place, culture and history, there is more to the Darug story than meets the eye. Many claims are experiential and uncanny, and cannot be proven through observable facts.[35] As Kristina Everett has discussed, drawing on anthropologist Elizabeth Povinelli, 'it is the non-Aboriginal historical records, ethnographies, reports, and interpretations that dominate ideas of [traditional] and authentic Aboriginal culture'.[36]

My research has explored ways of knowing and connecting with place with some of these people who identify as Darug. Many of the stories we have recorded are yet to be included in public history telling. These stories are being recorded on the landscape now, looking to the past, present and the future, framed as a history in the making.

32   McClennan 2012.
33   Foley 2007: 172.
34   Jacinta Tobin, oral history interview by Julia Torpey, 17 October 2012, Mount Victoria.
35   Boyd 2011: 186.
36   Everett 2006: 17.

Arriving on Country

For many of the people I have talked with, connection is everywhere; for those that believe in it, *it* has power, and gives *them* power. This connection is relayed through telling, talking of experience, and being in place, being in *it*. Directed by the storytellers who have accepted my invitation to talk about their history, in places which are connected to their wellbeing, identity and histories, many of the people I have encountered have been waiting for an opportunity to share their experiences of country, and regularly visit these places for respite, leisure, to inform their artistic productions, to care for the landscape, and to connect with family and ancestors. Our recordings, located in a specific place, are a reflection of established relationships and connections to place that have been developing for some time, that is, a reflection of the storytellers' past and their future in sound and video. So we visit diverse landscapes, and we talk about history – and record. These recordings were completed between 2011 and 2013.

Walking the landscape, the country is alive and the Aboriginal people I talk with sense history, the ghosts and spirits are all around us creating as we experience them, places that are of individual significance: the green moss growing under the rock ledge; the magpie elder who keeps a watchful eye on us; the feather presenting itself as Totem along a walking track answering a silent inner call; the whirling wind of the voices high above the valley – we are being noticed by the ancestors.

Sometimes, this belief or connection is shown and learnt by being with community, on cultural days and walking with elders. Many times, however, for the people I have talked with, their belief in a spiritual and intangible history is experienced in place, triggering a physical and/or emotional response from, and of, the past. History is sensed, felt, smelt and seen in visions and read on the landscape. It always has been. It is also protected. For many of the women I have talked with, this belief of experiencing history has run through generations of family. Belief is something that has been handed down, so the uncanny is not unusual or out of place or something to be frightened of, rather, it is a signal of belonging. It is a valued and recognised gift of cultural heritage and a trait, they say, of their history, Aboriginality and of being on landscape, in the right place at the right time, or sometimes, even the wrong place. It is a belief of spirit, religion, spiritual ancestors, haunting ghosts, and markers of identity. This is to me, and to the people I have talked with, more than mere genetics. Known heritage places are guarded or, in some cases, gated to keep the experience-seekers out; *knowledge* and *experience* of place on the landscape empowers and separates.

Locals have sought to protect, empower and separate an identified heritage place in the Blue Mountains; to mislead visitors they created a physical barrier to a place they know is of significant cultural value to their local Aboriginal community, and also of value to themselves. Signalling to inquisitive strangers that this place was out of bounds, it was hoped the physical marker (gate) would repel, and this is exactly what happened during my research and is an example of just how much we rely on these markers of 'place' to find welcoming and belonging or otherwise.

During my visit to this place of storytelling and significant cultural heritage, our immediate environment and the features of our expected destination were familiar to me. I had however not expected to see a 'gate' and to become 'locked out' of the destination I sought to visit.

Disoriented, I was unsure of how to proceed *into* this now unwelcoming place. I was concerned about what might be occurring beyond the gate so I waited for our storyteller to arrive. Perhaps we were not meant to be here after all I thought. Perhaps secret business was underway. Perhaps by being there we had upset or disturbed someone. Our storyteller had previously explained to us this place was being protected and managed to ensure past injustices to the site and the people it was connected to (both past and present) were rectified. I understood that not everything in and of this place could be explained to me. I knew in this location, which held secret and sacred heritage, *I* was out of place, and now I was literally locked out. Our storyteller pulled up in his car next to us. 'What are ya doing?' he asked sensing our unease. 'Oh don't worry,' he explained, 'that's just the neighbours, they're trying to protect this place. They know how significant it is to us. We didn't put it up!'[37] He laughed as he ushered us through.

Video available online: press.anu.edu.au/titles/aboriginal-history-monographs/long-history-deep-time/.

Jason Brown, 'Watching Over the Land'
Source: Oral history interview by Julie Torpey

Nikki Parsons-Gardiner has also relayed her experience travelling across country, 'being led by spirit, wherever they wanted to take me' to find her identity. She commented, 'everything around us gives us messages, whether it's the trees, whether it's the animals, and particularly the birds, they've always got messages for us'.[38] During this research, the intangible was introduced to us when we walked through the land and talked about history. When we visited places of

---

37 Nicole Parsons-Gardiner, oral history interview by Julia Torpey, 11 September 2012, Nurragingy Reserve, Blacktown.
38 Jo Clancy, oral history interview by Julia Torpey, 21 August 2012, Wentworth Falls.

refuge, escape, reflection, healing and meditation. On these journeys, the power was with the storyteller; places were brought alive, having the storyteller's needs and life experience placed upon it.

The ghosts of place include the ghosts of the living,[39] the energy and emotion of history that are held within a person's identity. Brought to place unwittingly or often unverbalised, ghosts are revealed – in body language and behaviour, positioned in relation to my own identity as a researcher, an unknown Aboriginal person 'wanting something'. So the angle of the camera and what it records, or does not record, matters. It records choice: choosing a landscape, choosing how to perform, choosing to answer questions, choosing what to reveal to me by directing me and telling me what I can and cannot film, choosing to trust and build a relationship with me, or choosing simply to engage with their place, reacting to what their place is showing them, and perhaps choosing not to talk with me at all.

These relationships to place point to a gap in the Aboriginal history of Western Sydney and the Blue Mountains that is only recently starting to be balanced. Going into a place, and choosing a site that is of personal significance, that may not be connected to wider stories of creation or colonial history, is validating because it acknowledges an alternative history that is being played out now. Diverse stories range from recognisable 'traditional' ancestral stories of the past that we have heard in recorded form before to more contemporary stories of spirituality and the uncanny, that is, survival. Steadfast and sure in excited, hushed conversation, a participant claimed 'it was a dreamtime event!'[40] One that was so special that the story could not be relayed on film; to more contemporary tellings of experiential and unbelievable events of family legend, ability and heritage 'the table walked out the door!'[41]

Other stories have expressed the temporal grief of what could have been, as storytellers imagine and romanticise a utopian Aboriginal lifestyle that was taken away from them.

Although widely discussed by many of the Darug people I was working with, Nikki Parsons-Gardiner was one of the first people to verbalise the impact of history making on her identity and those around her. She emphasised the fear of speaking up about her own experience of identity, history and place. She explains it like this:

---

39 Avery 1997: 823.
40 David King, oral history interview by Julia Torpey, 22 August 2012, Katoomba.
41 Jacinta Tobin, oral history interview by Julia Torpey, 17 October 2012, Mount Victoria.

I know that I am from here, and this is my rightful place, I'm able to honour, I'm able to speak for, and for the people that aren't able to do that … We know for a lot of Darug people, because we were hit first in this area, well in Sydney and then out in the Hawkesbury and Parramatta area, and a lot of people moved out, or a lot of people were moved in, and because we were the first to have the white bloodlines run through here and people were white skinned, and there was a lot of stigma in early days … when culture and all that was taken, that being Aboriginal was wrong. A lot of Darug people, and correct me if I'm wrong anyone out there, [she says] a lot of Darug people weren't able to speak up for themselves and I think still in a way, are unable to do that, or not do that properly …

Tapping into energy to remember the past, she continues:

A lot of us carry generational stuff of trauma. We may not have been affected by the stolen generation … didn't happen in my family, but I worked out not long ago that I carried the trauma of that, for the main reason being that what it meant to me, was that they didn't think my culture or my people were good enough. You know, so you carry that … they tried to extinct us. I believe that a lot of us carry trauma from colonisation because the family bloodline comes down … through birthing. You're mother held that; that comes through to us in emotion and in energy … you know, there is a lot of healing that needs to be done for our people …[42]

Video available online: press.anu.edu.au/titles/aboriginal-history-monographs/long-history-deep-time/.

Nicole Parsons-Gardiner, 'I've Always Been'
Source: Oral history interview by Julie Torpey.

Indeed, in this project, the power is with the storyteller and the believer. Our experience 'on location', places me in a relationship with the people I meet and work with, interlocking and in tension.[43] Together we begin and experience a conversation that is difficult to explain. We traverse a life story, spirituality, crises, and belonging. As Motz states, believing involves the specific choices and actions of individuals in particular historical, geographical, and social contexts,[44] and following De Certeau, 'the act of saying it and considering it as true'.[45] Even myself, the researcher, is caught unawares wondering, and eager to

---

42 Nicole Parsons-Gardiner, oral history interview by Julia Torpey, 11 September 2012, Nurragingy Reserve, Blacktown.
43 Avery 1997: 198.
44 Motz 1998: 349.
45 De Carteau 1984: 178, cited in Motz 1998: 349.

find truth in my experiences. 'I know who you are!', Robyn said as I began to introduce myself before we sat down to film in her home. 'They all followed you from your car to the balcony, through the front door. You have four [invisible] people with you.'[46]

Through our ghosts of belonging, we place ourselves in relation to one another. We place ourselves in relation to a physical place through our desire to belong, feeling a tie of kinship with that place. We experience a social tie to the spiritual and the physical world.

For some people, this is therapy; being together, they haven't talked before. In honouring this process, the experience of something barely visible, shrouded as another being, or seemingly not there at all, infiltrates place and story as defined by the storyteller:

> We're here in this place, Narragingy Reserve, across the bridge is Eastern Creek, my grandfather's country … energetically it just feels good and I will sit here, usually on this rock, and meditate. I'll just sit down here and connect with my ancestors.

> … Here we go, all the crows have turned up, in big numbers, they're a messenger, Wargan the crow. So even they think it's right to be down here. So any Aboriginal stuff I guess, is when crow come[s] along for me, and any angelic or spirit stuff that's not connected to Aboriginal, that when the white cockatoos come …

When I visited a billabong with Dianne Ussher behind Katoomba in the Blue Mountains, she expressed her belief in the Holy Ghost, surrounding her and guiding her decisions, this is her Aboriginality, her spirit and self:

> When Karen asked me for a place, I said on the telephone, I'll wait to be shown … quite literally just in my third eye, this [place] … was shown to me on Monday night … Don't question, don't waste time trying to think about things, because … there is something higher … if you just give time, you will be shown exactly the right time, in exactly the right place … and that is what I did and this is where I'm shown! … It feels very mystical, like its filled with good, holy sacred blood … and that there has been really happy times around this water … and when I've come down here in recent times, it maintains that place of joy … and that's the essence for me …[47]

46   Robyn Caughlan, oral history interview by Julia Torpey, 28 November 2012, Colyton.
47   Dianne Ussher, oral history interview by Julia Torpey, 8 August 2012, 'Billabong'.

Artist and playwright Leanne Tobin explains that upon moving to her home in the Blue Mountains:

> It's almost like the spirits are supporting my quest to put forward their story, you know ... everything I've done has been given like a big tick!
>
> I had my cousin who is a spirit woman. She sees spirits ... especially the old spirits ... she stepped out the back verandah and saw a young fella. She came to me afterwards and said, 'There's a young fella down the back there, he's pointing up to the gully here, he's saying Nullaway! Nullaway!' I finally went and looked it up and researched and found out it means 'camp', 'camp', 'to camp here' and it's just so apt because it's just the most perfect place to camp ...[48]

Her sister Jacinta continues: 'We were brought up with the spirit stuff'; familiar smells of people passing, of older women's rose perfume lingering in the air and the always identifiable smell of (smelly) 'rotten' feet of a much loved aunty; visionary dreams, hands hold the shoulders and a warning feeling inside that tells you you're in the wrong place.[49]

Nikki explains her experience:

> When I was younger, sitting on the side of the creek, and the fog would be coming up, and next minute you'd start to hear ... like ... a battle happening ... it was really bizarre. We'd all get up and run ...
>
> Next time we'd go down, the same things would happen. And of course latter on in life you'd find that that was where the battles or massacres had happened. Even back then, that energy, we were still picking up on it ...[50]

These sensations, as Motz explains, allow for individual interpretation and use.[51] These sensations however, are recognised within the community of people I have worked with, as a way of knowing. These lingering experiences give many of them something to hold onto that is their own experience, as well as perhaps presenting a history that is beyond a western view of what Aboriginal history might be.

---

48 Leanne Tobin, oral history interview by Julia Torpey, 3 April 2012, Springwood.
49 Jacinta Tobin, oral history interview by Julia Torpey, 17 October 2012, Mount Victoria.
50 Nicole Parsons-Gardiner, oral history interview by Julia Torpey, 11 September 2012, Nurragingy Reserve, Blacktown.
51 Motz 1998: 350.

The experiences and intuitions outlined above point to a gap in Aboriginal history of Western Sydney and the Blue Mountains that is only recently starting to be balanced. Going into a place, it has been reported back to me by the people I have worked with, and choosing a site that is of personal significance that may not be connected to wider stories of creation or colonial history, is validating because it acknowledges an alternative history that is being played out now.

As American author Toni Morrison in Avery encourages, 'that which appears absent can indeed be a seething presence'.[52] Through sight, sound, scent and movement, these experiences are reinforced by verbal storytelling, emotion, and the validation of identity. The stories that are coming to the surface are part of an energetic culture eager to share alternate ways of knowing.

Acknowledgements

Thank you to Peter Read, Mary Anne Jebb, Ann McGrath and Maria Haenga-Collins for your encouragement and editorial support. Thank you Karen Maber, Jo Clancy, Nikki Parsons-Gardiner, Jacinta Tobin, Leanne Tobin, Robyn Caughlan, Dianne Ussher, David King, and Jason Brown for sharing your stories with me.

Bibliography

Oral history interviews

Brown, Jason, interviewed by Julia Torpey, 8 August 2012, Kings Tableland.

Caughlan, Robyn, interviewed by Julia Torpey, 28 November 2012, Colyton.

Clancy, Jo, interviewed by Julia Torpey, 21 August 2012, Wentworth Falls.

King, David, interviewed by Julia Torpey, 22 August 2012, Katoomba.

Parsons-Gardiner, Nicole, interviewed by Julia Torpey, 11 September 2012, Nurragingy Reserve, Blacktown.

Tobin, Jacinta, interviewed by Julia Torpey, 17 October 2012, Mount Victoria.

Tobin, Leanne, interviewed by Julia Torpey, 3 April 2012, Springwood.

---

52   Avery 1997: 17.

Ussher, Dianne, interviewed by Julia Torpey, 8 August 2012, 'Billabong'.

Other sources

Archibald, Jo-Ann (Q'um Q'um Xiiem) 2008, 'An indigenous storywork methodology', in, J Gary Knowles and Ardra L Cole (eds), *Handbook of the arts in qualitative research: perspectives, methodologies, examples, and issues*, Sage Publications, Los Angeles.

Archibald, Jo-Ann (Q'um Q'um Xiiem) 2008, *Indigenous Storywork Methodology Educating the Heart, Mind, Body and Spirit*, UBC Press, Vancouver.

Ashcroft, Bill, Gareth Griffiths and Helen Tiffin (eds) 1995, *The Postcolonial Studies Reader,* Routledge, London and New York.

Avery, Gordon F 1997, *Ghostly Matters: Haunting and the Sociological Imagination*, University of Minnesota Press, Minneapolis.

Boyd, Colleen E 2011, '"We are standing in my ancestor's longhouse": learning the language of spirits and ghosts', in Colleen E Boyd and Coll Thrush (eds), *Phantom Past, Indigenous Presence: Native Ghosts in North American Culture and History*, University of Nebraska Press, Lincoln: 181–208.

Carlson, Bronwyn 2011, 'The Politics of Identity: Who Counts as Aboriginal Today?' PhD thesis, Social Sciences & International Studies, Faculty of Arts and Social Sciences, University of New South Wales.

De Carteau, Michel 1984, *The Practice of Everyday Life*, Steve Rendall (trans.), University of California Press, Berkeley.

Department of Aboriginal Affairs 1981, *Report on a Review of the Administration of the Working Definition of Aboriginal and Torres Strait Islanders*, Commonwealth of Australia, Canberra.

Everett, Kristina 2006, 'Impossible Realities: Indigenous and Non-Indigenous Relationships in a Sydney Aboriginal Community', PhD thesis, Macquarie University.

Everett, Kristina 2009, 'Welcome to country … not', *Oceania* 79(1): 53–64.

Foley, Dennis 2007, 'What has native title done to the urban Koorie in New South Wales who is also a traditional custodian?', in Benjamin R Smith and Frances Morphy (eds), *The Social Effects of Native Title: Recognition, Translation, Coexistence,* Centre for Aboriginal Economic Policy Research Monograph No. 27, ANU E Press, Canberra.

Gardiner-Garden, J 2000, *The Definition of Aboriginality: Research Note 18, 2000–01*, Parliament of Australia.

Gordon, F Avery 1997, *Ghostly Matters: Haunting and the Sociological Imagination*, University of Minnesota Press, Minneapolis.

Graham, Mary 1999, 'Some thoughts about the philosophical underpinnings of Aboriginal worldviews', *Worldviews: Global Religions, Culture and Ecology* 3(2): 105–118.

Healy, Chris 1997, *From the Ruins of Colonialism: History as Social Memory*, Cambridge University Press, Melbourne.

Hokari, Minoru 2003, 'History happening in/between body and place: journey to the Aboriginal way of historical practice', in John R Stephens (ed.), *Habitus: A Sense of Place: Proceedings of the Habitus 2000 Conference*, Curtin University of Technology, Perth, www.hokariminoru.org/pdfs/HistoryHappening.pdf (accessed 12 September 2014).

Kelleher, Matthew 2009, 'Aboriginal art in the Blue Mountains', in Eugene Stockton and John Merriman (eds), *Blue Mountains Dreaming, The Aboriginal Heritage*, Blue Mountain Education and Research Trust, Lawson, New South Wales, 73–102.

Kohen, James 1993, *The Darug and their Neighbours: The Traditional Aboriginal Owners of the Sydney Region*, Darug Link in Association with Blacktown and District Historical Society, Blacktown, New South Wales.

Langton, Marcia 1981, 'Urbanizing Aborigines: the social scientists' great deception', *Social Alternatives* 2(2): 16–22.

McClennan, Ben 2012, 'Blacktown Council suspends recognition of Darug Aborigines as Blacktown's Traditional Owners', *Blacktown Advocate*, 9 October 2012, www.dailytelegraph.ecom.au/news/national/blacktown-council-suspends-recognition-of-darug-aborigines-asblacktowns-traditional-owners/story-fndo28a5-1226491869900 (accessed 7 April 2015).

Mathews, Robert Hamilton 1902, 'The Thoorga language', *Queensland Geographical Journal* 17(3): 49–73.

Morgan, George 2006, *Unsettled Places: Aboriginal People and Urbanisation in New South Wales*, Wakefield Press, Kent Town, South Australia.

Motz, Marilyn 1998, 'The practice of belief', *The Journal of American Folklore* 111(411): 339–355.

Rowley, Charles D 1972, *Outcasts in White Australia*, Penguin, Sydney.

Taylor, Affrica 2000, '"The sun always shines in Perth": A post-colonial geography of identity, memory and place', *Australian Geographical Studies* 38(1): 27–35.

Thrush, Coll 2011, 'Hauntings as histories: indigenous ghosts and the urban past in Seattle', in Colleen E Boyd and Coll Thrush (eds), *Phantom Past, Indigenous Presence: Native Ghosts in North American Culture and History*, University of Nebraska Press, Lincoln.

9. Historyless People

Jeanine Leane

> *... theirs is a timelessness of men and women wandering around without recourse either to origin or destination ...*[1]

The construct of 'history' defines time as a space that can be measured. Time flows in a certain linear direction where people 'make' history. Historical discourse defines timelessness as an existence where time is not marked but melds in an unchanging, static environment. This chapter looks at the reconfiguration of time, place, history, memory, myth, magic and impossibility in Waanyi writer Alexis Wright's story *Carpentaria*.

Carpentaria is an Aboriginal narrative set in the fictional coastal town of Desperance by the Gulf of Carpentaria in north-western Queensland.[2] There are few familiar moorings for readers whose ethnocentric education presupposes that literature and history rely on inherently coherent and linear narratives. People with time and timeless people inhabit the space of the Gulf. Time and timelessness, history, memory and the sacred are central concerns of *Carpentaria*. Representations of deep and shallow time, notions of cosmos and chaos, history and memory, myth and reason are juxtaposed in Wright's narrative.

Who are the timeless people? *Carpentaria* begins with a chapter called 'From Time Immemorial', exposing different systems of time that exists in one place:

> A nation chants but we know your story already. The bells peal everywhere. Church bells calling the faithful to the tabernacle where the gates of heaven will open. But not for the wicked calling innocent little black girls from a distant community where the white dove bearing the olive branch never lands. Little girls who come back home after church on Sunday, who look around themselves at the human fallout and announce matter-of-factly, 'armageddon begins here'.[3]

Directly following this image of sharp and shallow Gregorian time, a deeper, languid and characterful world emerges:

---

1   Wright 2006: 58.
2   Wright 2006.
3   Wright 2006: 1.

> The ancestral serpent, a creature larger than storm clouds came down from the stars, laden with its own creative enormity. It moved graciously – if you had been watching with the eyes of a bird hovering in the sky far above the ground.
>
> Picture the giant serpent, scoring deep into – scouring down through – the slippery underground of mudflats, leaving in its wake the thunder of tunnels collapsing to form deep sunken valleys.
>
> The serpent travelled over the marine plains, over the salt flats, through the salt dunes, past the mangrove forests and crawled inland … When it finished creating the many rivers in its wake, it created one last river … a river which offers no apologies for … people who don't know it. This is where the giant serpent continues to live deep down under the ground in a vast network of limestone aquifers. They say its being is porous; it permeates everything. It is all around in the atmosphere and is attached to the lives of the river people like skin.[4]

Whose Armageddon are the opening lines referring to? When time and timeless meet, a warp occurs and cosmos becomes chaos. But whose cosmos and whose chaos? Is one people's chaos another people's cosmos?

Carpentaria is told from the third person omniscient perspective and in an Aboriginal storytelling style. To offer a plot summary would be reductionist, as the narrative is a complex layering of stories. It collapses time and space to honour Aboriginal past, present, memory, future and the sense of collectively experienced time like the serpent described in the opening passages, 'collapsing tunnels' that represent confined spaces to form 'deep sunken valleys' that are expansive and vast like the Aboriginal stories in the narrative.

Although fictional, Desperance is representative of small towns in the Gulf country, in terms of geography, climate, demographics, history and memory. It is home to a fractious Aboriginal community living on both the east and west sides of the town. The Pricklebush mob and their patriarch Normal Phantom make a life adjacent to the rubbish tip. A contrasting breakaway group, Joseph Midnight's mob lives in car bodies and they invent a fictitious Aboriginal identity to profit from a mine. Another group of separatist traditionalists led by Big Mozzie Fishman follow the ancient Dreaming tracks from across the Northern Territory border in battered Holdens and Fords that require constant maintenance and salvaging by bush mechanics 'using [the] tools and parts found only in nature'.[5] This group is inspired by another group of guerilla warriors, led by Will Phantom, who are intent on sabotaging the mine.

---

4 Wright 2006: 1–2.
5 Wright 2006: 120.

In between and surrounded by these Aboriginal groups live the Uptown Europeans, who continually resist the efforts of 'southern bureaucrats' to rename their town Masterton because they are intent on honouring their pioneer history. Underneath Desperance is a place of deep time that is out of the visual range of the settlers, but whose presence makes itself felt in ways that they cannot comprehend. The narrator points out that:

> The inside knowledge about this river and coastal region is Aboriginal Law handed down through [generations] since time began. Otherwise, how would one know where to look for the underwater courses in the vast flooding mud plains, full of serpents and fish in the monsoon season? ... Know the moment of climatic change better than they know themselves?[6]

Beneath Desperance, bits and pieces discarded from Uptown float to the bottom of the sea. The reefs are home to 'thousands of bits and pieces of chipped and broken China, sugar-bears, yellow chickens, spotted dogs and pink babies of lost cargo'.[7] The ancient sea reefs begin to archive settler history in their depths.

Beyond the town is the rubbish tip. It is home to the Pricklebush mob and one of the central characters in the story, Normal Phantom. Normal shares this home, built from all sorts of scraps thrown away by the white folk, with his wife Angel Day and their seven children. Normal was:

> an old tribal man who lived ... in the dense Pricklebush scrub on the edge of town ... They had lived in a human dumping-ground since the day Normal Phantom was born ... The descendants of the pioneer families, who claimed ownership of the town, said 'the Aboriginal was not really part of the town at all' ... 'Furthermore', they said, 'the Aboriginal was dumped here by the pastoralists, because they refused to pay the blackfellas equal wages, even when it came in. Right on the edge of somebody else's town, didn't they?'[8]

The Pricklebush mob fashion their dwellings from settler rubbish and in this way the settler waste takes on a different value. It becomes a layer of a deeper landscape and memory of place and is incorporated into the depth of the lands and waters. Like the bits and pieces under the sea, the Pricklebush transforms the tip; it becomes a layer of a deeper history. A record and an archive to the everyday life of the recent settler diaspora, they seem to undervalue it in favour of bigger, more important quests; for example, attempting to distinguish the town with a giant statue to celebrate local mining and cattle industries or

---

6   Wright 2006: 3.
7   Wright 2006: 61.
8   Wright 2006: 4.

local pastimes, such as drinking and fighting southern bureaucrats over the pioneer history. They are adamant that the town's name remains the same in honour of Matthew Flinders, who Uptown *insisted* discovered the deep port. To the Aboriginal residents it is a constant and quiet source of amusement to know that, 'no one in Uptown accepted that Matthew Flinders was a prize fool [for going around] saying he discovered a deep water port'.[9]

The Pricklebush mob knew that:

> Normal Phantom could grab hold of the river in his mind and live with it as his father's fathers did before him. His ancestors were the river people, who were living with the river before time began ... he came and went on the flowing waters ... out to the sea. He stayed away ... as long as he pleased. He knew fish, and was on friendly terms with gropers, the giant codfish of the Gulf sea, that swam in schools of fifty or more ... the prickly bush mob said he had always chased constellations: 'We watched him as a little boy running off into the night to try and catch stars'. They were certain he knew the secret of getting there ... right up to the stars in the company of groper fish ... when the sea and the sky became one ...[10]

Islands of floating debris, so large and so dense that they can support vegetation and human life, surround the waters around Desperance. In the final scene, one of these islands, largely formed of waste from a mine nearby, is used as a hideout for an Aboriginal guerilla warrior who eventually destroys the mine. This image of human-made islands floating in a wider, deeper, natural sea, provides us with a significant metaphor for reading between the contested space of Aboriginal memory and realism and western history and rationalism.

At this point a fair question may be to ask what has all this to do with history? Since its publication in 2006, *Carpentaria* has won a host of awards and attracted much critical attention from a largely non-Aboriginal readership. It has been described, for example, as a blurring of fact and fantasy, myth and history, a 'sprawling carnivalesque novel', a dreamscape of which magical realism is also associated, and 'a dreamscape'.[11] Literary scholar Ian Syson commented that while the novel had the 'bones of a contemporary realist plot' they are bones only – for they do not get fleshed out. Rather, the novel favours a 'more ornamental, magic-enabling mode'.[12] My interest as an Aboriginal reader is in

9   Wright 2006: 60.
10 Wright 2006: 6–7.
11 Delvin Glass 2007: 86; Molloy 2012: 1; Syson 2007: 86.
12 Syson 2007.

the use of descriptors such as these that defer to the magical, mythical and the incredible, and how such terms position Wright's narrative outside the realms of western realism.

Many of the incidents described revolve around Mabo-style native title claims in the far north. Clashes between Aboriginal communities and mining and pastoral leases are also reported in the colonial records, such as the sabotage of a mine in a similar setting by Aboriginal guerillas and the cyclone that levels the town in Armageddon-like circumstances. But what of that which is described as myth and fantasy, the unsubstantiated beyond the boundaries of western possibility? The epic sea journeys by Normal Phantom that are neither marked by days, weeks, months, years, fathoms, leagues or any other conventional marker of space or time; or the malfunctioning of every single watch, clock and timepiece owned by the settlers, thus suspending western time for the duration of the narrative?

Carpentaria is a working and weaving of many Aboriginal stories of place; the spiritual beliefs of the Waanyi passed down from Wright's grandmother, of whom she wrote:

> She had stories to explain everything – who we are, who each of us were and the place on our traditional country that was very deep.[13]

There are stories of place from elder storytellers and stories gathered from Wright's long career from the late 1960s onwards, working with political movements in Mount Isa and throughout north-west Queensland, including the Gulf – her traditional country. She draws upon her time at Mornington Island, when the Queensland Government, under Bjelke Petersen, wanted state control of the island after the Uniting Church mission withdrew. The Lardil people wanted self-determination and worked against the government. In this way, it is a work of Aboriginal realism.[14]

Wright recalls:

> I am still involved in campaigns for our rights. I am indebted to the generous spirit of men and women of great wisdom and knowledge ... they gave me the tool of writing. I felt literature, the work of fiction, was the best way to tell the truth ... more of a truth than non-fiction which isn't really true either. Non-fiction is often about the writer telling what it is safe to tell.[15]

---

13 Wright 2002: 13.
14 Alexis Wright resisted the term magic realism to describe *Carpentaria*. 'Some people call the book magic realism but really in a way it's an Aboriginal realism which carries all sorts of things.' Wright quoted by Dart 2007 and Ravenscroft 2010: 216.
15 Wright 2002: 13.

Furthermore, Alison Ravenscroft points out in relation to western categorisations of Wright's work, that when western translations of Aboriginal knowledge occur, the discourse surrounding it slips into familiar vocabulary and generic codes: magic, superstition, myth and the supernatural – western readings that label the knowledge of 'others' unexplainable and 'magic'; 'a move that paradoxically tames and familiarises'.[16]

Ravenscroft asks in relation to such terms: 'Whose magic, whose reality?' She refers to Toni Morrison's essay 'Rootedness: The Ancestor is Foundation'.[17] In response to interpretations of *Song of Solomon* as mythical and magical, Morrison stated: 'Among African Americans there are ways of knowing that might fall into the magic or superstitious in the eyes of white American readers.'[18] She went on to say: 'Flying was one of our [great] gifts. I don't care how silly it may seem ... it's in [our] spirituals and our gospels.'[19] What is taken by a white reader to be magic in texts such as Morrison's might not be so for the world of the author.

Ravenscroft's question is poignant as it draws attention to the frequency by white critics and scholars to refer to stories such as Toni Morrison's, and later Wright's, as magical or mythical. Morrison's, and later Ravenscroft's, reservations about these and similar descriptors are that the white western reality becomes the only reality.

Patrick Wolfe critiqued the term Dreamtime as an invention of anthropological discourse, where dreams are associated with the unconscious, imaginary and illusionary rather than what might rightly be called Aboriginal Law.[20] Wolfe argued that in the Australian colonising context, the combination of 'Aborigine' and 'dream' made for the dispossession of Aboriginal peoples by removing us from western historical time.[21] This makes colonial times and places the only reality. I am reminded here of Syson's comment that Wright may well have perfected the art of magical realism in Australia, pioneered in his view by Peter Carey and Richard Flanagan, by 'giving the magic more indigenous [sic] *and* Indigenous sources'.[22] Does this perfection lie in what the settler imagination insists and persists in reading as an ideal combination: the Indigenous and magic?

16 Ravenscroft 2010: 216.
17 Morrison 1984: 340.
18 Cited in Ravenscroft 2010: 200.
19 Quoted in Ravenscroft 2010: 200.
20 Wolfe 1991.
21 Wolfe 1991: 210.
22 Syson 2007.

What is at stake for Aboriginal writers of stories of place, deep time, present time and the future when contemporary historians, literary critics, cultural theorists, anthropologists continue to read our narratives via the constructs of 'the dream', 'the mythical' and the 'magical', thus making an association between Aboriginal storytelling and fantasy, the impossible, the illusory and the unreal? Or, as Ravenscroft asks, 'where Dreaming is translated as legend, myth or children's story ... the kind of dreaming one does on one's pillow, a fantasmatic distortion of everyday life without geographical or historical coordinates.'[23] From where I stand such readings assimilate our knowledge and stories of time and place to the familiar discourse of the settler readers' comfort zone.

Alexis Wright refuses such assimilation of Aboriginal experience and beliefs within western paradigms and exposes the dreams and beliefs of the settler residents of Desperance as impossible and a mere fantasy. It is the settlers who continually confront timeless un-belonging. From the Aboriginal perspective, Desperance is but a 'shared slither of similarity with others'.[24] Ironically, true Desperanians are described as 'blue-eyed, blond, nervy, skinny, freckled types belonging to old families whose origins in town stretched back several generations, not Johnny-come-latelies – no way'.[25]

The old people of the Pricklebush give their children, who they must send to Uptown for school, a job to do: '"Go", they told the schoolkids, "search through every single line of those whitefellas' history books"'. The children flicked through the damp pages of western history books to find that 'whitefellas had no secrets'.[26] At the end of the exercise, the 'little scholars' report on 'whitefella dreams' to their elders:

> These children stood full of themselves in front of the old people and proclaimed loudly, that the folk of Uptown could be masters of their own dreams. Yes, like stonemasons, who in a night could relay every single stone in an invisible boundary surrounding the town into a wall so solid it had the appearance of [an] important medieval palace. *But where were stones to be found in the claypans?* In these times it was assumed that any outsider to these dreams would never see the stones of Desperance, if he carried a different understanding of worldly matters originating from ancient times elsewhere. The outsider to these dreams only saw open spaces and flat lands.[27]

23 Ravenscroft 2010: 197.
24 Wright 2006: 55.
25 Wright 2006: 57.
26 Wright 2006: 57.
27 Wright 2006: 58–59.

The Aborigines are the outsiders to this dream, yet their deeper understanding of place, people and time make the settlers' certainty, and their dreams seem ridiculously impossible. Their faith in an invisible net that is 'made up of prayers and god-fearing devotion ... a protective shield, saving the town from a cyclone ... every November',[28] is juxtaposed over deeper Aboriginal knowledge of place and time. As the cyclone approaches, the omniscient voice of the Aboriginal storyteller speaks as the land itself and asks:

> The old, unanswerable question: [H]ow the heck were they going to keep themselves out of the water?[29]

For the Pricklebush mob: 'Crickets and frogs were the guardians of the night for generations of Pricklebush folk.'[30] The Pricklebush mob see not a boundary or a net or a fence but:

> huge, powerful, ancestral creation spirits occupying the land and sea moving through the town, even inside other folk's houses ... Nothing ... good was coming out of these puerile dreams of stone walls, big locked gates, barred windows, barbed wire rolled around the top to lock out the black demon. Pricklebush decided the Uptown boundary must be a gammon one. Then the Uptown folk showed their boundaries which they said had been created at the beginning of their time.[31]

The Pricklebush look on in disbelief at the settlers who believe that they can make and master their own dreams. This is a myth as the impending cyclone and destruction of the mine prove.

In the closing, highly symbolic passages of the novel, Desperance is levelled by a cyclone and Aboriginal activists use the settler chaos around the cyclone to carry out an attack on the mine. Settler rubbish in the form of a floating island of debris is used as a hideout for a guerilla warrior who survives for months floating around the Gulf of Carpentaria. For the settlers, the town is levelled and destroyed. For the Aboriginal residents, the town is transformed as part of the cosmos of the underground serpent. It never was a question of 'if', but 'when'. In this way, Wright challenges European arrogance and inexperience with the living land.

But like her refusal to accept a narrow and shallow definition of history, Wright also challenges the adequacy and accuracy of western terms like science to describe Aboriginal knowledge. In *Carpentaria*, Aboriginal knowledge

---

28   Wright 2006: 58.
29   Wright 2006: 55.
30   Wright 2006: 59.
31   Wright 2006: 59.

is grounded in its faithfulness and faith in a particular place, its ancestry, its people, its seas and skies, and the deep interpretation of these with the sacred – despite European efforts to consign this kind of knowledge to discourses of the irrational, superstitious and the pre-scientific. Aboriginal knowledge of sacred is summed up in the words of one of Wright's Aboriginal characters as already 'scientify enough'. This is a beautifully derisive term and the 'if-y-ness' of western science is contrasted throughout the narrative to the depths of Aboriginal knowledge of place. The question is posed in the opening passages as to how does a person who did not grow up in a place that is sometimes under water and sometimes dry as a bone, 'know the moment of climatic change better than they know themselves'.[32]

Carpentaria then is a continuing narrative of Aboriginal experience of place, people and of *all times*. Wright rejects the term history to describe the narrative for its confinement of Aboriginal people to victim spaces and its shallow view of time. Time is represented in *Carpentaria* by the resilience of ancient beliefs overlaying the inherited colonial experience that the author describes as 'nothing more than hot air passing through the mind'. And, of this shallow settler history,

> with no disrespect it is expedient to say at this point, that such little towns are apt to do one thing right, and this is how a town like Desperance shared a slither of similarity with others … it too sought glory in its own legends. A single, important legendary lore of place developed over a century or two …[33]

The irony that runs through the story is that while the settlers are intent on recording their history – the 'things that are safe to tell' – they fail to realise that they are already incorporated into a bigger past that is Aboriginal land and memory and that, in this scheme of things, they are the shallowest layer. The most striking contrast in Wright's narrative between deep and shallow time is arguably what the settlers cannot hear.

> Southern people who like noise would say that something north of the Tropic of Capricorn like Desperance, was just a quiet little town, but if you listened hard enough, you would have heard the silence screaming to be heard.[34]

---

32 Wright 2006: 3.
33 Wright 2006: 55.
34 Wright 2006: 55.

Long History, Deep Time

The silence that screams to be heard is the Aboriginal reality of past, present, belief and memory built over (albeit temporarily), and just below the surface of a literal and figurative colonial construction of a town and its settler foundation myths, superstitions and beliefs.

In reflecting on the lengthy process of telling an Aboriginal story of collective memories, Wright wrote:

> [The story] could not be contained in a capsule that was either time or incident specific. It would not fit into the English and therefore Australian tradition of creating boundaries and fences which encode the development of thinking in this country, and which follows through … the containment of thought and idea in the novel.[35]

And:

> I wanted to examine how memory is being recreated to challenge the warped creativity of negativity, and somehow becomes a … continuation of the Dreaming story.[36]

Aboriginal Dreaming is not a static place or time as western discourse often implies. *Carpentaria* challenges ideas of boundaries and confinement by exploring how ancient Aboriginal beliefs sit in the contemporary world as a continuation of our Dreaming stories.

So why, since much of what happens in this story could be substantiated by 'facts' that a western historian would have to accept, does the author reject 'history' as it is currently defined? Wright said she did not want to write a historical novel, even though Australia appears to be a land with a disappearing memory. She goes on to describe Australian history as 'the colonising spider' and certainly in a very short and shallow space of time it has woven a very tangled web and 'netted' (to use the author's own term from the novel) Aboriginal people within its colonising discourse. As Wright reminds us: 'History drags every Aboriginal person into the conquering grips of colonisation' – and it does! It brings us into someone else's time and that time has been written of as *the only time*. Wright goes on to say:

> the story does not only come from colonisation or assimilation or having learnt to write English, or arguing whether people with an oral history should write books, but is sung just as strongly from those of our ancestors who wrote our stories on the walls of caves and on the surface of weathered rock.[37]

---

35 Wright 2007: 81.
36 Wright 2007: 82.
37 Wright 2006: 13.

160

In trying to configure the history Wright knew, and the reality she understood, to tell an Aboriginal story of all times, she looked outside of Australia.[38] She was inspired and influenced by novelist Carlos Fuentes who described Mexico as a country of suspended times, where no time has been resolved. Fuentes explained that European writers assimilate and direct the past by writing with a sense of linear time that assumes a forward progression. He believed that novels were places where all times meet and 'past becomes memory, and the future, desire … The novel expresses things that history did not mention, did not remember or suddenly stopped imagining.'[39] Similarly, Uruguayan journalist and author Eduardo Galeano wrote in the introduction to his work *Genesis* that he 'wanted to contribute to the kidnapped memory of all America (Latin America) and to speak to his land, to talk to her, to share her secrets, ask of what difficult clays she was born, from what acts of love and violation she comes'.[40] The failure of history then, for Indigenous writers and storytellers is its containment, its selective memory and its general reluctance to recognise land as living.

Carpentaria closes with a different song to the one at the beginning. 'It was a mystery, but there was so much song wafting off the watery land, singing the country afresh.'[41] So Desperance is transformed, not destroyed. The settler disaster is reconfigured as Aboriginal cosmos. Land decides the destiny of people. People tell stories that existed before settler occupation and remember.

Historians write retrospectively and selectively. Wright reconfigures conventional meanings of time and timeless in a story of Aboriginal realism. More specifically, it is Waanyi realism as the story is born of Waanyi times and place and the Gulf of Carpentaria is a place for all times and memory − not just the last 225 years. The historyless people are those without deeper connections to the land that they occupy. Their timelessness is the vacuum of the short history they have made. The settler's belief in an invisible net protecting the town's colonial history from Aboriginal superstition and natural disaster proves to be but a slim veneer. In the face of a deeper, greater and more powerful force, *history* as currently defined is similarly a slim layer in Aboriginal memory and time.

---

38   Wright 2007.
39   Fuentes 2005: 178.
40   Galeano 1987: xv.
41   Wright 2006: 519.

Bibliography

Dart, Jonathan 2007, 'Alexis' book helps break the mould', *Central Advocate*, 25 May 2007.

Delvin-Glass, Frances 2006, 'Broken songs and ecology: writing about the Gulf of Carpentaria', *TAIN* 44(Dec. 2006 – Feb. 2007): 28–29.

Delvin-Glass, Frances 2007, 'Review essay: Alexis Wright's *Carpentaria*', *Antipodes: A North American Journal of Australian literature* 21(1): 82–85.

Fuentes, Carlos 2005, *This I Believe: An A to Z of a Life*, Random House, London.

Galeano, Eduardo 1987, *Genesis*, Metheun, London.

Molloy, D 2012, 'Finding hope in the stories: Alexis Wright's *Carpentaria* and the carnivalesque search for a new order', *Journal for the Association for the Studies of Australian Literature* 12(3): 1–8.

Morrison, Toni 1984, 'Rootedness: the ancestor is foundation', in Mari Evans (ed.), *Black Women Writers*, Anchor Books, New York.

Ravenscroft, Alison 2010, 'Dreaming of others *Carpentaria* and its critics', *Cultural Studies Review* 16(2): 194–224.

Syson, Ian 2007, 'Uncertain magic', *Overland* 187: 85–86.

Wolfe, Patrick 1991, 'On being woken up: the Dreamtime in anthropology and in Australian settler culture', *Comparative Studies in Society and History* 33: 197–224.

Wright, Alexis 2002, 'The politics of writing', *Southerly* 62(2): 10–20.

Wright Alexis 2006, *Carpentaria*, Giramondo, Sydney.

Wright, Alexis 2007, 'On writing *Carpentaria*', *HEAT* (NS) 13: 79–95.

10. Panara

The grain growers of Australia[1]

Bruce Pascoe

In 1844 Charles Sturt's party was dying in what was to become known as Sturt's Stony Desert. One of them, Poole, was so badly afflicted by scurvy that he had been sent back to the base camp. But he died on the way. Most of the others were not much better off and the horses could barely walk.

The men climbed countless sand hills and on reaching the summit of another they were hailed by a party of Aboriginal people. Sturt estimated that there were almost 300 people and they seemed to be welcoming them. As Sturt recorded, if they had been in any way aggressive his group could not have defended themselves as the men were too ill and the horses so weak they could only stumble forward to the bottom of the hill, but there the Aborigines approached them with coolamons of well water.

After the 'explorers' had drunk their fill, the Aborigines, who had never seen a horse, held out the coolamons so that the animals could drink. Sturt remarked on their courage in doing so. Sturt's party were fed on roast duck and cake, and Sturt, who was to eat similar cakes over the next few months, referred to them as the best he had ever eaten. The Europeans were then offered the pick of the houses in a new estate built on the bank of the Warburton River. The privations of 'explorers' in the Australian desert can never be overestimated: sweet well water, roast duck, fine cakes and a new house.

In the nights to follow, it was Sturt's delight to listen to the singing and laughter as the town prepared its meals. The whispering of whirring grain mills made a captivating sound in the twilight, but around 10 o'clock the town fell silent as it prepared for sleep. Sturt remarks on the modest civility of the people of this town.

The Warburton River people referred to themselves as the Panara or grain people. They were probably a clan of the Arrernte but their reference to Panara was to associate themselves with all the other groups within what Norman Tindale referred to as the Aboriginal grain belt, an area more than twice the size of the

---

1   Based on Pascoe 2014.

current Australian wheat belt.[2] The languages of these inland people have over a dozen words based on the word *panara*, and all of them have both a spiritual and practical connotation. The importance of agriculture to the Aboriginal economy is demonstrated by language.

In 1839 Lt Grey was thwarted in his attempt to cross some land near Hutt River, Western Australia.[3] The ground had been so thoroughly cultivated it was impossible to walk across and it reached as far as the eye could see. Grey attempted to skirt the area, but on ascending a small rise came across another area of the same size and the same degree of cultivation. On the next day another and then another. The scale of the operation was massive.

Grey remarked on the housing, the wells and the beaten roads, which provided access to the cultivated area where the Nhanda had been growing 'warran' or yam. Some historians and agriculturalists wonder if the remnants of the Batavia mutiny may have been responsible, but that seems unlikely given the existence of more or less identical yam production in most suitable Australian climate zones. Colonists reported on the vast yam terraces close to Melbourne where the soil was so deeply cultivated that it 'ran through the fingers like ashes'. Explorers in all corners found either grain fields or tons of stored grain and flour or massive yam pastures and stored starch and preserved dough cakes.

Peter Beveridge and Thomas Kirby were the first to 'settle' the area near Swan Hill on a station they called Tyntynder.[4] They were astounded by the huge steaming mounds found right through the district. It took them weeks to discover that this industry was to cook cumbungi prior to the removal of the starch and other processes in the plant's utilisation.[5]

One morning, Kirby came across a man reclining on one of the miles of earthen weirs that the local Aboriginal people had erected everywhere on the river system. Tons of earth were required for every barrier. The Aboriginal man was using a machine to catch fish. In the wall of this dam, several fish apertures had been built. In them a noose had been placed, and this was attached to a long sling tied under tension to a pole, which was anchored to the river bottom and fixed in place with a peg.

When a fish swam through the gate and into the noose, it was caught around the gills and this action caused the peg to release, which in turn allowed the tension of the pole to swing the fish from the bottom of the river onto the wall beside

---

2   Tindale 1974.
3   Grey 1841.
4   Beveridge 1889.
5   Cumbungi is a kind of bulrush and the base was cooked and eaten.

the Aboriginal, who flung the fish into a basket. You'll have to agree this is insouciance. The man was studiously refusing to acknowledge Kirby's existence but made sure he was aware of his prowess.

How did Kirby describe this remarkable process? 'I have often heard of the indolence of the blacks and soon came to the conclusion after watching a blackfellow catch fish in such a lazy way, that what I had heard was perfectly true.'[6]

What of the industry required to build those weirs throughout the entire Riverina? What of the engineering required to invent and build the automatic fishing machine?

When Beveridge and Kirby first arrived they were accosted by Aborigines yelling out to them, throwing dirt in the air and waving branches aggressively. Beveridge reports that the men nearly yelled themselves hoarse screaming 'cum-a-thunga, cum-a-thunga'. Beveridge interpreted this to mean 'you are welcome to our land'.

I have experience in language recovery myself, but after failing to find 'cum-a-thunga' in the Wati Wati dictionary that Beveridge wrote during his retirement, I wondered why he had left it out. Perhaps it showed that his desperation to claim legitimacy had been proven untenable by later knowledge. Better leave it out than have people think the Wati Wati had resisted his right to the land.

I spoke to linguists, Dr Christina Eira and Dr Stephen Morey, to try and unravel the mystery of this word. Their study of language reveals a far more plausible possibility: 'Get up and go away or we will spear you in the guts' seems the most likely meaning. Our study of this group of words requires more work, but the example shows that if you alter your view by 15 degrees to accommodate Aboriginal knowledge, your doubts would be aroused simply by the reference to the kicking up of dirt and the vigorous thrashing of branches – universal signs of Aboriginal hostility. Unless, of course, you are hoping to legitimise your occupation of another sovereign nation's land.

I used to run tours of the Cape Otway Lighthouse. The pay was lousy and the stairs were many, but you got a free ice cream at the end of every shift. I saw a lot of overseas visitors and many were fixated by the stories of migrant ships and their 15-week journey from England. One family of Vietnamese knew a lot about arrival by boat. They studied the interior plan of the convict ships and cried.

---

6   Beveridge 1889.

We all cried. The story they told me of their years in refugee camps sounded like a picnic compared to the eight days on the 30-foot fishing boat with 150 people on board.

I also saw a lot of French, Germans, Italians and Dutch at the lighthouse. I watched closely as they read the story of Australia's 'settlement' which the acceptable historians had prepared. They muttered amongst themselves and turned to me in disbelief. Some were direct in expressing that disbelief. They knew a lot about colonial methods and were caught between laughter and indignation at the fables that had been prepared for their edification. Some collusion between Governor LaTrobe and 'settlers' like Roadknight ensured that every Aboriginal person for 80 kilometres around the lighthouse site was attacked, killed or incarcerated in prisons or missions to guarantee the safety of the light and the keepers.

If you were in charge of that construction, you may arrive at the same conclusion. If the white community was to prosper, the black had to be eliminated. The Blacks wanted to retain their real estate: unlimited protein resources, sheltered bays and views to die for. Position, position, position. My goodness, there were some interesting conversations on those tours of the lighthouse.

Australia still has a gift for nursery rhyme. Tim Winton's *Cloudstreet* is officially Australia's favourite novel. It has a black ghost which informs the Pickles family that he is glad they have come to take the land. I love Tim Winton's writing, I published one of his first stories, but I don't like myopia. It may be a novel, but it should come with a warning that it supports the great Australian fairy story of a peaceful handover from thankful Aboriginal people.

A second famous book and a text for Australian high schools and universities is Kate Grenville's *Secret River* (2005), where Aboriginal people barely speak and remain foils for the progress of the story's reconciliation of white occupation. Australians have leapt at art which legitimises occupation.

If you looked at the paintings of acclaimed nineteenth-century artist Fred Williams from an Aboriginal perspective, rather than an artistic innovation, his scenes of white pioneers in richly treed landscapes may well seem to be another form of appropriation and occupation. If you read the journals of explorers and the contemporary writing of non-Aboriginal Australian historians and alter your perspective by as little as 15 degrees toward an Aboriginal point of view, you will see some surprising things: you might see the ground Lt Grey couldn't walk across as evidence of cultivation, you might see Kirby's indolent black as a genius of design and industrial innovation, and you might see the earthen terraces around Melbourne as an intriguing social, spiritual and economic puzzle that we have steadfastly refused to contemplate.

I am not a genius or morally superior. I came by my opinions as an 18-year-old after a very similar education and socialisation to many, but when my uncle told me about our Aboriginal family history and insisted I sit down in fishing boats and kitchens with Aboriginal relatives and elders, I saw the history of the country I loved in a harsh new light and I was ashamed – ashamed at believing a history an intelligent 13-year-old would scorn if she were given the encouragement to explore and question.

The facts don't change, but if we look at those facts with a tiny bit of compassion and scepticism, we might alter what we think of the history accepted by most Australians.

When you study the 450 Aboriginal languages of Australia, will you approach them as the blinkered horse approaches the race track or will you be wondering about Aboriginal opinion then and now? How is it possible to conduct national affairs for 60,000 years without territorial war? Look at the languages and how they reflect not just age but single location. Which languages talk about volcanism, which describe mangroves, which talk sea level rise, desertification or the appearance of strange wooden objects on the shore?

The languages by and large develop and remain in a single location. Recently, language scientists were talking about a north to south thrust of language 5,000 years ago as if driven by Asian invasion, but the latest essays throw doubt on the theory and suggest instead a spiritual and social language trajectory with the people remaining where they were.

There will be many theories posited and argued, but my interest is in how such a large number of languages could co-exist in such unparalleled harmony. The world has never known a civilisation to last so long. Do you wonder about the basis of that government? Bill Gammage in *The Biggest Estate on Earth* (2011) speculates on the diplomacy required to organise environmental burns across the continent. Don't burn my crops, cemetery, sacred trees, ceremonial idylls. That diplomacy must have engaged thousands of people for thousands of hours over thousands of years.

The Brewarrina fish traps are thought to be the oldest human structure on earth, and yet they have had very little research interest and are not part of any school curriculum. Does this omission reflect a desire to hide the wonders of Aboriginal Australia?

Imagine if a Texan was in possession of such an artefact. Planes, bus fleets, health spas and snake oil salesmen would descend on the place. It would become the tourist hub of Australia and every child in Year 5 would build fish trap replicas.

Stonehenge, Angkor Wat, the Mayan cities, we all know them, but who has heard of Brewarrina? I searched high and low for the proof for the claim that they were the oldest structures on earth but could only find one brief analysis of the stone bedding technique, which is where the figure of 40,000 years came from. This is Australia's contribution to the birth of engineering. It's not just the labour or the engineering wizardry that is important; it's the spiritual and social ethic to which we have devoted almost none of our attention.

The scientists who have examined the structure are still not sure how the locking principle works. How come the stones don't wash away in a flood? They know it has something to do with the node on the keystones but are not sure on which element of physics it relies. We know a lot about the design of Greek and Roman columns, we can all recall Ionic if needed for a crossword puzzle, but in 2013 we don't know the science of the Brewarrina fish traps.

Even more incredibly, the structures were designed so that any trapping ensured that people upstream and down from any site would retain access to fish.

Within months of European arrival, however, the traps were breached to provide sail boat, and later, steam boat access. Two types of fish, which the earliest photographs record in the hands of Brewarrina fisher-people, become extinct within one season of the destruction of the traps.

When Sir Thomas Mitchell rode through the area in 1831 he passed large villages, many with populations he estimated at over 1,000. He envies the comfort of the homes and the pleasing aesthetic of the construction and location. These people are sustained by a multifarious economy for, as Mitchell notes, he also rode through one field of harvested grain for 9 miles and the hayricks reminded his men of home. The fish capturing system was an important, but not the only, method of production. As Veronica Frail told me during my visit to Brewarrina, her ancestors weren't hunters and gatherers they were Festival Caterers. And they weren't catering just for their own selfish needs, they designed a system that would allow the satisfaction of needs of people they would never see.

Do you wonder at a people who could design an economic system based on care for the economies of clans unknown to each other except in dream and story? Might that egalitarian diplomacy be a handy tool in the modern world? What about the restraint imposed on territorial aggression? Syria? Gaza? The Amazon? Korea? This is a society with skills we need today.

Those ideas are in the language too; they are in the words for earth and people, and they are in the names of the plants and animals that sustained life. They are in the concepts which expressed the fastidious responsibility and care for the land.

Even in the area of linguistics, a battle still rages over the ownership of Aboriginal languages. Some professional linguists continue to take possession of the words while presenting themselves as saviours of dying languages. One instance involves an Aboriginal clan led by a man who has devoted his entire life to this recovery. You will not find a man of greater grit or generosity. He is old now. A few weeks ago he had to hold up his chin in order to turn around, but his wicked sense of humour lit up his face when he told his latest joke.

He is the language champion. He sent his daughter across two states to make sure I corrected an error I'd made in translation. Another of his countrywomen recovered from a substance dependency and, despite being a single mother of three primary school aged children, introduced language teaching into two schools. This process led to the recovery of a mountain of words and grammar as she drew in old Aboriginal people, some of whom had not spoken a word of their language in 50 years. It was she, in between making school lunches and coaching the hockey team, who saved that language. We must break our necks to ensure women like that are not marginalised by those with a far bigger ego, massive professional ambition and a gift of the gab. That woman and her sisters were mistreated and insulted by every linguist that descended on her town.

I'm hopeful that Aboriginal languages will be respected as the words of other people are and not just grist for the academic mill. This will require management protocols to ensure Aboriginal language organisations are supported and our young Aboriginal people nurtured into language positions. Is this impossible; is it too difficult to have a person of low initial educational attainment on university staff?

One of our language workers never finished school, and when her community begged her to help recover their language she could neither speak a word of it nor had a clue what syntax, morphology or suffix meant. That woman drove herself to learn – because it was her language. Generous linguists supported her, but she did it out of the fierce will of her bones. It was an astonishing achievement.

When an Aboriginal person graduates, they are hunted by Aboriginal and non-Aboriginal organisations. There are too few for the positions we need to fill. We acknowledge that training and retaining Aboriginal graduates is difficult, but in a world where Canadians sing David Bowie songs in space, it should not be impossible.

When I visited the University of Jayewardene in India to talk with students about my fiction, I was called to a secret meeting of Dalit students. They were afraid to meet with me in front of university authorities. Even though the course had been established to 'study their culture', they feared that the government's interest in their world was in order to consume and assimilate it. They'd seen it happen all too often. A bit dramatic? They cited instance after instance of villages following the old cultural ways which, after accepting government money for schools and health, had seen their culture stripped of all sovereignty and turned into a dozen artefacts in a museum.

This is the history of colonial interaction with subjugated cultures. Fortunately, Charles Darwin wasn't entirely right. The weak don't meekly give way to the strong on every occasion because sometimes the strong discover that their ethos and civility is not indestructible. Think Atlantis, Persepolis, Machu Picchu, Petra, Palmyra and Perth.

Jared Diamond believes the collapse of civilisations can be predicted by their level of waste. In our case, think the Murray Basin, Mallee soil, Burrup Peninsula, Tasmanian rainforests and bi-lingual Aboriginal schools. The model we are following so slavishly has every chance of being a laughable indulgence within the century. We may not survive our excess.

Consider instead the economic and philosophical culture of the world's oldest civilisation. The tools used to create that egalitarian longevity are far better tested than those of Keynes, Machiavelli, Churchill and Lincoln. They have kept a people together and the continent healthy and deserve respect even if just for their liberal-conservative philosophy. The benefits derived from the concepts of diplomacy, sustainability and love are treasures and once mined would naturally be shared with the inventors, the Aboriginal people. Wouldn't they?

Australia will discover those treasures, but hopefully it will insist they remain Aboriginal property.

If this is a moral country.

Bibliography

Beveridge, Peter 1889, *The Aborigines of Victoria and Riverina*, ML Hutchison, Melbourne.

Grey, George 1841, *Journals of Two Expeditions of Discovery in North-West and Western Australia, During the Years 1837, 1838 & 1839*, Vols 1 & 2, T & W Boone, London.

Pascoe, Bruce 2014, *Dark Emu: Black Seeds: Agriculture or Accident?*, Magabala Books, Broome.

Tindale, Norman B 1974, *Aboriginal Tribes of Australia: Their Terrain, Environmental Controls, Distribution, Limits, and Proper Names*, University of California Press and Australian National University Press, Canberra.

11. The Past in the Present?

Archaeological Narratives and Aboriginal History

Harry Allen

Introduction

'Deep Time and Deep Histories' represents more than our ability to accurately measure time or to construct new versions of human history based on genetics and molecular biology. As such, seeking to understand the human place in nature is to undertake a significant political task.[1] For humans living in the twenty-first century, exploring these issues is central to our self-understanding and our aspirations for the future.

This review of archaeological accounts of the past has as its subject the transcendental idea of human progress, which presents human history as passing through a series of progressive stages defined by essentialist criteria. A great number of theories based on these ideas have been placed before the public over the past 200 years. However, despite differences in subject matter and emphasis, it is apparent that these are of the same basic nature and follow the same historical logic. While archaeologists are stringent critics of many of these ideas, the historical schemes they have attempted to replace them with, based on newer evidence, are often variations on the same theme. Through repetition, the newer schemes constantly reinforce the older ones.

In presenting a review of archaeological versions of human progress, the aim is to come to grips with their ideological basis and to further the process of mapping out more accurate accounts of the human story.

Historicising human variability

One of the earliest attempts to explain human variability began as a psychological rather than a historical theory. This was based on Aristotle's ideas as transmitted through the writings of Thomas Aquinas to the Catholic Church. Aristotle considered that non-Greek peoples were 'natural slaves' on the grounds that, while they had the capacity to think rationally, they chose not to. He did,

---

1 Huxley 1906; Mulvaney 1971b.

however, consider that Greek male children could develop a rational facility after correct tuition. The Catholic Church in Spain grappled with these problems in trying to decide the legal position of Amerindian people. Should the Indians be considered slaves and incapable of learning, or as children, who could be denied their civic rights until they demonstrated rationality? In the event, the Church accepted that the South American Indians should be considered 'natural children' under the tutelage of the Church and Civil authorities.[2]

Locating ethnographic peoples in this manner fitted with the idea of the 'Ages of Man', a metaphor frequently used by classical authors. The concept transferred seamlessly into Christianity, and Augustine made complex use of it:

> The earliest period of the human race, when men first began to enjoy the light, can be compared ... to the first day of creation ... We must consider this age as the infancy of the world, for the world in this instance is to be thought of as a single human being ...[3]

In later historical works, the secular goal of continuous human progress replaced spiritual improvement, transforming Aristotle's psychological/developmental theory into a historical one. The evolutionary historian Peter Bowler notes that the Victorians were deeply attracted to the idea that human social development paralleled the progression of an individual from the simplicity of a single cell to the complexity of a mature adult:

> Once we begin thinking of the history of civilization, or of life on earth, as following the same pattern as the growing embryo, we are locked into a model in which evolution is seen as the ascent of a ladder towards ever-higher states of development.[4]

Such ideas have been applied to all ethnographic peoples and conceptualising the Australian Aborigines as children during the late nineteenth and early twentieth-centuries was common across the scientific, religious and political spectrum.[5] Such teleological and organic ideas have little to do with an archaeological understanding of the past. However, in incorporating growth from simple beginnings to a more complex maturity with time broken up into Ages, they form a template for the historicist theories which follow.[6]

2   Adams 1998: 141–142; Heath 2008; Pagden: 60–79; Smith 1983: 109–122.
3   Quoted in Archambault 1966: 203.
4   Bowler 1989: 10.
5   See Gsell 1955; Broome 1982: 104; Spencer 1914: 38; Staniland Wake 1872: 82.
6   Both Broome and Stanner document that these ideas had a profound impact on public policy directed towards Aboriginal people. Broome 1982; Stanner 1979 [1962]: 152–153.

A second set of influential ideas arranged human societies into a temporal sequence in terms of their economic form: hunters, pastoralists, gardeners, and finally, mercantilists.[7] Adam Smith was the most important of the Scottish Enlightenment writers to advance such a materialist theory of human development.[8] Smith's scheme began with an 'Age of Hunters' followed by an 'Age of Shepherds', noting:

> when a society becomes numerous they would find difficulty in supporting themselves by herds and flocks. Then they would naturally turn themselves to cultivation of land and the raising of such plants and trees as produced nourishment ... And by this means they would gradually advance into the Age of Agriculture ...[9]

These speculative schemes combined *stage theory* with the idea that human history moves through a sequence of successive stages, *conjectural prehistory,* a speculative account of the past based on the logical premise that movement is from simple beginnings to a more complex present and, the *comparative method,* which used accounts of contemporary societies as both analogues for past societies and as the evidence for sequential change.[10] To this list might be added the functionalist idea that the manner in which a society gained its livelihood determined its social and legal arrangements.[11] Although not writing within an evolutionary framework, the French political philosopher Montesquieu classified the political systems of 'nations' as belonging either to Savagery, Barbarism or Civilization. That this classification represented progressive and successive stages of development emerged only later.[12]

In 1800, Joseph Marie, Baron de Gérando (Degérando) published his *Considération sur les diverses méthodes à suivre dans l'observation des peuples sauvages,* which interpreted the emergence of political systems in developmental terms. Degérando gave the following advice to members of Nicholas Baudin's scientific expedition to the Southern Ocean:

> The philosophical traveller, sailing to the ends of the earth, is in fact travelling in time; he is exploring the past; every step he makes is the passage of an age. The unknown islands that he reaches are for him the cradle of human society. [They] ... recreate for us the state of our own ancestors, and the earliest history of the world.[13]

---

7   Burrow 1966; Bryson 1945; Meek 1976.
8   Barnard 2004.
9   Smith 1762–3 quoted in Meek 1976: 117–178.
10   Adams 1998: 29–34.
11   Meek documents the influence that the Scottish Utilitarian philosophers had on the development of Karl Marx's ideas. Meek 1954.
12   Meek 1976: 32–35; Montesquieu 1949 [1748]: 275.
13   Degérando 1969 [1800]: 63; see also Jones 1992. Fabian and Gamble observe that such theories arrange coeval societies along a scale turning space and economic form into a temporal difference. Fabian 1983; Gamble 1992.

Approaches based on technology or social evolution

Towards the end of the eighteenth century, the popularity of speculative theories waned in favour of those based on physical evidence. As a result, the findings of practical science became a significant element in the creation of a universal natural history.[14] It was in this milieu that CJ Thomsen, working at the Danish National Museum in 1819, reorganised the collections in terms of the Ages of Stone, Bronze and Iron – a set of generalisations about successive developments in Danish prehistory which he presented to museum visitors.[15]

Historians of archaeology suggest that Thomsen's Three Ages was an empirically based scheme that relied on the evidence placed before him.[16] In her analysis of the Three Ages, Judith Rodden, however, argues that the Three Ages closely paralleled approaches used by the Utilitarian philosophers as it was based on the notion of ideal or essential types, it used comparative ethnography as an analogue for prehistoric behaviour and it reflected an underlying belief that change in the human past was directional, occurring as a series of technological stages through time, each defined in terms of artefact types.[17]

Thomsen's scheme was the first of many to make use of the data of archaeology to create a sequential account of human history based on changes in technology. A series of further elaborations followed. John Lubbock, author of the influential *Prehistoric Times*, divided the Stone Age into the Palaeolithic and Neolithic periods,[18] further modified when the anthropologist Hodder Westropp inserted the Mesolithic, or advanced hunting era, between the two, using microlithic stone tools as the criteria.[19] In addition, there was the division of the Palaeolithic into Lower, Middle and Upper Palaeolithic divisions (Table 11.1), and the French Upper Palaeolithic into the cultural sequence Châtelperonian, Aurignacian, Gravettian, Solutrean and Magdalenian, each defined on the basis of particular tool types.[20]

---

14 Mokyr 2009; Yeo 2003.
15 Thomsen's usage included both 'Age of Stone' and 'Stone Age' for his earliest period. The formulation 'Age of Stone' invokes a sense of a *World of Stone*, somewhat different in meaning to the contemporary usage of 'Stone Age' (for geological use of the term 'World' see Rudwick 1995). Thomsen 1848: 64–69.
16 Daniel 1943: 16; Gräsland 1987: 20–21, 27–28.
17 In a letter in 1825, Thomsen compared the Stone Age of Europe with the 'Wild North Americans' noting 'They were war-like, lived in the forest, [and] were not acquainted with metals (or only sparingly so)…' (quoted in Rodden 1981: 58). See also Thomsen 1848: 64. Klindt-Jensen also quotes Thomsen as noting that triangular Danish arrow points were quite like those used by the 'savage North American Indians'. Rodden 1981: 51–68; Klindt-Jensen 1981: 15.
18 Palaeolithic is glossed as the Old Stone Age and the Neolithic as the New Stone Age. The older terms were considered to parallel geological usage, for example, the Pleistocene. Lubbock 1865: 2–3; Daniel 1978: 125–126, 251.
19 Westropp 1872: xxiii.
20 Chazan 1995: 462–463; Clark 1969: 51; Daniel 1978: 125; De Mortillet 1872.

Table 11.1: Palaeolithic chronology based on de Mortillet (1872)

Epoque	Industry	Age
Magdélien, Epoque de la Madeleine	Stone blades and bone points	Upper Palaeolithic
Solutréen, Epoque de Solutré	Laurel leaf points, bifaces	Upper Palaeolithic
Moustérien, Epoque de Moustiers	Mousterian points and scrapers	Middle Palaeolithic
Acheuléen, Epoque du Saint Acheul	Handaxes	Lower Palaeolithic

Source: After de Mortillet 1872.

The various ideas discussed above were brought together by Lewis Henry Morgan in *Ancient Society* (1877). Morgan demonstrated human progress by combining Montesquieu's terminology 'Savagery, Barbarism and Civilization' with information about economy, technology and social relations.[21] He presented a scheme of a progression of stages, each divided into lower, middle and upper parts. Thus for Morgan, humans moved from Savagery to the lower stage of Barbarism when they began to make pottery. A middle stage came with the domestication of animals and plants and the final stage of Barbarism saw the introduction of iron smelting.[22] Morgan considered that the Australian Aborigines remained at the stage of 'middle Savagery', while he believed there were no contemporary examples of 'lower Savagery', which he termed 'the infancy of the human race'.[23] Furthermore, Morgan was explicit about the connection between geological periods and the use of uniformitarian principles to document human progress through the classification of contemporary tribal peoples. He explained:

> Like the successive geological formations, the tribes of mankind may be arranged according to their relative conditions, into successive strata. When thus arranged, they reveal with some degree of certainty the entire range of human progress from savagery to civilization.[24]

Through Marx, Morgan's view of human history had a direct influence on the archaeology of V Gordon Childe.[25]

---

21 Hiatt provides a detailed analysis of evolutionary theories concerned with social relationships as they related to Australian Aboriginal people. Hiatt 1996.

22 Morgan 1877: 10–13.

23 Morgan 1877: 10, 12.

24 Morgan 1877: 422, quoted in Keen 2000.

25 Childe states that he took Morgan's categories from Marx, as they were compatible with the functionalist idea that the economy was determinative of social relations. Engels used his Morgan's *Ancient Society* as the basis of essay 'The Origin of the Family, Private Property and the State'. Engels 1972 [1884]; Childe 1958.

Childe's *What Happened in History*

The English-trained Australian archaeologist Gordon Childe was largely responsible for the development of culture-historical archaeology, one of the major archaeological approaches of the first half of the twentieth century. Childe worked at two levels. The first was the definition of individual cultures and culture sequences based on assemblages of artefact types. Childe thought artefacts in a culture system were analogous to words in a language, where similarities and differences allowed relationships to be traced through time and space. It was assumed that an archaeologically defined culture was representative of 'a people' who resided within a defined territory. Commenting on Childe's archaeological theories, Andrew Sherratt notes their Romantic basis whereby cultural ancestry and relationships follow the form of a genealogical tree.[26]

Childe's second level is found in his general historical works, in which he presents a universal history demonstrating development through time from Palaeolithic beginnings to the end of the Iron Age.[27] This step required abstracting essential elements, such as technology, economy or settlement form from individual archaeological cultures, and grouping these into higher order entities, ages or stages without reference to genetic relationships. The narrative structure of his general historical works presented a progressive sequence of techno-evolutionary stages punctuated by 'revolutions'.[28] When it came to creating a framework for these stages however, Childe fell back on ideas put forward by Thomsen, Lubbock and Morgan.[29] In *Man Makes Himself* (1936), Childe presented his materialist ideas in terms of successive economic stages beginning with Food Gatherers, the Neolithic Revolution, and the Urban Revolution, later reformulating these stages as Palaeolithic Savagery, Neolithic Barbarism, Bronze Age Civilization, and finally, The Iron Age.[30] Childe considered that combining them in this manner represented 'a useful scaffolding'.[31] Through the use of these ideas, Childe was able to present a historical account that was immediately familiar to his readers.[32]

---

26 Greene documents that Childe projected ideas about the Industrial Revolution onto the past, firstly in terms of the Urban Revolution and later the Neolithic Revolution. Childe was careful to state that these represented processes rather than events. The terminology, however, took on a life of its own. Sherratt 1989: 165–168; Greene 1999.

27 Allen, 2000: 109–111.

28 Greene: 97–109.

29 Allen 2000: 109–111; Childe 1958: 72.

30 Childe 1954 [1942].

31 Childe 1956a: 93.

32 Childe exemplified Marx's dictum that at the moment of creating a new version of history, we disguise the fact by conjuring up 'the spirits of the past'. Childe was also returning to an evolutionary view of history, one which had lost favour during the 1920s and 1930s. Grahame Clark was critical of Childe's later books and considered that he contributed little of importance to archaeology after 1930 (but for an opposing view see Thomas 1982). Clark 1976: 3; Marx 1926; Piggott 1958; Sherratt 1989: 178–182.

While his Stages or Ages followed the same sequential order, Childe warned that this did not mean that they were everywhere synchronic.

> The distinctive assemblages of tools have been shown stratigraphically to follow one another in the same order wherever they occur. But the archaeologist is fortunate in having to hand independent time scales with which to compare each local sequence. So he has come reluctantly ... to realise that his Ages are in fact not everywhere contemporary; they are just homotaxial and might therefore more legitimately be called Stages.[33]

Australian Aboriginal people and culture presented an example. Childe accepted that their gathering economy corresponded with the Palaeolithic period and with Morgan's Savagery, noting that the Old Stone Age lasted until the present in Central Australia, 'at least in economic terms'.[34] On the other hand, Childe warned against thinking that any savage tribe was primitive, unchanging or unthinking.[35]

Childe was too good a historian to write a Whig history of the world. He thought that the historical process could be disorderly and was neither automatic nor inevitable, that the outcome lay in our own hands.[36] Childe's *What Happened in History* was written at the height of World War Two, partly to provide readers with a lesson of hope during a time of despondency about the future:

> Progress is real if discontinuous. The upward curve resolves itself into a series of troughs and crests. But ... no trough ever declines to the low level of the preceding one; each crest out-tops its last precursor.[37]

The weakness of versions of history organised in stages lies in the fact that all change has to occur in that abstract moment when one stage shifts to the next.[38] This leaves the process of change under-theorised and amenable to either an evolutionary or a particularist understanding of history. Most archaeologists of the nineteenth and early twentieth centuries invoked both evolutionary and particularist approaches, arguing that while overall human progress might be assumed, movement from one culture to another, or from one stage to the next, could be abrupt, attributable to ethnic replacement, the diffusion of ideas

---

33 Childe 1944: 7. Homotaxial relates to relative position in a geological sequence rather being contemporaneous, thus allowing that the Stone Age might continue in some places into the twentieth century.
34 Childe 1936: 43; Childe 1954 [1942]: 24.
35 Childe 1936: 46–47.
36 Childe 1947: 60, 65–67; Childe 1956a: 164–165.
37 Childe 1954 [1942]: 282.
38 Groube 1967.

or trade, or individual inventions stimulated by biological or environmental change.[39] This understanding of history survived the challenge of Darwinian thought almost unscathed.[40]

The deep history emerging in these accounts creates its own sense of time, and as a result, could equally fit Biblical or geological time frames. Prior to the discovery of radiocarbon dating, archaeologists were forced to connect their sequences with the chronologies of Egypt or the Middle East, or to use differing proportions of artefacts (seriation), or to make assumptions based on artefact styles in order to date their sites.[41] There was, however, a chronological blind spot between the Pleistocene dating of geological fossils and the emergence of written records and dynastic lists; a period of prehistory that is highly significant as it was during this time that the domestication of plants and animals, the advent of metallurgy and the beginnings of urban settlement took place.

The radiocarbon revolution

The advent of radiocarbon dating in 1949 provided a dating mechanism independent of artefacts and their typology.[42] Since that time, the archaeologist's arsenal has been augmented by an increasing range of chronological methods based on isotopic and luminescence dating techniques.[43] This has freed archaeology from the necessity to date sites through artefact types, and it ultimately allowed archaeology to move beyond culture-history to approaches that are less taxonomic in nature.[44]

Given our enhanced ability to date the material evidence of archaeology plus the sophisticated methods of recovery and analysis now available, it might be considered that progressive staged versions of a universal human history should have collapsed under the weight of critical evidence arraigned against them. Two examples will demonstrate, however, that this has not been the case.

There continues to be a debate as to whether the Neolithic represented a rapid and abrupt shift, or alternatively, the slow emergence of a range of food procurement techniques. Smith argues against the concept of a 'Neolithic Revolution', noting that the apparently sharp boundary between hunting-gathering and agriculture is a construct, produced by reclassifying anomalous societies as 'Complex

---

39   Breuil 1912: 174; Chazan 1995: 451–452; Clark 1976: 15; Daniel 1978: 45; Murray 2007: 245.
40   Bowler 1988; Bowler 1989: 175–219; Freeland 1983.
41   Childe 1956a: 57–83.
42   Arnold and Libby 1949; Renfrew 1976 [1973].
43   Macdougall 2008; Roberts 1997.
44   Hodder 1991.

hunter-gatherers' or 'Incipient agriculturalists'.[45] Smith does not entirely avoid the pitfall of considering low-level food production as an intermediate phase between hunting and gathering and agriculture. His emphasis, however, is on the variability of human economic responses to individual circumstances. Harris has similarly modified the concept of a Neolithic Revolution seeking to replace it with an ecological understanding of human–plant interactions across a broad spectrum of occurrences.[46]

The second case involves Grahame Clark's proposal that stone tool technology could be divided into a succession of modes dating from the Lower Palaeolithic to the Mesolithic.[47] Clark, and more recently Foley, argue that the shift from one mode to another is associated with progressive changes in hominin speciation and cognition.[48] Clark's sequence of modes is shown in Table 11.2 below. Within this scheme, artefacts act as typological and staged markers, blades in the case of the Upper Palaeolithic and microliths for the Mesolithic, just as polished stone axes and pottery were previously taken to be indicators of the Neolithic.

Table 11.2: Modes of stone tool technology

Mode	Technology	Dating and Association
Mode 5	Microliths	Mesolithic, modern *Homo sapiens*
Mode 4	Blades	Upper Palaeolithic, modern *Homo sapiens*
Mode 3	Levalloisian prepared core technology	Middle Palaeolithic, Neanderthals and archaic *Homo sapiens*
Mode 2	Acheulian handaxes	Lower Palaeolithic, *Homo erectus*
Mode 1	Oldowan – cobble tools and simple flakes	Lower Palaeolithic, Australopithecus and early *Homo sp.*,

Source: After Foley 1987.

This model of progressive techno-evolutionary development was linked to the 'Human Revolution', the idea that many aspects of modern human behaviour, including developed cognition and symbolic communication, originated in Europe with the Middle to Upper Palaeolithic transition. Palaeoanthropologists Sally McBrearty and Alison Brooks have challenged this idea, documenting how the types defining the European Upper Palaeolithic sequence can be found at earlier dates in Africa during the Middle Stone Age (MSA).[49] They argue that

---

45 Smith 2001.
46 Harris 1990: 18.
47 Clark 1969.
48 Foley 1987.
49 Foley now accepts that most of the defining elements of Modes 4 and 5 developed in Africa during the Mode 3/ MSA period. McBrearty and Brooks 2000; Foley and Lahr 1997.

the classic European sequence, against which other tool making traditions have been compared, is anomalous, being the result of a discontinuous archaeological record in the remote *cul de sac* of Pleistocene Western Europe.[50]

Attempts to locate Australian Aboriginal stone technologies within this modal sequence have proven difficult, as Australian technologies equally represent aspects of both Mode 1 and Mode 3 technologies.[51] A number of archaeologists now argue that it is a mistake to attempt to measure human cultural development in terms of stone tools.[52]

The 'Out of Africa' hypothesis and increased knowledge of the African Middle and Late Stone Ages have undermined much of the archaeological understanding of the origins of modern *Homo sapiens*. This compels us to reconsider afresh the manner in which the past has been conceptualised as a series of progressive stages. It is now time to turn our attention more directly to Australian archaeology.

Historicising the Australian past

Historical schemes about Indigenous peoples predate both knowledge of Aboriginal peoples and the archaeological discovery of deep time, having previously been applied to both North and South American Indians, and to different groups of Africans. However, once the Australians, and especially the Tasmanians, were discovered they were taken as representatives of primordial man by theorists of human development.[53]

In the years following the development of anthropology and archaeology in Europe, a number of attempts were made to locate the Australian Aborigines within the frameworks discussed above. The British anthropologist Edward Burnett Tylor compared the Australians with Palaeolithic peoples, referring to them as the 'lowest savages'.[54] In his paper 'On the Tasmanians as Representatives of Palaeolithic Man', he observed technical similarities between Tasmanian Aboriginal stone artefacts and those recovered from Le Moustier in the Dordogne,[55] arguing that stone tool types indicated that the Tasmanians were:

> living representatives of the early Stone Age, left behind in industrial development even by the ancient tribes of the Somme and the Ouse ... the condition of modern savages illustrates the condition of ancient stone

---

50   McBrearty and Brooks 2000: 454.
51   Foley and Lahr 1997: 18, 20, 24; Brumm and Moore 2005: 162.
52   Gamble 1995: 179; Oppenheimer 2003: 97; White 1977.
53   Mulvaney 1958: 297.
54   Tylor 1865: 136–138, 363.
55   Tylor 1894: 147.

age peoples, representatives of a stage of culture at once early in date and low in degree. The Tasmanian specimens and records now place us in full view of the state of a people in the Palaeolithic stage, who may have lasted on their remote and unvisited home from the distant ages when rudely chipped stones grasped in the hand were still the best implements of mankind.[56]

In his book *Ancient Hunters and Their Modern Representatives*, Sollas placed the Tasmanians at the very dawn of history, a Palaeolithic, even 'eolithic' race, considering them to be an autochthonous primitive people. They were thought to have survived in isolation on the island of Tasmania – having been destroyed, driven from or absorbed on the Australian mainland by the later arrival of Australian Aborigines.[57] While he considered that the Australians had made substantial cultural advances compared to the Neanderthals, Sollas still described the Australians as 'the Mousterians of the Antipodes'.[58] An argument followed as to whether the Tasmanians and Australian Aborigines represented either a Middle or Upper Palaeolithic technological stage, that is, whether they should be considered archaic Mousterians or members of modern *Homo sapiens*?[59]

By 1953, Frederick McCarthy could confidently state 'there is no such thing in Australia as distinct stages of culture or time periods corresponding to the Eolithic, Palaeolithic or Neolithic'.[60] Our confidence in his finding, however, is shaken a few lines later, when McCarthy notes:

> The most archaic traces of culture in Australia comprise a few Palaeolithic stone-working techniques and types ... Another early relationship is that of pebble-choppers chipped on one side ... They belong to the late Pleistocene and Mesolithic periods between five and ten thousand years ago.[61]

A survey of anthropological and archaeological books published during the twentieth century reveals that the term 'Stone Age' was commonly used to describe contemporary Australian Aboriginal peoples. Such works included *The Stone Age Men of Australia, Back in the Stone Age: The Natives of Central Australia; Exploring Stone Age Arnhem Land; Stone-Age Craftsmen: Stone Tools and Camping Places of the Australian Aborigines; Steel Axes for Stone Age Australians;* and most recently, *Stone Age Economics*.[62]

---

56 Tylor 1894: 148–149, 152.
57 Sollas 1911: 85.
58 Sollas 1991: 170, 207.
59 Balfour 1926.
60 McCarthy 1953: 246.
61 McCarthy 1953: 249.
62 British Pathé 1933; Chewings 1937; Mountford 1949; Mitchell 1949; Sharp 1952; Sahlins 1974.

In many cases, the term 'Stone Age' was used to gain a reader's attention, much as Karl Lumholtz (1889) used the title *Among Cannibals*. However, there was also a clear relationship between title and content in many of these books. The pre-eminent student of Australian Aboriginal culture in the early twentieth century, W Baldwin Spencer, in the Preface of *The Arunta: A Study of a Stone Age People,* claimed it was possible in Australia to study human beings 'that still remain on the cultural level of men of the Stone Age'.[63]

Figure 11.1: A fine portrait of an Aboriginal man, probably from central Australia by Charles P Mountford, which appeared as the frontispiece to Ion Idriess's book *Our Living Stone Age* (Angus and Robertson, Sydney, 1963) with the caption 'Stone Age Man'.
Source: State Library of South Australia.

63 Spencer and Gillen 1927. Attwood argues that such statements supported anthropology's bid for legitimacy and he reiterates Fabian's point that the denial of coevalness plays a significant role in maintaining colonial relationships between Aboriginal peoples and the white colonists. Attwood 1996; Fabian 1983: 31–34.

Figure 11.2: A photograph appearing in Charles Barrett's *Coast of Adventure* (Robertson and Mullens, 1941) showing some boys preparing a lunchtime meal and captioned in the original 'Primitive boys prepare a primitive meal on Wessel Island'.
Source: Photograph by Charles Leslie Barrett in *Coast of Adventure*.

The essentialist notion that Australian Aboriginal people inhabited the Stone Age remained commonplace. In his assessment of Australian archaeology, *The Stone Age of Australia* (1961), John Mulvaney noted: 'In 1788, Australia emerged from a stone age society of hunters and gatherers into the era of the Industrial revolution.'[64] Similarly, Peterson in his 'Ethno-archaeology in the

---

64   Mulvaney 1961b: 57.

Australian Iron Age' suggests that the years between 1939 and 1976 'saw the end of the Stone Age in Australia: [as] everywhere stone tools have been replaced by those of iron'.[65]

There is a considerable archaeological literature criticising the idea that Australian Aboriginal people in any way represented Palaeolithic survivals or Stone Age peoples.[66] However, it is difficult for archaeologists to conceive of the past outside the Three Age system.[67] Archaeologist Clive Gamble similarly observes, 'Today's prehistorians reject progress as a guiding principle, but continue to follow the agenda into human origins ... set over 150 years ago'.[68]

The Neolithic problem

There are two dimensions to the 'Neolithic Problem' in Australian archaeology. The first involves attempting to explain why Australian Aborigines had not, in this formulation, 'achieved' agriculture.[69] The second attempts to account for the presence of polished stone axes in Australia. Polished stone was the defining artefact of 'Neolithic' gardeners, yet the Australians were clearly hunters and gatherers. The latter problem, however, only emerges when archaeologists approach stone artefacts from an essentialist point of view, as the defining criteria of a stage of human development.

Tylor, previously discussed in reference to the Tasmanian question, argued the presence of stone axes was evidence for cultural degeneration.[70] On the other hand, he explained the absence of hafted tools, including axes, from Tasmania in terms of isolation and of stalled development, observing 'in their remote corner of the globe they have gone on little changed from early ages'.[71] The majority opinion was that the Australians had obtained their axes through external contacts, from Neolithic New Guineans, Oceanic peoples or through a migratory wave of settlers.[72] The most extreme view was that of WJ Perry, who believed that polished stone axes had come from Carthage to Australia aboard Egyptian triremes.[73]

---

65   Peterson 1976: 265.
66   Mulvaney 1961b: 5–107.
67   Rowley-Conwy 2007: 3.
68   Gamble 1995: 3, 244.
69   Allen 1974; White 1971.
70   Tylor 1865: 186.
71   Tylor 1894: 148.
72   Heine-Geldern 1932 quoted in Skinner 1957: 206; McCarthy 1953: 246; Sollas 1911: 179, 209.
73   Perry 1923: 99, 501–502.

Summarising the position, Mulvaney pointed to the different contexts of axe use in Australia and Melanesia, that edge-grinding was the sole 'Neolithic' component of Aboriginal culture and concluded their presence represented a recent addition, one that had 'diffused to Australia from New Guinea or other islands to the north'.[74]

Similar problems involved explanations for the presence of small stone spear points and microliths in Australia. For example, small, leaf-shaped stone points are a hallmark of the Upper Palaeolithic Solutrean culture in Europe, while microliths and various other backed implements first appear in Europe during the European Mesolithic and are definitional for this period.[75] Because of their status as markers of progress in the European sequence, their presence in Australia has been taken to indicate Aboriginal advancement to a higher level of technical production and social organisation.

That polished axes, small stone points and microliths might be associated with hafted tools (with a handle), together with the fact that the Tasmanians only used hand-held tools, led John Mulvaney to divide the Australian archaeological record into two phases: a *nonhafted phase* followed by a *hafted phase*.[76] He argued that the hafted phase, which began at about 5,000 years BP, represented a major shift in technical ability and initiated an accelerated pace of change in Australia.[77]

The discovery of Pleistocene axes with hafting grooves in contexts dating back to 35,000 years BP in northern Australia provoked serious questioning of the hafted phase concept.[78] Conceptually, however, the sequence proposed to supersede it, 'The Australian core tool and scraper tradition' followed by the 'Australian small tool tradition' used the same evidence and replaced the hafted/non-hafted sequence in everything but name (Table 11.3).[79] Based on the presence of new types of stone artefacts post 5,000 years BP in Australia, Mulvaney reiterated his belief that there were at least two widespread and major technological stages in prehistoric Australia and he, along with a number of authors, continue to argue that the presence of Pleistocene axes in northern Australia does not invalidate the 'Hafted Phase' concept.[80]

---

74 Mulvaney 1961b: 93.
75 Phillips 1981: 88–90, 137–141.
76 Mulvaney 1966; Mulvaney and Joyce 1965: 192–193.
77 Mulvaney 1966: 89–90, 93.
78 Geneste et al. 2011; Mulvaney and Kamminga 1999: 220–221; White 1967.
79 Bowler et al. 1970; Gould 1973: 18–20.
80 Mulvaney 1971a: 374; Gould 1973: 19; Smith 2013: 289.

Table 11.3: Technological stages proposed for Australia

Defining artefacts	Technological stages, proposed by Mulvaney 1966	Technological stages, proposed by Jones and Allen in Bowler et al. 1970; Gould 1973
Backed artefacts, polished stone axes	Hafted Phase	Small Tool Tradition
Core tools, flakes, scrapers	Non-hafted Phase	Core Tool and Scraper Tradition

Source: Mulvaney 1966; Jones and Allen in Bowler et al. 1970; Gould 1973.

While the presence of Pleistocene axes is discounted in some contexts, in others they are given a prominence beyond their technical significance. Firstly, there are claims that the Australians either 'invented' edge grinding, or at least that they were one of the first people in the world to adopt the process.[81] Secondly, it is claimed that the manufacture and use of polished stone artefacts involved a higher investment of labour and more complex relations of production than is evidenced by the flaked artefacts that make up the bulk of the Australian archaeological record.[82] Polishing stone and attaching handles are techniques that are likely to have a technical explanation. Within current understanding of Australian archaeology, it does not necessarily follow that polished axes and microliths should be treated as indicators of a stage of human advancement as they have been elsewhere in the world.[83]

The Intensification debate

In 1953, Joseph Birdsell, an American palaeoanthropologist, set out a number of propositions concerning Australian Aboriginal populations which have proved to be very influential. Firstly, that Aboriginal hunter-gatherers were relatively uniform both in their material culture and the efficiency with which they utilised their environment. Secondly, that the population of inland tribes was proportional to the rainfall. Thirdly, that the population densities of Australian tribes were rigorously subject to environmental determinism. And, finally, Aboriginal populations were in equilibrium with their environment.

---

81 Diamond 1997: 297; Geneste et al. 2011: 11–12.
82 Sutton locates the claims of Morwood and Tresize as a part of an earlier 'proto-intensification' debate which argued that the Australians were moving from an expedient technology associated with a foraging economy to a curated technology associated with collecting. Sutton 1990: 102; Balme et al. 2009: 197; Geneste et al. 2011: 10; Morwood and Trezise 1989: 82.
83 Hiscock 2008.

A number of Australian archaeologists were dissatisfied with this approach, which appeared to lock Australian hunter-gatherers into an environmental determinacy without the possibility of change due to Aboriginal agency or inventiveness.[84] In a series of articles published in the 1980s, a young Australian archaeologist, Harry Lourandos, argued that the division between hunter-gatherers and food producers was overdrawn, and that a number of Mid to Late Holocene changes in the Australian archaeological record was evidence of 'Intensification', an increase in the complexity of Aboriginal social arrangements, which moved Aboriginal societies in the direction of agriculture. Most controversially, Lourandos argued that such changes were the result, not of environmental circumstances, but of humanly induced changes in the social relations of production.[85]

Lourandos placed these shifts within a progressive trajectory believing that the move towards higher levels of resource use and social complexity was 'nipped in the bud by the coming of the Europeans', though elsewhere he denied he was suggesting that Australian hunter-gatherers were 'one step away' from food production.[86]

The evidence in favour of the increased complexity argument was drawn from multiple sources and regions in Australia. When looked at in finer detail, most instances of directional or cumulative change turned out to be either a product of the manner in which the data was analysed, or else, reflected short-term adjustments to local conditions.[87] Many archaeologists considered the changes Lourandos was talking about represented technical adjustments or adaptations that were compatible with a degree of environmental determinism rather than a shift towards more complex relations of production.[88] Lourandous' arguments failed to convince on empirical grounds and Australian archaeology returned to the status quo, where Aboriginal populations, technology and social complexity were considered to be in balance with the prevailing environmental conditions.

---

84 Thomas 1982.
85 Lourandos 1980, 1983, 1985, 1988. Bowdler 1981: 109–110 puts forward a similar argument.
86 Lourandos 1983: 92; Lourandos 1980: 258.
87 Bird and Frankel 1991; Hiscock 2008: 197–198.
88 Beaton 1983: 94–97.

'Out of Africa' and Australian Aboriginal history

The 'Out of Africa' hypothesis and the development of new theories regarding anatomically modern *Homo sapiens* and the emergence of 'modernity' has engendered a reassessment of how and when Aboriginal people moved from Africa to Australia, the nature of the material culture they brought with them, and the changes that took place subsequent to arrival to Sahul.

Studies of the distribution of mtDNA and Y Chromosome lineages of human populations suggest the Australians were a part of the earliest wave of modern *Homo sapiens* to leave Africa, making a rapid transit along the 'Southern Arc' route, where multiple colonising groups utilised boats to cross the water gaps between Sunda and Sahul.[89] This has stimulated a debate about whether Australian Aborigines, as anatomically modern humans, were also materially modern before they left Africa. There is, as yet, little consensus on this issue. Two camps have emerged.

The first argues that the early presence of art and complex tools, the rapidity of the move to Australia and the possession of boats suggests that complex information exchange systems and symbolic conceptualisation were present from the time the Aborigines made their first steps towards Australia.[90] The second view is that major changes in the Australian archaeological record occurred after arrival during the Mid Holocene, paralleling the Middle to Upper Palaeolithic transition in Europe.[91] This view returns us to the vision of Aboriginal people making slow but upward progress *after* arrival. Neither camp can claim a decisive victory as the archaeological record of Pleistocene Australia is marked by inadequate sampling and poor preservation.[92]

The Out of Africa debate allows us to reconsider many of the ideas discussed in this chapter and to work towards new solutions for old problems. However, the genetic findings also have the potential to return us to older modes of thought without resolving the ideological implications involved. Rasmussen and colleagues suggest that contemporary Aboriginal Australians are:

---

89 Oppenheimer 2003: 2–13; van Holst Pellekaan 2011; Redd and Stoneking 1999.
90 Balme et al. 2009: 59–68.
91 Brumm and Moore 2005.
92 Langley et al. 2011; McBrearty and Brooks 2000.

the direct descendants from the first humans to be found in Australia, dating to ~50,000 years B.P. This means that Aboriginal Australians likely have one of the oldest continuous population histories outside sub-Saharan Africa today.[93]

However, the conservativeness of Aboriginal genetic lineages should not be interpreted as supporting the case for the conservativeness of Aboriginal cultural traditions.

Primacy, continuity and antiquity are aspects of the human story that deserve to be highly valued. On the other hand, isolation, an underdeveloped technology and continuity from the earliest emergence of human culture are ideas which have been used to place Australian Aboriginal people on the lowest rung of the ladder of progress. In the context of colonial relationships in Australia, these findings present the danger that the 50,000 years of Aboriginal *change* will be lost sight of.

Conclusion

Over the past 100 years, Australian archaeologists have struggled to come to terms with the archaeological record and to understand the Aboriginal past in its own terms. Part of this struggle has consisted of unsuccessful attempts to apply the findings of European archaeology to the Australian situation. Even where distinctive ideas and terminologies have been applied, such as the concept of hafting, the intensification debate, or documenting movement towards agriculture, they have for the most part replicated the form, if not the content, of the imported approaches. In seeking to demonstrate that the Aboriginal past was dynamic and changing, Australian archaeologists have been on the side of the angels, creating a historical account of the past that was not prejudicial to Aboriginal people. But in giving these changes a linear direction, organising their data into stages and treating artefacts in an essentialist manner, they have left the door open for a return to theories that are demonstrably inadequate.

In 1997, Jared Diamond described the Australians as 'Stone Age nomadic hunter-gatherers' and posed the question, 'Why did the human societies of … Greater Australia remain so "backward"?'[94] Tylor asked a similar question a century earlier and Diamond's answer is Tylorian in its scope, noting that isolation, a poor environment and a low population means that the Australians were 'left behind' and, in their isolation their technology regressed.[95] Diamond is writing

---

93 Rasmussen et al. 2011: 95; Hudjashov et al. 2007: 8729.
94 Diamond 1997: 298, 316.
95 Diamond 1997: 308–311.

in a populist mode. However, similar terminology continues to be used in both the popular press and the adventurist offerings of tourist brochures. The point is not one of political correctness but rather that a narrative based on concepts of staged history, differential temporal dimensions and the idea of an evolutionary progression from the prehistoric world to the modern state, has entered deeply into the language.

Popular use of terms such as Stone Age, Palaeolithic, Prehistory, Prehistoric and Hunter-Gatherer gained their original meanings during the eighteenth and nineteenth centuries. The archaeologist's dilemma lies in the fact that they continue to use the same terms but argue that these have new meanings. The rub, however, is the singular lack of success archaeologists have had in convincing the public to accept new and technical meanings for long familiar terms. Archaeology cannot easily free itself from concepts which represent a nineteenth-century metaphysic and *episteme*.[96] In claiming that his stages were 'Homotaxial', Childe illustrates the chronological confusion that arises from mixing archaeological instances with ethnographic observations of contemporary peoples.[97] Seen in essentialist terms, the continued use of stone tools by Australian Aboriginal people qualified them as a Stone Age people.[98] Similarly, the classification of their lithic technology as Mode 1 or Mode 3 places them at the lower end of the sequence of human technological development.[99] Yet Australian Aboriginal use of stone tools is hardly definitive of their culture – a fact that stimulated Mulvaney to remark: 'For a stone age people, the Otway aborigines were singularly loathe to fashion stone implements.'[100]

No Australian archaeologist would consider that use of the term 'hunter-gatherer' implies substantive continuity from the deep past. However, the term ambiguously straddles both the period when hunting and gathering was a universal mode of economy and the ethnographic present. At the root of this problem is the conception of history as a series of progressive steps, where hunting and gathering takes on an essentialist meaning, locking the Aboriginal past and present into a continuous temporal dimension. Rather than illustrating the application of uniformitarian principles to understanding the past, this represents the projection of an archaeological understanding onto extant peoples. Apart from the scale of social units and the necessity for mobility, the degree to which hunting and gathering should be considered definitive of Aboriginal society can also be questioned. Within the Australian context, a false distinction is drawn between the simplicity of hunting and gathering

96 Clarke 1973: 14; McNiven and Russell 2005: 218–222; Preucel and Mrozowski 2010: 18–19; Rowe 1962; Shryock and Smail 2011: 44–45; Taylor 2008: 13–14.
97 Childe 1944: 7.
98 Childe 1936: 43; Childe 1954 [1942]: 24.
99 Foley and Lahr 1997: 18, 20, 24.
100 Holdaway and Douglass 2012; Mulvaney 1961a: 11.

as an economic system and the complexity of Aboriginal social and ritual life – a separation of the technical economy from relations of production.[101] Given these ambiguities, archaeologists question whether 'hunter-gatherer' is a meaningful term, one which places unlike societies with distinctive histories within a single, historically determined category.[102]

Towards the end of his book *Society and Knowledge*, Gordon Childe observed that archaeology did not 'increase the production of guns or butter' and hence questioned its ultimate usefulness to society.[103] This is an interesting comment from an archaeologist who stressed that knowledge was socially constructed, and who was a leading figure opposing the Nazi use of archaeology for ideological purposes.[104]

Nineteenth-century ideas and historical schemes criticised above are profoundly ideological. They continue to support a hierarchy of relations between Aboriginal and non-Aboriginal populations in Australia. In these theories, the nature of these hierarchical relations is portrayed as natural, the outcome of a compelling conceptualisation of history where European Australians drape the mantle of progress and modernity on their own shoulders and give Aboriginal people the burden of 'catching up'. Aboriginal people have rightly expressed outrage at these ideas.[105]

Escaping the ideological baggage of our colonial past represents a daunting task. Anthropologists have long attempted to confront the biological essentialism represented by the term 'race'. The archaeological task of creating new understandings of human history will prove equally difficult. However, if we are to remain true to our discipline and its responsibilities, challenging the essentialisms of the past is a task that must be undertaken.

Andrew Shryock and Daniel Smail argue that to comprehend the immensity of human time and its dynamic of change, we need new frameworks based on kinshipping, webs, trees, fractals, spirals, extensions and scalar integration.[106] Through the recognition that material changes through time reflect multiple processes and adjustments, Australian archaeologists are moving towards new understandings of the past. Some of these are directional and cumulative, others are nonlineal, all, however, are filtered through environmental changes and population responses.[107]

---

101 Jones 1990; Sahlins 1974.
102 Hamilton 1982; Head 2000; Panter-Brick et al. 2001.
103 Childe 1956b: 127.
104 Childe 1933: 410.
105 Gilbert 1977: 194, 268, 301; Langford 1983.
106 Shryock and Smail 2011: 119.
107 Hiscock 2008; Holdaway and Douglass 2012; Smith 2013.

In colonising this continent 50,000 years ago, Aboriginal people opened the chapter of human history in Australia. In tending the light of human culture in Australia and creatively responding to the difficult times which followed, they fulfilled all the requirements we could ask of any people. I remain optimistic that we can arrive at a new history of our human world – one that accepts that *all* twenty-first century human cultures are exactly the same age. And where every history is one of continuities and changes. If humans have progressed, then this is the result of the labour of all individuals, all human societies, all times and all places.

Acknowledgements

This is a revised version of a paper presented at the symposium 'Deep Time and Deep Histories: A Trans-disciplinary Collaboration', in June 2013. The symposium was hosted by the Australian Centre for Indigenous History (ACIH) at The Australian National University and organised by Ann McGrath, Malcolm Allbrook and Mary Anne Jebb. I thank them for their invitation to participate in this symposium. I would also like to acknowledge my debt to John Mulvaney, Jim Bowler and Rhys Jones at ANU, and the many colleagues who over the years have engaged in discussions about Australian archaeology. Simon Holdaway, in particular, is an implacable foe of essentialism in all its many forms. I would also like to thank members of the Mutthi Mutthi, Paakantji (Barkindji) and Ngyiampaa tribes, traditional owners of the Willandra Lakes, for their comments and feedback. My wife Jenny kept telling me that what was wanted was a fun paper about Mungo, instead I felt the need to bang on once again about archaeological abstractions and their impact on contemporary peoples. I hope the end result is not entirely disappointing. I thank Maria Haenga-Collins for her helpful comments and Tim Mackrell, Anthropology, University of Auckland, for the image scans.

Bibliography

Adams, Williams Y 1998, *The Philosophical Roots of Anthropology*, CSLI Publications, Stanford, CA.

Allen, Harry 1974, 'The Bagundji of the Darling Basin: cereal gatherers in an uncertain environment', *World Archaeology* 5: 309–322.

Allen, Harry 2000, 'Particular and universal explanations in the work of V. Gordon Childe', in Atholl Anderson and Tim Murray (eds), *Australian Archaeologist: Collected Papers in Honour of Jim Allen,* Coombs Academic Publishing, Canberra: 109–111.

Archambault, Paul 1966, 'The Ages of Man and the Ages of the World: a study of two traditions', *Revue des etudes augustinennes* 12: 193–228.

Arnold, JR and WF Libby 1949, 'Age determination by radiocarbon content: checks with samples of known age', *Science* 110(2869): 678–680.

Attwood, Bain 1996, 'Introduction: The past as future: Aborigines, Australia and the (dis) course of history', in Bain Attwood (ed.), *In the Age of Mabo: History, Aborigines and Australia,* Allen and Unwin, St Leonards, New South Wales.

Balfour, Harry 1926, 'Stone implements of the Tasmanians and the culture-status which they suggest', in L Keith Ward (ed.), *Report of the Seventeenth Meeting of the Australasian Association for the Advancement of Science. Australia and New Zealand. Adelaide Meeting, August, 1924,* Published by the Association. REE Rogers, Government Printer, Adelaide, South Australia.

Balme, Jane, I Davidson, J McDonald, N Stern, and P Veth 2009, 'Symbolic behaviour and the peopling of the southern arc route to Australia', *Quaternary International* 202: 59–68.

Barnard, Alan 2004, 'Hunting-and-gathering society: an eighteenth-century Scottish invention', in Alan Barnard (ed.), *Hunter-Gatherers in History, Archaeology and Anthropology,* Berg, Oxford.

Beaton, Jim 1983, 'Does intensification account for changes in the Australian Holocene archaeological record', *Archaeology in Oceania* 18: 94–97.

Bird, Caroline FM and David Frankel 1991, 'Problems in constructing a prehistoric regional sequence: Holocene south-east Australia', *World Archaeology* 23: 179–191.

Bowdler, Sandra 1981, 'Hunters in the highlands: Aboriginal adaptations in the Eastern Australian uplands', *Archaeology in Oceania* 16: 109–110.

Bowler, Jim M, R Jones, H Allen, and A Thorne 1970, 'Pleistocene human remains from Australia: a living site and human cremation from Lake Mungo, western New South Wales', *World Archaeology* 2: 39–60.

Bowler, Peter J 1988, *The Non-Darwinian Revolution: Reinterpreting a Historical Myth,* John Hopkins University Press, Baltimore.

Bowler, Peter J 1989, *The Invention of Progress: The Victorians and the Past,* Basil Blackwell, London.

Breuil, H 1912, 'Les subdivisions du Paléolithique supérieur et leur signification', XIV Congrés International d'Anthropologie et d'Archéologie Préhistoriques, Geneva 1, 174.

British Pathé 1933, *The Stone Age Men of Australia* (Parts 1 and 2), with the Mackay Aerial Survey Expedition to Central Australia, Described by Commander HT Bennett DSO, FRGS, RN, video.

Broome, Richard 1982, *Aboriginal Australians: Black Response to White Dominance, 1788–1980,* George Allen and Unwin, Sydney,

Brumm, Adam R and Mark W Moore 2005, 'Symbolic revolutions and the Australian archaeological record', *Cambridge Archaeological Journal* 15: 157–175.

Bryson, Gladys 1945, *Man and Society: The Scottish Inquiry of the Eighteenth century,* Princeton University Press, Princeton, New Jersey.

Burrow, John W 1966, *Evolution and Society: A Study in Victorian Social Theory,* Cambridge University Press, Cambridge.

Chazan, Michael 1995, 'Conceptions of time and the development of Paleolithic chronology', *American Anthropologist* 97: 462–463.

Chewings, Charles 1937, *Back in the Stone Age: The Natives of Central Australia,* Angus & Robertson, Sydney.

Childe, V Gordon 1933, 'Is Archaeology practical?', *Antiquity* 7, 410–418.

Childe, V Gordon 1936, *Man Makes Himself,* Watts and Co., London.

Childe, V Gordon 1944, 'Archaeological Ages as technological Stages', *Journal of the Royal Anthropological Institute of Great Britain and Ireland* 74: 7–24.

Childe, V Gordon 1947, *History,* Corbett Press, London.

Childe, V Gordon 1954 [1942], *What Happened in History,* Penguin Books, Harmondsworth, Middlesex.

Childe, V Gordon 1956a, *Piecing Together the Past: The Interpretation of Archaeological Data,* Routledge and Kegan Paul, London.

Childe, V Gordon 1956b, *Society and Knowledge,* George Allen and Unwin, London.

Childe, V Gordon 1958, 'Retrospect', *Antiquity* 32: 69–79.

Clark, Grahame 1969, *World Prehistory: A New Outline,* Cambridge University Press, Cambridge.

Clark, Grahame 1976, 'Prehistory since Childe', *Bulletin of the Institute of Archaeology* 13: 1–21.

Clarke, David 1973, 'Archaeology: the loss of innocence', *Antiquity* 47, 6–18.

Daniel, Glyn 1943, *The Three Ages-an Essay on Archaeological Method,* Cambridge University Press, Cambridge.

Daniel, Glyn 1978, *150 Years of Archaeology,* second edition, Duckworth, London.

Degérando, Joseph Marie, Baron de Gérando 1969 [1800], *Observation of Savage Peoples*, trans. by FCT Moore [*Considération sur les diverses méthodes à suivre dans l'observation des peuples sauvages*, Société des Observateurs de l'Homme], Routledge & K Paul, London.

De Mortillet, Gabriel 1873, 'Classification des diverses périodes de l'âge de la pierre', *Congrés International d'Anthropologie et d'Archéologie Préhistorique, Compte rendu de la 6e Session, Bruxelles, 1872,* Librairie JB Balliére et Fils, Paris, 432–444.

Diamond, Jared 1997, *Guns, Germs, and Steel: The Fates of Human Societies,* WW Norton and Company, New York.

Engels, Frederick 1972 [1884], *The Origin of the Family, Private Property and the State,* Pathfinder Press, New York.

Fabian, Johannes 1983, *Time and the Other: How Anthropology Makes Its Object,* Columbia University Press, New York.

Freeland, Guy 1983, 'Evolutionism and arch(a)eology', in David Oldroyd and Ian Langham (eds), *The Wider Domain of Evolutionary Thought*, D. Reidel Publishing Company, Dordrecht, 175–219.

Foley, Robert 1987, 'Hominid species and stone-tool assemblages: how are they related?' *Antiquity* 6: 3–36.

Foley, Robert and Marta Mirazón Lahr 1997, 'Mode 3 technologies and the evolution of modern humans',*Cambridge Archaeological Journal* 7: 3–36.

Gamble, Clive 1992, 'Archaeology, history and the uttermost ends of the earth – Tasmania, Tierra del Fuego and the Cape', *Antiquity,* 66: 712–720.

Gamble, Clive 1995, *The Timewalkers: The Prehistory of Global Colonization*, Penguin Books, London.

Geneste, Jean-Michel, B David, H Plisson, J Delannoy, and F Petchey 2011, 'The origins of ground-edge axes: new findings from Nawarla Gabarnmang, Arnhem Land (Australia) and global implications for the evolution of fully modern humans', *Cambridge Archaeological Journal* 22: 1–17.

Gilbert, Kevin 1977, *Living Black: Blacks Talk to Kevin Gilbert*, Allen Lane, The Penguin Press, London.

Gould, Richard A 1973, *Australian Archaeology in Ecological and Ethnographic Perspective*, Warner Modular Publication, Andover, MA.

Gräsland, Bo 1987, *The Birth of Prehistoric Chronology: Dating Methods and Dating Systems in Nineteenth-Century Scandinavian Archaeology*, Cambridge University Press, Cambridge.

Greene, Kevin 1999, 'V. Gordon Childe and the vocabulary of revolutionary change', *Antiquity* 73: 97–109.

Groube, LM 1967, 'Models in prehistory: a consideration of the New Zealand evidence', *Archaeology and Physical Anthropology in Oceania* 2: 1–27.

Gsell, Francis Xavier 1955, *The Bishop with 150 Wives: Fifty Years as a Missionary*, Angus and Robertson, London.

Hamilton, Annette 1982, 'The unity of hunting and gathering societies: reflections on economic forms and resource management', in Nancy M Williams and Eugene S Hunn (eds), *Resource Managers: North American and Australian Hunter-Gatherers*, 229–248.

Harris, David R 1990, 'Settling down and breaking ground: rethinking the Neolithic Revolution', *Twaalfde Kroon-voordracht Gehouden Voor de Stichting Nederlands Museum Voor Anthropologie en Praehistorie Te Amsterdam*.

Head, Lesley 2000, *Second Nature: The History and Implications of Australia as Aboriginal Landscape*, Syracuse University Press, Syracuse, New York.

Heath, M 2008, 'Aristotle on natural slavery', *Phronesis: A Journal for Ancient Philosophy* 53: 243–270.

Hiatt, LR 1996, *Arguments about Aborigines: Australia and the Evolution of Social Anthropology*, Cambridge University Press, Cambridge.

Hiscock, Peter 2008, *Archaeology of Ancient Australia*, Routledge, London.

Hodder, Ian 1991, *Reading the Past: Current Approaches to Interpretation in Archaeology*, Cambridge University Press, Cambridge.

Holdaway, Simon and Matthew Douglass 2012, 'A twenty-first century archaeology of stone artifacts', *Journal of Archaeological Method and Theory* 19: 101–131.

Hudjashov, Georgi, T Kivisild, P Underhill, P Endicott, J Sanchez, A Lin, P Shen, P Oefner, C Renfrew, R Villems, and P Forster 2007, 'Revealing the prehistoric settlement of Australia by Y chromosome and mtDNA analysis', *PNAS* 104: 8726–8730.

Huxley, Thomas Henry 1906, *Man's Place in Nature and Other Essays*, JM Dent and Sons, London.

Jones, Rhys 1990, 'Hunters of the Dreaming: some ideational, economic and ecological parameters of the Australian Aboriginal productive system', in DE Yen and JMJ Mummery (eds), *Pacific Production Systems: Approaches to Economic Prehistory*, Department of Prehistory, Research School of Pacific Studies, The Australian National University, Canberra, 25–53.

Jones, Rhys 1992, 'Philosophical time travellers', *Antiquity* 66:744–757.

Keen, Ian 2000, 'The anthropologist as geologist: Howitt in colonial Gippsland', *The Australian Journal of Anthropology* 11: 78–97.

Klindt-Jensen, Ole 1981, 'Archaeology and ethnography in Denmark: early studies', in Glyn Daniel (ed.), *Towards a History of Archaeology,* Thames and Hudson, London.

Langford, Rose F 1983, 'Our heritage – your playground', *Australian Archaeology* 16: 1–6.

Langley, Michelle C, C Clarkson and S Ulm 2011, 'From small holes to grand narratives: the impact of taphonomy and sample size on the modernity debate in Australia and New Guinea', *Journal of Human Evolution* 61: 197–208.

Lourandos, Harry 1980, 'Change or stability? Hydraulics, hunter-gatherers, and population in temperate Australia', *World Archaeology* 11: 245–264.

Lourandos, Harry 1983, 'Intensification: a late Pleistocene-Holocene archaeological sequence from southwestern Victoria', *Archaeology in Oceania* 18: 81–97.

Lourandos, Harry 1985, 'Intensification and Australian prehistory', in T Price and J Brown (eds), *Prehistoric Hunter-Gatherers: The Emergence of Complexity*, Academic Press, London, 385–414.

Lourandos, Harry 1988, 'Palaeopolitics: resource intensification in Aboriginal Australia and Papua New Guinea', in Tim Ingold, David Riches and James Woodburn (eds), *Hunters and Gatherers 1: History, Evolution and Social Change*, Berg, Oxford.

Lubbock, John 1865, *Pre-Historic Times: As Illustrated by Ancient Remains and the Manners and Customs of Modern Savages*, Williams and Norgate, London.

MacDougall, Doug 2008, *Nature's Clocks: How Scientists Measure the Age of Almost Everything*, University of California Press, San Diego.

Marx, Karl 1926, *The eighteenth Brumaire of Louis Bonaparte*, G Allen & Unwin Ltd, London.

McBrearty, Sally and Alison Brooks 2000, 'The revolution that wasn't: a new interpretation of the origin of modern human behaviour', *Journal of Human Evolution* 39: 453–563.

McCarthy, Frederick D 1953, 'The Oceanic and Indonesian affiliations of Australian Aboriginal culture', *Journal of the Polynesian Society* 62: 246.

McNiven, Ian J and Lynette Russell 2005, *Appropriated Pasts: Indigenous Peoples and the Colonial Culture of Archaeology*, AltaMira Press, Lanham, MD, 218–222.

Meek, Ronald M 1954, 'The Scottish contribution to Marxist sociology', in John Saville (ed.), *Democracy and the Labour Movement*, Lawrence and Wishart, London, 84–102.

Meek, Ronald L 1976, *Social Science and the Ignoble Savage,* Cambridge University Press, Cambridge.

Mitchell, SR 1949, *Stone-Age Craftsmen: Stone Tools and Camping Places of the Australian Aborigines*, Tait Book Co., Melbourne.

Mokyr, Joel 2009, *The Enlightened Economy: An Economic History of Britain 1700–1850*, Yale University Press, New Haven.

Montesquieu, Charles-Louis de Secondat 1949 [1748], *The Spirit of the Laws,* Vol. 1, translated by Thomas Nugent, Hafner Library of Classics, Hafner, New York.

Morgan, Lewis H 1877, *Ancient Society: Researches in the Lines of Human Progress from Savagery through Barbarism to Civilization,* Charles H Kerr and Company, Chicago.

Morwood, Mike and Percy J Trezise 1989, 'Edge-ground axes in Pleistocene greater Australia: new evidence from S.E. Cape York', *Queensland Archaeological Research* 6: 77–90.

Mountford, Charles P 1949, 'Exploring Stone Age Arnhem Land', *National Geographic* 96: 745–782.

Mulvaney, Derek John 1958, 'The Australian Aborigines 1606–1929: opinion and fieldwork', *Historical Studies* 8: 131–151, 297–315.

Mulvaney, Derek John 1961a, 'Archaeological excavations on the Aire River, Otway Peninsula, Victoria', *Proceedings of the Royal Society of Victoria* 75: 1–15.

Mulvaney, Derek John 1961b, 'The Stone Age of Australia', *Proceedings of the Prehistoric Society* 27: 56–107.

Mulvaney, Derek John 1966, 'The prehistory of the Australian Aborigine', *Scientific American* 214: 83–93.

Mulvaney, Derek John 1971a, *Discovering Man's Place in Nature*, Sydney University Press for the Australian Academy of the Humanities, Sydney.

Mulvaney, Derek John 1971b, 'Aboriginal social evolution: a retrospective view', in Derek John Mulvaney and Jack Golson (eds), *Aboriginal Man and Environment in Australia*, Australian National University Press, Canberra.

Mulvaney, Derek John and E Bernie Joyce 1965, 'Archaeological and geomorphological investigations at Mt. Moffatt Station, Queensland, Australia', *Proceedings of the Prehistoric Society* 31: 192–193.

Mulvaney, Derek John and Johan Kamminga 1999, *Prehistory of Australia*, Allen and Unwin, St Leonards.

Murray, Tim 2007, *Milestones in Archaeology: A Chronological Encyclopedia*, ABC-Clio, Santa Barbara, California.

Oppenheimer, Stephen 2003, *Out of Eden: The Peopling of the World*, Constable, London.

Pagden, Anthony 1982, *The Fall of Natural Man: The American Indian and the Origins of Comparative Ethnology*, Cambridge University Press, Cambridge.

Panter-Brick, Catherine, R Layton and P Rowley-Conwy 2001, 'Lines of inquiry', in Catherine Panter-Brick, Robert H Layton and Peter Rowley-Conwy (eds), *Hunter-Gatherers: An Interdisciplinary Perspective*, Cambridge University Press, Cambridge.

Perry, William James 1923, *The Children of the Sun: A Study of in the Early History of Civilization,* Methuen and Co., Ltd, London,.

Peterson, Nicolas 1976, 'Ethno-archaeology in the Australian Iron Age', in Gale de G Sieveking, Ian H Longworth and Kenneth E Wilson (eds), *Problems in Economic and Social Archaeology,* Duckworth, London, 265–275.

Phillips, Patricia 1981, *The Prehistory of Europe,* Penguin Books, Middlesex.

Piggott, S 1958, 'The dawn: and an epilogue', *Antiquity* 32: 77–79.

Preucel, Robert W and Stephen Mrozowski (eds) 2010, *Contemporary Archaeology in Theory: The New Pragmatism,* second edition, Wiley-Blackwell, New York.

Rasmussen, Morten, X Guo, Y Wang, K Lohmueller, S Rasmussen, A Albrechtsen, L Skotte, S Lindgreen, M Metspalu, T Jombart, T Kivisild, W Zhai, A Eriksson, A Manica, L Orlando, F De La Vega, S Tridico, E Metspalu, K Nielsen, M Ávila-Arcos, J Moreno-Mayar, C Muller, J Dortch, M Gilbert, O Lund, A Wesolowska, M Karmin, L Weinert, B Wang, J Li, S Tai, F Xiao, T Hanihara, G van Driem, A Jha, F Ricaut, P de Knijff, A Migliano, R Gallego, K Kristiansen, D Lambert, S Brunak, P Forster, B Brinkmann, O Nehlich, M Bunce, M Richards, R Gupta, C Bustamante, A Krogh, R Foley, M Lahr, F Balloux, T Sicheritz-Pontén, R Villems, R Nielsen, J Wang, and E Willerslev 2011, 'An Aboriginal Australian genome reveals separate human dispersals into Asia', *Science* 334(6052): 94–98.

Redd, Alan J and Mark Stoneking 1999, 'Peopling of Sahul: mtDNA variation in Aboriginal Australian and Papua New Guinean populations', *American Journal of Human Genetics* 65: 808–828.

Renfrew, Colin 1976 [1973], *Before Civilization: The Radiocarbon Revolution and Prehistoric Europe,* Penguin Books, Middlesex.

Roberts, Richard G 1997, 'Luminescence dating in archaeology: from origins to optical', *Radiation Measurements* 27: 819–892.

Rodden, Judith 1981, 'The development of the Three Age System: archaeology's first paradigm', in Glyn Daniel (ed.), *Towards a History of Archaeology,* Thames and Hudson, London.

Rowe, John Howland 1962, 'Stages and periods in archaeological interpretation', *Southwestern Journal of Anthropology* 18: 40–54.

Rowley-Conwy, Peter 2007, *From Genesis to Prehistory: The Archaeological Three Age System and its Contested Reception in Denmark, Britain, and Ireland,* Oxford University Press, Oxford.

Rudwick, Martin 1995, *Scenes from Deep Time: Early Pictorial Representations of the Prehistoric World,* University of Chicago Press, Chicago.

Sahlins, Marshall 1974, *Stone Age Economics*, Tavistock Publications, London.

Sharp, Lauriston 1952, 'Steel axes for Stone-Age Australians', *Human Organization* 11: 17–22.

Sherratt, Andrew 1989, 'V. Gordon Childe: archaeology and intellectual history', *Past and Present* 125: 165–168.

Shryock, Andrew and Daniel Lord Smail 2011, *Deep History: The Architecture of Past and Present*, University of California Press, Berkeley.

Skinner, HD 1957, 'Migrations of culture in South-east Asia and Indonesia', *Journal of the Polynesian Society* 66: 206–207.

Smith, Bruce D 2001, 'Low-level food production', *Journal of Archaeological Research* 9: 1–43.

Smith, Mike 2013, *The Archaeology of Australia's Deserts,* Cambridge University Press, Cambridge.

Smith, Nicholas D 1983, 'Aristotle's theory of natural slavery', *Phoenix* 37: 109–122.

Sollas, William Johnstone 1911, *Ancient Hunters and Their Modern Representatives*, Macmillan, London.

Spencer, Baldwin W 1914, *Native Tribes of the Northern Territory of Australia,* Macmillan and Co. Limited, London.

Staniland Wake, C 1872, 'On the mental characteristics of primitive man, as exemplified by the Australian Aborigines', *Journal of the Anthropological Institute of Great Britain and Ireland* 1: 74–84.

William Edward Hanley Stanner, 1979 [1962], 'Caliban discovered', in WEH Stanner (ed.), *Whiteman Got No Dreaming: Essays 1938-1973*, Australian National University Press, Canberra, 152–153.

Sutton, Stephen A 1990, 'Pleistocene axes in Sahul: a response to Morwood and Tresize', *Queensland Archaeological Research* 7: 95–109.

Taylor, Timothy 2008, 'Prehistory vs. archaeology: terms of engagement', *Journal of World Prehistory* 2: 13–14.

Thomas, Nicholas 1982, 'Childe, Marx and archaeology', *Dialectical Anthropology* 6: 245–252.

Thomsen, Christian Jürgensen 1848, *Guide to Northern Archæology* by the Royal Society of Northern Antiquaries of Copenhagen; edited for the use of English readers by the Earl of Ellesmere, James Bain, London, 64–69.

Tylor, Edward Burnett 1865, *Researches into the early history of mankind and the development of civilization,* John Murray London.

Tylor, Edward Burnett 1894, 'On the Tasmanians as representatives of palaeolithic man', *Journal of the Anthropological Institute of Great Britain and Ireland* 23: 141–152.

Van Holst Pellekaan, Shelia 2011, 'Genetic evidence for the colonization of Australia', *Quaternary International* 285: 44–56.

Westropp, Hodder M 1872, *Pre-Historic Phases; or, Introductory Essays on Pre-Historic Archaeology*, Bell & Daldy, London.

White, Carmel 1967, 'Early stone axes in Arnhem Land', *Antiquity* 41: 149–152.

White, Peter, J 1971, 'New Guinea and Australian prehistory: the "Neolithic Problem"', in Derek John Mulvaney and Jack Golson (eds), *Aboriginal Man and Environment in Australia*, Australian National University Press, Canberra, 182–195.

White, Peter J 1977, 'Crude, colourless and unenterprising? Prehistorians and their views on the Stone Age of Sunda and Sahul', in Jim Allen, Jack Golson and Rhys Jones (eds), *Sunda and Sahul: Prehistoric Studies in Southeast Asia, Melanesia and Australia*, Academic Press, London, 13–30.

Yeo, Richard 2003, 'Classifying the sciences', in Roy Porter (ed.), *The Cambridge History of Science, Vol. 4: Eighteenth Century Science*, Cambridge University Press, Cambridge, 241–266.

12. Lives and Lines

Integrating molecular genetics, the 'origins of modern humans' and Indigenous knowledge

Martin Porr

Introduction

Within Palaeolithic archaeology and palaeoanthropology a general consensus seems to have formed over the last decades that modern humans – people like us – originated in Africa around 150,000 to 200,000 years ago and subsequently migrated into the remaining parts of the Old and New World to reach Australia by about 50,000 years ago and Patagonia by about 13,000 years ago.[1] This view is encapsulated in describing Africa as 'the cradle of humankind'. This usually refers to the origins of the genus *Homo* between two and three million years ago, but it is readily extended to the processes leading to the origins of our species *Homo sapiens sapiens*.[2]

A narrative is created that consequently imagines the repeated origins of species of human beings in Sub-Saharan Africa and their subsequent colonisation of different parts of the world. In the course of these conquests other human species are replaced, such as the Neanderthals in western and central Eurasia.[3] These processes are described with the terms 'Out-of-Africa I' (connected to *Homo ergaster/erectus* around two million years ago) and 'Out-of-Africa II' (connected to *Homo sapiens sapiens* about 100,000 years ago). It is probably fair to say that this description relates to the most widely accepted view of 'human origins' both in academia as well as the public sphere.[4]

Analysis of ancient DNA, historical DNA samples and samples from living human populations molecular genetics increasingly contributes to our understanding of the deep past and generally, and seems to support this 'standard model of human origins', beginning with the establishment of the mitochondrial 'Eve' hypothesis from the 1980s onwards.[5] In 2011 an Australian Indigenous genome was for the first time analysed – a 100-year-old hair sample from the Western Australian

---

1   Oppenheimer 2004, 2009.
2   Antón 2003; Mellars and Stringer 1989; Schwartz and Tattersall 2010; Stringer 2011.
3   Stewart and Stringer 2012
4   Klein 2009; Roebroeks et al. 2012; Tattersall and Schwartz 2000.
5   Crawford 2007; O'Rourke 2007.

Goldfields region held in the British Museum — with a range of results and implications, which impact not only on the narrative of the earliest colonisation of what is now Australia, but also the timing and character of successive waves of early modern humans' assumed journeys out of Africa and into Asia and beyond.[6] The analysis also concluded that 'present-day Aboriginal Australians descend from the earliest humans to occupy Australia, likely representing one of the oldest continuous populations outside Africa'.[7]

The understanding of modern human origins in Africa and replacement scenarios elsewhere had to be further revised with genetic evidence for inter-breeding within Africa of supposedly archaic and modern humans, as well as the persistence of archaic populations until a surprisingly recent date.[8] Although one of the researchers involved in these studies claims that latest results signal a 'paradigm shift', this does not go so far as to question the fundamentals of current views.[9] The latter are firmly based on the existence of separate lineages of human beings, such as modern humans, Neanderthals, Denisovans or 'archaic humans', who interacted with each other over time and to a different degree. Despite these latest complications, current views seem not to question the boundaries between species or sub-species within recent human evolution, although this was a major issue of contention in debates during the twentieth century.[10] In this context, the evidence from molecular genetics is mainly regarded as having influenced the debate between the Multiregional and Out of Africa views of recent human evolution in favour of the former.

One thing that all scientific and western narratives about human origins appear to have in common, however, seems to be that they are well removed from traditional Indigenous world-views, concepts of history and the past. These issues are relevant for the relationship between western and traditional knowledge systems in all parts of the globe. However, the particularities of Australia's deep and more recent history and geography make some of these aspects particularly visible. The presence of human beings in Greater Australia (or Sahul, which encompasses present-day Australia and the island of New Guinea) is seen and explained as an episode of the more general narrative of modern human's colonisation of the world. The scientific view reconstructs the first arrival of human beings at a particular point in time or, rather, having occurred during a specific period in the deep past. The initial colonisation is currently estimated to have been between about 45,000 to 60,000 years ago.[11] Before this time Sahul was uninhabited by humans or their ancestors.

---

6   Rasmussen et al. 2011.
7   Green et al. 2010.
8   Hammer et al. 2011; Harvati et al. 2011.
9   Michael Hammer quoted in Gibbons 2011: 167.
10 Caspari and Wolpoff 1994; Mayr 1963; Wolpoff and Caspari 1997.
11 Davidson 2013; O'Connell and Allen 2004.

This view stands in contrast to some fundamental features of traditional Australian Indigenous world-views and knowledge systems, which stress a close connection to 'Country', timelessness of identity and an ongoing presence of a mythological past. Famously (but not without its problems), this understanding has been encapsulated in the academic and popular literature in the term 'the Dreaming'.[12] While this term is discussed in more detail in chapters by James, Paton, Hughes and Leane, it generally is taken to imply that people are so intimately connected to Country that they are one and the same, and thus neither 'arrived' nor came from somewhere else.[13] The stories that bind people and Country together are timeless and always present, and the people who know the stories have always been in the Country. The Indigenous notions of Country and Dreaming are of great relevance here for an understanding of a large range of issues. This applies particularly to the ways of perceiving, experiencing and understanding the dialectic, fundamental and inseparable interrelationships between people, their life ways and the land. Millroy and Revell have elaborated that 'the individual is born to Country, not just in Country, but from Country, and his or her identity is inextricably and eternally linked to the Dreaming'.[14] The relationship between persons and Country is dialectic and social:

> People talk about Country in the same way that they would talk about a person … Country is a living entity with a yesterday, a today and tomorrow, with consciousness, action, and a will toward life. Because of this richness of meaning, Country is home and peace: nourishment for body, mind and spirit; and heart's ease.[15]

Personally, I was exposed to these perspectives during my recent fieldwork in the Kimberley region of north-west Australia, and during a workshop meeting 'Gwion Gwion rock art of the Kimberley' that I co-organised in 2010.[16] In the course of this workshop it became increasingly clear to me how different the perception of the rock art between western and Indigenous people is on many levels. Kim Doohan, who has worked as an anthropologist many years in the Kimberley, participated in this workshop together with Donny Woolagoodja and Leah Umbagai from the Dambimangari Aboriginal Corporation, and Valda Blundell. Since the workshop we have had many conversations about Indigenous viewpoints and the implications for research into knowledge systems, heritage management, the interpretation of archaeological evidence and rock art. During a conversation in Kalumburu, Kim mentioned that she recently was asked by young Indigenous men the following: 'The scientists said that Aborigines only

---

12 Stanner 1958; Wolfe 1991.
13 Kolig 2000; Porr and Bell 2012; Stanner 1968.
14 Milroy and Revell 2013.
15 Rose 1996: 7.
16 See Porr and Bell 2012; McNiven 2011; Aubert 2012.

arrived in Australia 50,000 years ago, but our Elders have told us that we have always been here. Have our Elders been lying to us all the time?' Kim said that she was not sure how to respond, and when I heard this I was dismayed by the fact that so-called 'modern science' continues to undermine (and potentially destroy) Indigenous knowledge systems – which are inseparably intertwined with and connected to art and rock art in Country, as well as a solid sense of individual and collective identity.[17]

It is probably fair to say that for most people the so-called scientific version of historical events and the Indigenous view seem to be separated by an abyss of conceptual differences and epistemologies. I want to argue that it is possible to integrate so-called scientific and Indigenous knowledge in this context, but this will necessitate some deconstruction of the foundations of current scientific narratives of human origins.

Narratives of human origins and their representation

The Out of Africa and multiregional explanations of modern human origins have been subject to much debate, as well as attempts to unpack their inherent epistemological assumptions and structures. In this respect, major analyses have been provided by science historian Landau and social anthropologist Stoczkowski.[18] Both concentrated on narratives of human origins in general, rather than on the origins of modern humans in particular. However, elements of their analyses are also applicable to the latter field. A thorough critical and reflective assessment of the assumptions that are guiding present models of modern human origins is a major research topic that still needs to be addressed.[19] Landau has emphasised the structural similarities between narratives of human evolution and folk tales to draw attention to the fact that these are fundamentally guided by deep, mostly implicit cultural convictions and motives.[20] Stoczkowski has criticised this approach, emphasising that Landau has not succeeded in unravelling the philosophical and historical origins of the structures that she described.[21] He identifies four 'complementary assumptions' that have structured explanations and narratives of human origins and evolution since the eighteenth century, and have produced surprisingly

---

17   Blundell 2003; Blundell and Woolagoodja 2012; Layton 1992; Milroy and Revell 2013; Porr and Bell 2012; Redmond 2001; Vinnicombe and Mowaljarlai 1995.
18   Landau 1984, 1993; Stoczkowski 2002.
19   See for example Porr 2014.
20   Landau 1993.
21   Stoczkowski 2002: 188.

similar approaches despite vastly increasing archaeological and anthropological evidence. The most important assumptions are environmental determinism, materialism, utilitarianism and individualism.[22] As will become clear, these elements are key to addressing the status of scientific knowledge in relation to Indigenous knowledge and the question of human origins and evolution.[23]

I am interested in how these narratives are graphically represented in the literature, an analysis which takes some inspiration from Tim Ingold's exploration of lines across different historical and cultural contexts.[24] Graphic representations of the process of modern human origins are dominated by two elements: an area or point of origin, and lines in the form of arrows pointing away from the former.[25] It would be intriguing to analyse closely how differences in representation actually correlate with ideas and concepts proposed by the respective authors. However, in this chapter a more general question will suffice – what do these different elements represent in the assumed processes of biological evolution in the context of 'modern human origins'? Clearly, the area or point of origin has to be understood as the origin location of our species, *Homo sapiens sapiens*, if 'people like us' or modern humans supposedly originated in one area and spread from there all over the world. This assertion immediately runs into the problem that there is actually no morphological definition of our own species that allows us to clearly identify what an anatomically modern human is in biological taxonomic terms. For example, physical anthropologists Schwartz and Tattersall have drawn attention to the fact that this view has a long history in western thought, and was also a feature in the original Linnean formulation of the modern taxonomic system (first published in 1735).[26] In the case of humans, Carolus Linnaeus 'abandoned his usual practice of providing a [morphological] diagnosis for each taxon' and stated that to recognise a member of this species you should simply look at yourself: *Nosce te ipsum*.[27] Much more recently, one of the most prominent biologists of the twentieth century, Ernst Mayr, also argued that the identity of modern humans is not a matter or physical appearance or morphology:

> If groups of apparently disparate morphology are more or less universally agreed on to be members of the same species, it is scientifically ludicrous (and racist) to attach biological, systematic, and thus evolutionary meaning to the differences between them.[28]

22 Stoczkowski 2002: 16–17.
23 Ingold 2004.
24 Ingold 2007.
25 Klein 2008: 270; Oppenheimer 2009: 3.
26 Schwartz and Tattersall 2010.
27 Schwartz and Tattersall 2010: 95.
28 Schwartz and Tattersall 2010: 97.

After all, with the atrocities that were inflicted in the name of racism during the nineteenth and twentieth centuries there can be little doubt that from an ethical point of view this should be the case. The Australian colonial experience clearly demonstrates this in the most painful way.[29] But in the context of human evolution, this orientation causes a range of conceptual problems. It seems that in Palaeolithic archaeology this view is reflected by the fact that anatomical features have largely been rejected to define modern humans, and their actual origins are now supposedly to be found in 'modern human behavioural features' – hence, the often used terminology of 'behaviourally modern humans'.[30] However, as material reflections of behaviours that are seen to signal 'full behavioural modernity' do not occur at one point in time but rather are scattered patchily across Europe and Africa over the next 100,000 years, this origin point is now increasingly and implicitly seen as the origin of the 'capacity' for modern behaviour or thinking.[31]

As you cannot observe a 'capacity' – neither in fossil human remains nor in archaeological artefacts – this point of origin gains an almost mystical quality and becomes completely defined by later history, by qualities that are regarded by different authors as specifically human and modern, creating a narrative that sees humanity as a slow unfolding of an essential human capacity or endowment.[32] Drawing on Derrida's writings, Gamble and Gittins have eloquently argued that the whole study of the Palaeolithic is a reflection of western *logocentrism* (from the Greek *Logos*, meaning logic, reason, the word, God), a metaphysical desire for foundation and therefore tied to the notion of origins from single points in time and space.[33] These centres, as *logos*, are considered whole and indivisible and provide coherence for the structure of the argument. However, because they are considered indivisible, they escape structure and as such the origins for any phenomenon consequently become unanalysable. Like the 'big bang' in physics, it seems as if at the point of origin of modern humanity causality and analysis can no longer be applied, because the whole justification of the origin of the phenomenon comes from its later unfolding.

In fact, the current discussion about the so-called modern human origins – although supposedly grounded in modern evolutionary theory and modelling – is very much anti-evolutionary, because it assumes the creation of a capacity without a material or behavioural (phenotypic) expression that is then transmitted in essentialist and unchanged form through the generations without variation. The justification for its success and transcendental quality

29 Anderson 2007.
30 Henshilwood 2007.
31 McBrearty 2007.
32 Ingold 2004.
33 Gamble and Gittins 2004: 105–107.

[Handwritten margin notes:]
Palaeolithic archaeology (species!) drifts to now according behaviour rather than anatomy

Archaeologists look across time to observe a 'capacity' for behaviour that has been scattered across history

The study of the Palaeolithic is a reflection of western logocentrism

a metaphysical desire for foundation,

The study is thus tied to the notion of origins) from single points in time and space.

Modern evolutionary theory is actually essentialist, not evolutionary is rarely explained and seems to lie rather in its ultimate ability to produce modern culture and technology (as evidenced by modern human's success in colonising all environments around the globe). It is clear that there are distinct links with deep essentialist western traditions of thought, which are more thoroughly addressed elsewhere.[34] Here, I want to concentrate instead on the current amalgamation with a reductionist view of molecular genetics and the role of genes in processes of evolution.

Genes and lifelines

Returning to the notion of graphic representations, the lines and arrows that are drawn across the maps radiating outwards from the 'epicentre' of modern human origins are drawn solid and unidirectional, and the question arises about what they actually represent. I would argue here that the similarity with maps of military operations or the journeys of early European explorers is not accidental.

They collapse the depth of time of Upper Pleistocene human movements to a scale of an individual and directional narrative. They refer to the idea that modern humans originated at one point in time and in one place – where they acquired their essential identity – and that these humans remained *essentially* modern humans, because they carried a genetically fixed potential or capacity for modern behaviour or modern humanity.

This narrative of modern human origins is ultimately a reflection of the general view of biological evolution as established by Darwin and refined over the last 150 years. Darwin included only one graphic representation or diagram in *The Origins of Species*, but it is very telling in this context.[35]

GRAPHIC REPRESENTATIONS OF
MODERN HUMAN ORIGINS ARE
DRAWN SOLID & UNIDIRECTIONAL
AKIN TO MILITARY MAPS & EXPLORATION
MAPS

---

34 Ingold 2004, 2006; Marks 2008, 2009.
35 Ingold 2007: 114.

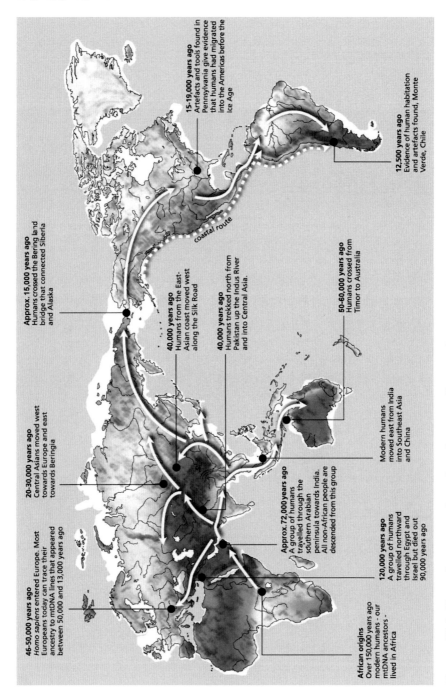

Figure 12.1: Narrative map of modern human dispersals.

Source: (c) Stephen Oppenheimer (modified from Oppenheimer 2003, 2009).

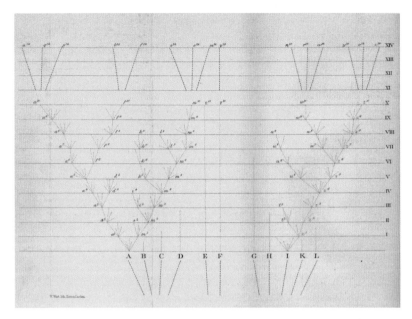

Figure 12.2: Diagram from Darwin's *The Origin of Species by Means of Natural Selection* (1859) to illustrate the evolutionary process.
Source: Reproduced with permission from John van Wyhe (ed.) 2002– , 'The Complete Work of Charles Darwin Online' (darwin-online.org.uk/).

The cornerstone of Darwin's book was the notion of 'descent with modification'. In Darwin's diagram, no solid lines are drawn to signify evolutionary processes. Darwin's original evolutionary branching trees consist of rows of single dots aligned to form lines that stand for successive generations of organisms in relations of descent. Each individual is seen as an essential representative of a genetic configuration inherited from its parents with added genetic variation or modification over time. While Darwin recognised in this way the necessity to view evolutionary processes as successions of separate and changing individuals and populations over time, he also assumed that each individual represents an inherited biological or cognitive capacity or potential in the same way as it appears in the current standard model of the origins of modern humans, the notion of universal capacity that defines and characterises our species.[36] This capacity supposedly encapsulates the identity of our species and the core of each and every individual human being. This view transports the idea that identity is preformed *before* a human being is actually developing within and into a specific environment.

[handwritten: DARWIN DOESN'T USE SOLID LINES TO SIGNIFY EVOLUTIONARY PROCESSES]

36   Renfrew 1996.

In this chapter it is not possible to discuss the complex links between the dramatic discoveries and advances within the fields of molecular biology and genetics over the last 50 years and evolutionary theory.[37] However, it has to be recognised that the observations outlined above for the fields of palaeoanthropology and Palaeolithic archaeology are to a large extent reflections of a highly influential strand within biological evolutionary thinking that continues to have an important impact on academic and popular discussions.[38] With reference to the above-mentioned analysis by Stoczkowski, it can be argued that interpretations of human evolution seem to have explicitly, or implicitly, accepted the respective fundamental deterministic assumptions about genetic information and its relationships with human morphological, cognitive and behavioural characteristics.[39] In contrast, the extensive critique that has been put forward in this context on different levels has only made minor impacts on views of human evolution and 'modern human origins'. These latter approaches raise concerns about the notion of genetic 'information' as such, the contingency of developmental processes, the complexities of organism-environment interactions and a lack of anthropological reflection of terminologies and concepts.[40] Consequently, the fields of palaeoanthropology and Palaeolithic archaeology appear very selective and restrictive in their choice of evolutionary models and concepts – a situation that contributes to the opposition between 'interpretative' and 'evolutionary' approaches within archaeological research as a whole.[41]

To overcome the division between these perspectives it seems particularly worthy to concentrate on dynamic aspects of individual and social development and situated learning. The importance of all these aspects is that they do take place in the real world and one might say are constantly locally negotiated and re-negotiated. Most importantly, they cannot be separated from growth and movement in the landscape or in Country. What emerges then is a world-view that is not essentialist, but relational, recursive and bound to processes of growth and movement within a particular environment.[42]

In my understanding, so-called Indigenous world-views concentrate on these aspects of life in which people, animals and so on are not realisations of essential categories, but are different forms of narratives that constantly develop along interrelated and enmeshed pathways. Building onto terminology by philosopher Henri Lefebvre, Ingold has put forward the notion of 'meshwork' to capture this way of looking at the world and to describe the lines that create places in Country

37 Gould 2002.
38 Dawkins 1995; Dennett 1995.
39 Stoczkowski 2002; Bird and O'Connell 2012; Shennan 2008, 2012.
40 García-Sancho 2006; Griffiths 2001; Oyama 1985; Oyama et al. 2001; Griffiths and Stotz 2006; Jablonka and Lamb 2005; Stotz 2006; Ingold 2006, 2011; Marks 2003, 2009, 2013.
41 Cochrane and Gardner 2011; Hodder 2012a, 2012b.
42 Ingold 1998, 2004, 2011.

as life-lines along which particular narratives develop.[43] In this reading, places are locations where lines meet and art marks places within narratives; indeed, artistic expressions are narratives themselves, just as the Country and its myriad inhabitants are narratives and stories. To learn about the art and to learn about Country are consequently the same thing. But to learn about their significance you have to go there and experience it yourself. It is in this sense that art and rock art are 'time-archives' because they reflect the ongoing interrelationships between people's life-lines and Country. Any engagement with art or rock art in Country is irreducibly a process of growth and learning. This is why – in my understanding – knowledge is actually *in* Country and it cannot be separated from it. People and Country are inseparably and irreducibly intertwined.[44]

In this sense, modern scientific knowledge and Indigenous knowledge are not exclusive. In the realm of understanding human beings and their identity, they address different aspects of each living and growing organism. Beyond the powerful essentialist discourse of molecular biologists, who try to create momentum to receive funding for their expensive research, one should not forget that biology itself has for some time in fact moved into a post-genomic era and recognises the limitations of a very narrow genetic view of biology, and also recognises that the notion of 'the gene' has indeed mostly mystical and mythological qualities in current discourses and narratives.[45] Neuroscientist Steven Rose has compared this view with ideas surrounding the discovery of the mechanisms of human reproduction by the Dutch tradesman and pioneer microbiologist Antonie van Leeuwenhoek in the seventeenth century:

> Genes and genomes neither contain the future of the organism, in some preformative modern version of the homunculi van Leeuwenhoek thought he saw in the sperm, nor are they regarded, as in modern metaphors, as architects' blueprints or information theorists' code-bearers. They are no more and no less than an essential part of the toolkit with and by which organisms construct their futures.[46]

Human beings develop and grow through these relationships, which provide both potentials and constraints. What humans are and can do is not a reflection of internal essences of human nature. It is a product of situated growth, reflection and interaction with people, places, materials, art. The 'origin' of modern humans did not happen at one point a long time ago. It is still, and continuously, happening.

---

43 Ingold 2007: 80.
44 Blundell 2003; Blundell and Woolagoodja 2012; Milroy and Revell 2013.
45 Griffiths and Stotz 2006; Marks 2013; Stotz 2006.
46 Rose 2005: 137.

Bibliography

Anderson, Kay 2007, *Race and the Crisis of Humanism*, Routledge, New York.

Antón, Susan C 2003, 'Natural history of *Homo erectus*', *Yearbook of Physical Anthropology* 46: 126–170.

Aubert, Maxime 2012, 'A review of rock art dating in the Kimberley, Western Australia', *Journal of Archaeological Science* 39: 573–577.

Bird, Douglas W and James F O'Connell 2012, 'Human behavioral ecology', in Ian Hodder (ed.), *Archaeological Theory Today*, Polity Press, Cambridge, 37–61.

Blundell, Valda 2003, 'The art of country: aesthetics, place, and Aboriginal identity in north-west Australia', in David Trigger and Gareth Griffiths (eds), *Disputed Territories: Land, Culture and Identity in Settler Societies*, Hong Kong University Press, Hong Kong, 155–185.

Blundell, Valda and Donny Woolagoodja 2012, 'Rock art, aboriginal culture, and identity: the Wandjina paintings of northwest Australia', in Peter Veth and Jo McDonald (eds), *A Companion to Rock Art*, Wiley-Blackwell, Chichester, 472–488.

Caspari, Rachel and Milford H Wolpoff 1994, 'Weidenreich, Coon, and multiregional evolution', *Human Evolution* 11(3–4): 261–268.

Cochrane, Ethan E and Andrew Gardner (eds) 2011, *Evolutionary and Interpretive Archaeologies: A Dialogue*, Left Coast Press, Walnut Creek.

Crawford, Michael H (ed.) 2007, *Anthropological Genetics: Theory, Methods and Applications*, Cambridge University Press, Cambridge.

Davidson, Iain 2013, 'Peopling the last new worlds: the first colonisation of Sahul and the Americas', *Quaternary International* 285: 1–29.

Dawkins, Richard 1995, *River out of Eden*, Basic Books, New York.

Gamble, Clive S and Erica Gittins 2004, 'Social archaeology and origins research: a Paleolithic perspective', in Lynn Meskell and Robert W Preucel (eds), *A Companion to Social Archaeology*, Blackwell, Malden, MA, 105–107.

Dennett, Daniel 1995, *Darwin's Dangerous Idea*, Simon and Schuster, New York.

García-Sancho, Miguel 2006, 'The rise and fall of the idea of genetic information (1948–2006)', *Genomics, Society and Policy* 2: 16–36.

Gibbons, Ann 2011, 'African data bolster new view of modern human origins', *Science*, 334(6053): 167.

Gould, Stephen J 2002, *The Structure of Evolutionary Theory*, Harvard University Press, Cambridge, MA.

Green, Richard E et al. 2010, 'A draft sequence of the Neandertal genome', *Science* 328(5979): 710–722.

Griffiths, Paul E 2001, 'Genetic information: a metaphor in search of a theory', *Philosophy of Science* 68: 394–412.

Griffiths, Paul E and Karola Stotz 2006, 'Genes in the postgenomic era', *Theoretical Medicine and Bioethics* 27: 499–521.

Hammer, Michael F et al. 2011, 'Genetic evidence for archaic admixture in Africa', *Proceedings of the National Academy of Sciences* 108(37): 15123–15128.

Harvati, Katerina, C Stringer, R Grün, M Aubert, P Allsworth-Jones, and C Folorunso 2011, 'The Later Stone Age Calvaria from Iwo Eleru, Nigeria: morphology and chronology', *PLoS ONE* 6(9) e24024.

Henshilwood, Christopher Stuart 2007, 'Fully symbolic *sapiens* behaviour: innovations in the Middle Stone Age at Blombos Cave, South Africa', in Paul Mellars et al. (eds), *Rethinking the Human Revolution: New Behavioural and Biological Perspectives on the Origin and Dispersal of Modern Humans*, McDonald Institute for Archaeological Research, Cambridge, 123–132.

Hodder, Ian (ed.) 2012a, *Archaeological Theory Today*, Polity Press, Cambridge.

Hodder, Ian 2012b, *Entangled: An Archaeology of the Relationships between Humans and Things*, Wiley-Blackwell, Chichester.

Ingold, Tim 1998, 'From complementarity to obviation: on dissolving the boundaries between social and biological anthropology, archaeology and psychology', *Zeitschrift für Ethnologie* 123: 21–52.

Ingold, Tim 2004, 'Between biology and culture: the meaning of evolution in a relational world', *Social Anthropology* 12(2): 209–221.

Ingold, Tim 2006, 'Against human nature', in Nathalie Gontier et al. (eds), *Evolutionary Epistemology, Language and Culture*, Springer, Dordrecht, 259–281.

Ingold, Tim 2007, *Lines: A Brief History*, Routledge, New York.

Ingold, Tim 2011, *Being Alive: Essays on Movement, Knowledge and Description*, Routledge, London.

Jablonka, Eva and Marion J Lamb 2005, *Evolution in Four Dimensions: Genetic, Epigenetic, Behavioral and Symbolic Variation in the History of Life*, MIT Press, Cambridge, MA.

Klein, Richard G 2008, 'Out of Africa and the evolution of human behavior', *Evolutionary Anthropology* 17(6): 267–281

Klein, Richard G 2009, *The Human Career: Human Biological and Cultural Origins*, University of Chicago Press, Chicago.

Kolig, Erich 2000, 'Social causality, human agency and mythology: some thoughts on history-consciousness and mythical sense among Australian Aborigines', *Anthropological Forum* 10(1): 9–30.

Landau, Misia 1984, 'Human evolution as narrative', *American Scientist* 72: 262–268.

Landau, Misia 1993, *Narratives of Human Evolution*, Yale University Press, New Haven.

Layton, Robert 1992, *Australian Rock Art: A New Synthesis*, Cambridge University Press, Cambridge.

Marks, Jonathan 2003, *What it means to be 98% Chimpanzee: Apes, People, and Their Genes*, University of California Press, Berkeley.

Marks, Jonathan 2008, 'Race. Past, present, and future', in Barbara A Koenig, Sandra Soo-Jin Lee and Sarah S Richardson (eds), *Revisiting Race in a Genomic Age*, New Brunswick, Rutgers University Press, London, 21–38.

Marks, Jonathan 2009, 'The nature of humanness', in Barry Cunliffe, Chris Gosden and Rosemary A Joyce (eds), *The Oxford Handbook of Archaeology*, Oxford University Press, Oxford, 237–253.

Marks, Jonathan 2013, 'The nature/culture of genetic facts', *Annual Review of Anthropology* 42: 247–267.

Mayr, Ernst 1963, 'The taxonomic evaluation of fossil hominids', in Sherwood L Washburn (ed.), *Classification and Human Evolution*, Aldine, Chicago, 332–346.

McBrearty, S 2007, 'Down with the revolution', in Paul Mellars et al. (eds), *Rethinking the Human Revolution*, 453–563.

McNiven, J 2011, 'The Bradshaw debate: lessons learned from critiquing colonialist interpretations of Gwion Gwion rock paintings of the Kimberley, Western Australia', *Australian Archaeology* 72: 35–44.

Mellars, Paul and Chris Stringer (eds) 1989, *The Human Revolution: Behavioural and Biological Perspectives in the Origins of Modern Humans*, Edinburgh University Press, Edinburgh.

Milroy, Jill and Grant Revell 2013, 'Aboriginal story systems: remapping the west, knowing country, sharing space', *Occasion: Interdisciplinary Studies in the Humanities* 5: 1–24.

O'Connell, Jim F and Jim Allen 2004, 'Dating the colonization of Sahul (Pleistocene Australia-New Guinea): a review of recent research', *Journal of Archaeological Science* 31: 835–853.

Oppenheimer, Stephen 2004, *Out Of Eden: The Peopling of the World*, Robinson, London.

Oppenheimer, Stephen 2009, 'The great arc of dispersal of modern humans: Africa to Australia', *Quaternary International* 202(1–2): 2–13.

O'Rourke, Dennis 2007, 'Ancient DNA and its application to the reconstruction of human evolution and history', in Michael Crawford (ed.), *Anthropological Genetics: Theory, Methods and Applications*, Cambridge University Press, Cambridge.

Oyama, Susan 1985, *The Ontogeny of Information: Developmental Systems and Evolution*, Cambridge University Press, Cambridge, 210–231.

Oyama, Susan, Paul E Griffiths and Russell D Gray (eds), 2001, *Cycles of Contingency: Developmental Systems and Evolution*, MIT Press, Cambridge, MA.

Porr, Martin 2014, 'Essential questions: "modern humans" and the capacity for modernity', in Robin Dennell and Martin Porr (eds), *Southern Asia, Australia and the Search for Human Origins*, Cambridge University Press, Cambridge, 257–264.

Porr, Martin and Hannah Rachel Bell 2012, '"Rock-art", "animism" and two-way thinking: towards a complementary epistemology in the understanding of material culture and "rock-art" of hunting and gathering people', *Journal of Archaeological Method and Theory* 19(1): 161–205.

Rasmussen, Morten, X Guo, Y Wang, K Lohmueller, S Rasmussen, A Albrechtsen, L Skotte, S Lindgreen, M Metspalu, T Jombart, T Kivisild, W Zhai, A Eriksson, A Manica, L Orlando, F De La Vega, S Tridico, E Metspalu, K Nielsen, M Ávila-Arcos, J Moreno-Mayar, C Muller, J Dortch, M Gilbert, O Lund, A Wesolowska, M Karmin, L Weinert, B Wang, J Li, S Tai, F Xiao, T Hanihara, G van Driem, A Jha, F Ricaut, P de Knijff, A Migliano, R Gallego, K Kristiansen, D Lambert, S Brunak, P Forster, B Brinkmann, O Nehlich, M Bunce, M Richards, R Gupta, C Bustamante, A Krogh, R Foley, M Lahr, F Balloux, T Sicheritz-Pontén, R Villems, R Nielsen, J Wang, and E Willerslev 2011, 'An Aboriginal Australian genome reveals separate human dispersals into Asia', *Science* 334(6052): 94–98.

Redmond, Anthony 2001, 'Rulug wayirri: Moving Kin and Country in the Northern Kimberley', PhD thesis, Department of Anthropology, University of Sydney, Sydney.

Renfrew, Colin 1996, 'The sapient behaviour paradox: how to test for potential?', in Paul Mellars and Kathleen Gibson (eds), *Modelling the Early Human Mind*, McDonald Institute for Archaeological Research, Cambridge, 11–15.

Roebroeks, Wil, M Sier, T Nielsen, D De Loecker, J Parés, C Arpsd, and H Müchere 2012, 'Use of red ochre by early Neandertals', *Proceedings of the National Academy of Sciences* 109(6): 1889–1894.

Rose, Debra 1996, *Nourishing Terrains: Australian Aboriginal Views of Landscape and Wilderness*, Australian Heritage Commission, Canberra.

Rose, Steven 2005, *Lifelines: Life beyond the Gene*, Vintage, London.

Schwartz, Jeffrey H and Ian Tattersall 2010, 'Fossil evidence for the origin of *Homo sapiens*', *Yearbook of Physical Anthropology* 53: 94–121.

Shennan, Stephen J 2008, 'Evolution in archaeology', *Annual Review of Anthropology* 37: 75–91.

Shennan, Stephen J 2012, 'Darwinian cultural evolution', in Ian Hodder (ed.), *Archaeological Theory Today*, Polity Press, Cambridge, 15–36.

Stanner, William Edward Hanley 1958, 'The Dreaming', in William Lessa and Evon Vogt (eds), *Reader in Comparative Religion: An Anthroplogical Approach*, Harper and Row, New York, 158–167.

Stanner, William Edward Hanley 1968, *After the Dreaming*, Australian Broadcasting Commission, Sydney.

Stewart, JR and CB Stringer 2012, 'Human evolution out of Africa: the role of refugia and climate change', *Science* 335(6074): 1317–1321.

Stoczkowski, Wiktor 2002, *Explaining Human Origins: Myth, Imagination and Conjecture*, Cambridge University Press, Cambridge.

Stotz, Karola 2006, 'With "genes" like that, who needs an "environment"? Postgenomic's argument for the "ontogeny of information"', *Philosophy of Science* 73(5): 905–917.

Stringer, Christopher 2011, *The Origin of our Species*, Allen Lane, London.

Tattersall, Ian and Jeffrey H Schwartz 2000, *Extinct Humans,* Westview Press, Boulder, CO.

Vinnicombe, Patricia and David Mowaljarlai 1995, 'That rock is a cloud: concepts associated with rock images in the Kimberley region of Australia', in Knut Helskog and Bjomar Olsen (eds), *Perceiving Rock Art: Social and Political Perspectives*, Instituttet for sammenlignende kulturforskning, Oslo, 228–246.

Wolfe, Patrick 1991, 'On being woken up: the Dreamtime in anthropology and in Australian settler culture', *Comparative Studies in Society and History* 33: 197–224.

Wolpoff, Milford H and Rachel Caspari 1997, *Race and Evolution: A Fatal Attraction*, Simon & Schuster, New York.

13. The Archaeology of the Willandra
Its empirical structure and narrative potential

Nicola Stern

Efforts to extend history into deep time have been driven largely (though not exclusively) by historians interested in breaking the apparently artificial barrier that separates historical narratives based on written or oral testimonies from those based on the study of material remains.[1] However, to achieve this goal, historians and archaeologists will have to grapple with the substantive implications of studying the unique material archives that are the particular purview of the historical sciences. This chapter explores some of the issues involved in doing so by investigating the empirical characteristics of an archaeological record that spans the entire known history of human settlement on the Australian continent. As such, it holds out the promise of writing a narrative of the continent's earliest history as well as exploring the dynamics of long-term change that followed the colonisation of a previously unpeopled and unfamiliar country.

Archaeological perspectives on human action

The long time span of the archaeological record is often identified as the critical factor underpinning the potentially unique contribution the discipline can make to an understanding of human actions and their consequences. This is argued in part because material remains are the only record of humanity's first 2.5 million years, and in part because the bracketing age determinations available for most archaeological sites means that they can be assigned only to broad intervals of time.[2] This is viewed by many as an opportunity to investigate the dynamics of changes that take place over long periods of time and which were not necessarily perceptible to the individuals who contributed to or lived through them. By identifying those changes, exploring the dynamics that drove them and understanding how they interact with processes of change that operate over the time span of individual lives, archaeologists believe they have an opportunity to offer unique insights into human action.[3]

---

1 Shryock and Smail 2011; see also Chapter 1 of this volume.
2 Bailey 1983, 2007; Stern 1993.
3 Murray 1997, 2008; Holdaway and Wandsnider 2008: 2.

However, the idea that archaeology is unique amongst the social sciences derives not only from the long time span of the record and the temporal resolution of its data, but from the fact that material remains represent the consequences of human action, not human action *per se*.[4] The behavioural information embedded in these remains is not intuitively obvious, and neither the naïve ethnographic analogies employed during the late nineteenth and early twentieth centuries or the material-behavioural correlations advocated during the late twentieth century have generated interpretations of the past whose validity can be assessed using archaeological data itself. This results partly from the complex interplay that exists between material objects and a people's world-view, and that material-behavioural relationships are context dependent and not universal. There is also a complex interplay between the loss and discarding of material remains and the depositional processes that cover them with sediment, ensuring their preservation, but also influencing the patterns and associations of surviving material remains.[5] The complexity of these relationships means that there is often a mismatch between the time spans of the observations that underpin the ecological and the social theories used to make sense of these remains, and the time spans involved in the accumulation of the archaeological debris under investigation. As a result, long chains of inference connect material traces to the historical narratives written from them.[6]

Historical narrative versus empirical validation

Since the inception of the discipline, archaeologists have employed historical narratives as a way of summarising what they know and understand about the human past. However, from the outset, scholars were torn between their desire to present intuitively satisfying narratives of the remote human past and their dependence on scientific methods to generate the information from which those accounts were written, and which also provided the basis for assessing their empirical validity.[7]

The tensions between the goals and methods of the fledgling discipline are manifest in its founding text, John Lubbock's *Prehistoric Times*, published in 1865.[8] On the one hand, the long time span of the archaeological record was viewed as an opportunity to document the evolution and differential success of European societies from the durable traces of their technologies. On the

---

4   Stern 2008a.
5   Stern 2008b.
6   Stern 2008a; Grayson 1986; Schiffer 1982.
7   Stoczkowski 2002.
8   Lubbock 1865.

other hand, life could only be breathed into those material traces by appealing to burgeoning ethnographic information about the habits, customs, tools and weapons of an array of primitive societies employing similar technologies. Explanations for the patterns of increasing technological complexity were derived from recently developed evolutionary theory. As a result, archaeological data in itself was not the primary source of novel insights into the human past.

Similar tensions haunt contemporary archaeological practice. Critical evaluations of the evolutionary scenarios that purport to account for humanity's origins show that they contain some remarkably tenacious cultural constructs whose appropriateness have not been assessed using the discipline's own database. Many of these have deep roots that can be traced back to the discussions of the Enlightenment scholars, and to the philosophical speculations of the Ancient Greeks and Romans, who themselves were undoubtedly drawing on the ideas of the preliterate societies who preceded or lived alongside them.[9]

Anthropologist Wiktor Stoczkowski argues that the persistence of these long-standing cultural constructs reflects the priority that researchers have given to establishing the plausibility of their evolutionary narratives at the expense of developing empirical validation of them. There is tension between the empirical characteristics of archaeological data, the methods available for studying it, and the discipline's goal of making sense of the remote past in the same way as the contemporary world is understood. Stoczkowski's solution to this dilemma is to exhort practitioners to attempt empirical validation of their evolutionary narratives as they are formulated.[10]

In the discussion that follows, some of the issues involved in striving to achieve this balance are illustrated through a discussion of the archaeological traces preserved at Lake Mungo, in south-east Australia. These are being studied with the ultimate goal of writing a dynamic account of Australia's early history, and of exploring long-term patterns of change and their relationship to changes in landscape and climate. Writing a historical narrative whilst subjecting its elements to empirical validation is a multi-stage research endeavour and this project is still in its infancy. This discussion thus focuses on a burgeoning understanding of the empirical characteristics of this record, the categories of information that can be generated from it, and the way in which these can contribute to the writing of a deep time narrative.

---

9   Stoczkowski 2002: 3–28.
10 Stoczkowski 2002: 191–198.

The study area

Lake Mungo is one of a series of dry lake basins making up a large, relict overflow system on the edge of Australia's arid core.

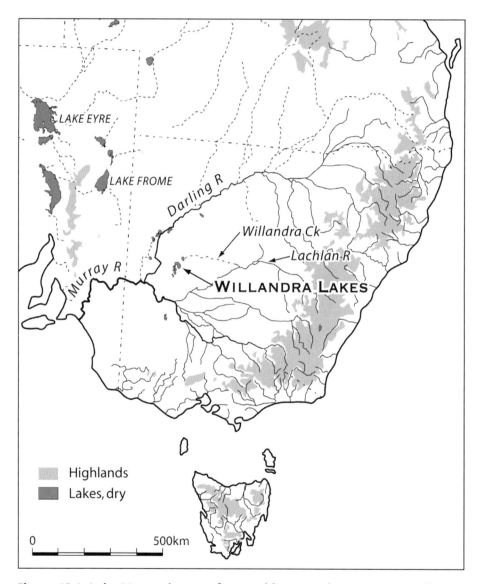

Figure 13.1: Lake Mungo is one of several large and numerous smaller lake basins making up the Willandra Lakes, a relict overflow system in south-eastern Australia.

When active, the overflow system was fed by waters that flowed westward from the south-east Australian highlands towards the continent's arid interior, via the Lachlan River and its former channel, the Willandra Creek.

Source: Base map from Geoscience Australia.

At times in the past when there was more effective precipitation in the Australian Alps, increased discharge in the Lachlan River and its former channel, the Willandra Creek, filled these lakes from north to south. When effective precipitation was reduced, the lakes fluctuated or dried out completely.[11] Each lake in the system has a unique depositional history, recorded in the sediments that built up on its floor; the lunettes bounding its eastern margin and the disrupted linear dunes forming its western margin.

The lunettes have been the main focus of efforts to document the palaeoenvironmental history of the Willandra Lakes region, partly because severe erosion of some lunettes provides a window into their internal structure and partly because their alternating layers of sand and clay reflect conditions that prevailed in the adjacent lakes. Jim Bowler's pioneering geomorphological research in the Willandra provided the key to the relationship between sediment characteristics and hydrological conditions.[12]

Bowler showed that when the lakes in this system were at overflow level, waves driven by the prevailing south-west winds washed sediments to the eastern margin and created high-energy beaches. Sands blown from those beaches contributed to the build up of low, vegetated quartz fore-dunes. When the lakes fell below overflow level, water levels fluctuated, exposing part of the lake floor. Salts precipitated from saline groundwater broke up the lake floor sediments into sand-sized aggregates that were picked up by the prevailing winds and draped across the landscape, forming pelletal clay dunes.[13] When the landscape was stable, soils formed. The sedimentary sequence thus records changes taking place in a distant catchment in the Australian Alps, which were being driven by regional and global shifts in climate.

Traces of human activity were incorporated into the lunette sediments as they accumulated, and recent erosion, which accelerated following the establishment of the pastoral industry in the late nineteenth century, has exposed many of these on the modern land surface. Once exposed, most features disperse and disintegrate within two to three years, unless they lie in micro-topographic and sedimentary settings that provide protection from the impact of water flow during heavy rains. Highly visible clusters of debris lie on the lunette surface towards its lake-ward margin, but these are predominantly accumulations of material whose encasing sediment has blown away (i.e. lags) or that have been reworked and redeposited through erosion of older sediments (i.e. transported).

---

11 Bowler 1998.
12 Bowler 1971, 1976, 1998; Bowler et al. 2012.
13 Clay particles are so light that they are usually blown hundreds of kilometres from their source before being redeposited. However, in the Willandra, the efflorescence of salts on the partly exposed lake floor caused the clay particles to aggregate around sand grains. The resulting sand-sized particles were picked up by the prevailing winds and deposited on the lunette building up along the lake's eastern margin. Bowler, 1973, describes the mechanism involved in the formation of clay dunes in the Willandra Lakes.

Continuing erosion of the lunette means that *in situ* features weather, disintegrate and disperse whilst new ones are being exposed. As a result, any attempt to document the archaeological traces preserved in the Mungo lunette can only provide a snapshot of what was exposed at the time the survey was undertaken.

These activity traces have long been regarded as a potential treasure trove of information about changing patterns of land use in this swathe of semi-arid savannah on the margins of the continent's arid core. However, a paucity of systematic archaeological research over the past 30 years means that not much is actually known about these activity traces or their context, making it difficult to characterise their empirical characteristics and to assess their potential for contributing to a narrative about the settlement of the Australian continent. To build an understanding of this record, and to assess its information potential, a systematic foot survey of the central Mungo lunette was initiated in 2009.

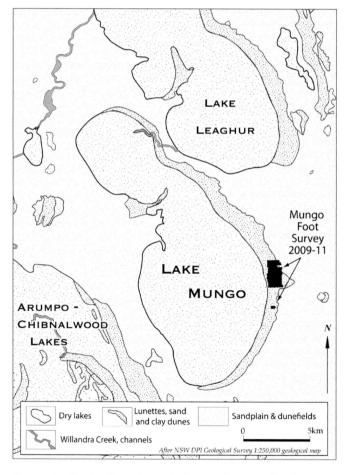

Figure 13.2: The location of the study area in the central Mungo lunette.
Source: After NSW DPI Geological Survey 1:125,000 geological map.

Foot survey of the central Mungo lunette

This systematic foot survey of the central portion of the Mungo lunette was designed to generate information that could be used to assess the empirical structure of this record. To achieve this, three interrelated sets of information are collected: information about the types of activity traces preserved in different depositional settings and stratigraphic units; the time span represented by individual hearths or clusters of stone-working debris; and the time span represented by the stratigraphic units containing large numbers of those activity traces. The latter establishes the time span represented by all the archaeological traces that accumulated on the landscape when the same palaeoenvironmental[14] conditions prevailed.

Together, these data provide a basis for assessing how depositional processes have impacted on the survival of material traces, and on the configuration and associations of those remains. They also lay a foundation for investigating changes in the types of activities in which people engaged during different time spans and corresponding environmental conditions, and thus for exploring changes in the technological, economic and social strategies employed over time.

To collect these data, the foot survey focuses on cultural features whose sedimentary context and stratigraphic provenience can be established without ambiguity. This includes features that remain at least partially embedded in sediments as well as tight clusters of surface debris whose encasing sediment has been removed but which have not yet dispersed, weathered or disintegrated, indicating that they were only recently exposed on the modern surface. Ongoing erosion of the Mungo lunette, together with ongoing aeolian and alluvial deposition of reworked sediments, means that the boundaries between networks of rills and gullies, slope wash surfaces, alluvial fans and deflation surfaces are constantly shifting. Systematic coverage of the lunette is therefore facilitated by the use of a grid system superimposed on digital air photos taken in 2007. The corners of each 50m x 50m grid square are located on the ground using a hand-held GPS.

A great many of the archaeological features exposed on the surface of the lunette are extremely subtle, so to assist their identification, each grid square is walked by a 'police-line', with team members pacing in two directions so that the exposures can be observed in different light conditions. The features being observed include a variety of heat retainer and baked sediment hearths, discrete clusters of burned and unburned animal bone, clusters of chipped stone tools,

---

14 Past environmental conditions, including temperatures, rainfall, circulation patterns and evaporation, are not the same as those currently experienced; palaeoenvironmental conditions are those that prevailed during some defined time interval in the past.

together with debris from their manufacture and/or repair, and isolated *in situ* finds (mostly animal bones and artefacts). It also includes rare finds, like ochre pellets, grinding stones and shell tools, which lie on the surface, but whose stratigraphic unit of origin can be established. Information about the content and the context of each feature is recorded in the field, using a palm top or tablet computer. This includes information about the type of hearth or stone cluster and the materials of which they are comprised, as well as information about associated material lying within that cluster of debris. Records are also made about the sediment in which the feature is encased, its ancient topographic context (beach, fore dune, dune crest, back dune) and its modern topographic setting (flat erosional bench, low angle slope, high angle slope, rill, gully, etc).

Most of the activity traces recorded so far are small and discrete and contain a limited array of debris. Arguably, each consist of debris generated during a single activity or related set of activities, like the striking of a few stone tools from a nodule of raw material (Figure 13.3), the cooking of an emu egg (Figure 13.4), and the lighting of a fire to cook a bettong, along with the manufacture of a few stone tools (Figure 13.5).

Figure 13.3: A silcrete core and refitting flakes, representing at least part of a single knapping event.
Source: Caroline Spry, Mungo Archaeology Project.

Figure 13.4: A partially burned emu egg in the position in which it was cracked open after cooking.
Source: Rudy Frank, Mungo Archaeology Project.

Figure 13.5: A fireplace comprising ash and lightly baked sediment, with an associated scatter of bettong bones representing a single individual (white flags) and a scatter of stone tools struck from the same nodule of silcrete (black flags). The artefact scatter includes six sets of refits.
Source: Rudy Frank, Mungo Archaeology Project.

Ultimately, the suggestion that these represent single events can be validated through analysis of the debris they contain and/or the materials from which they were made. For example, archaeomagnetic data[15] are being used to establish the number of times a baked sediment hearth was lit as well as the temperature to which it was lit. Refitting chipped stone artefacts or broken up animal bones scattered around a hearth can be used to identify what was brought into that location, in what form, as well as the activities undertaken at that location. The baked sediment hearth in Figure 13.4 has an associated scatter of bettong bones that represent a single individual and a scatter of artefacts struck from the same nodule of silcrete. An initial study of the archaeomagnetic properties of the baked sediments suggest that the hearth may have been heated to high temperature only once.

Each of these features is embedded in sediments (a sand or clay, sandy clay or soil), which record the conditions that prevailed in the lake at the time that debris accumulated. Each is also contained within a stratigraphic unit that records the environmental conditions that prevailed during a specific time interval, for example, between circa 55,000 and 40,000 years BP conditions across the continent resulted in more effective precipitation and in the Willandra, a long phase of sustained lake-full conditions prevailed; between circa 25,000 and 14,000 years BP conditions were cooler and more arid but seasonal snow-melt brought large volumes of water down the Lachlan River, resulting in oscillating lake conditions throughout the Last Glacial Maximum.

The type of sediment in which each feature is encased is documented as part of the site record, while its stratigraphic context is established by mapping the boundaries of the stratigraphic units exposed on the surface of the lunette and through optically stimulated luminescence (OSL) dating of the mapped units.[16] The locations of all dating samples, stratigraphic boundaries and archaeological features and isolated finds are recorded using the GDA (Geocentric Datum Australia – Australian mapping grid) coordinates; these data are then uploaded into GIS software (MAPINFO) to facilitate integration of the archaeological and geological data sets. Both the sediments encasing each archaeological feature and the strata in which those features are preserved can be used as analytical units to generate commensurate behavioural and palaeoenvironmental information. They thus provide the initial framework for writing a narrative account of the history of human settlement in the Willandra.

---

15 Heating of sediments that contain magnetic minerals can result in the formation of new magnetic minerals, enhancing the magnetic properties of those sediments. Reheating of samples in the laboratory can identify the temperature to which those sediments were heated in the past. See Herries 2009: 245–246.

16 Fitzsimmons et al. 2014.

The history of human settlement

So far, the systematic survey has located and documented 1,442 cultural features over a 2 km² area in the central portion of the Mungo lunette. Although Mungo's archaeological record has been characterised as one of middens and stone artefacts,[17] 50 per cent of the features recorded in the study area are hearths, approximately half of which are associated with food remains or tools or both. Isolated finds, clusters of chipped stone artefacts and clusters of burned animal bones make up the remainder of the sample.

Geological mapping of the survey area, combined with OSL dating of mapped units, shows that the stratigraphic sequence in this part of the lunette is similar but not identical to that recorded at the southern end of the lunette during Bowler's earlier work.[18]

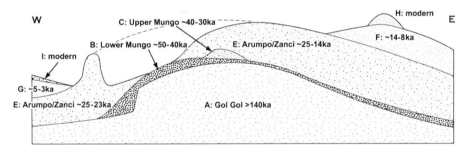

Figure 13.6: A schematic cross-section summarising the stratigraphic sequence in the central Mungo lunette.

Here as elsewhere, the core of the lunette is formed by the Golgol unit, which was deposited during a lake sequence that predates the Last Interglacial (< 130,000 years BP). Units E–B were laid down during a lake sequence that spans the time interval from circa 55,000–14,000 years BP, while Units F and G were deposited after the lake dried out. Units H and I are modern depositional units resulting from ongoing erosion and reworking of the older lunette sediments. Age estimates for each unit are based on those reported in Fitzsimmons et al. 2014, Bowler 1998 and Bowler et al. 2012.

Source: Based on Fitzsimmons et al. 2014, Figure 5 and Mungo Archaeology Project data.

Units B and C, which lie at the base of the present lake sequence, are the lateral equivalents of Bowler's Lower and Upper Mungo units[19] but in the central portion of the lunette they are thin and laterally discontinuous. Unit B represents a long phase of sustained lake-full conditions (from circa 50,000 until circa 40,000 years BP), while Unit C represents the establishment of a fluctuating lake in response to the onset of continental aridity (circa 40,000 until circa 30,000 years BP).[20]

---

17 Allen et al. 2008; Allen and Holdaway 2009.
18 Bowler 1998.
19 Bowler's description of the stratigraphic units making up the Mungo lunette was based on geological sections recorded in the southern end of the lunette. Although there are similarities between the stratigraphic sequences in the southern and central portions of the lunette, there are also some differences. The units defined by Fitzsimmons et al. in 2014 can be correlated with those described by Bowler in 1998 on the basis of age and sediment characteristics and are thus their lateral equivalents.
20 Bowler 1998; Fitzsimmons et al. 2014.

Unit E, which was deposited between about 25,000 and 14,500 years BP, makes up the greatest volume of sediment in the central Mungo lunette and is the lateral equivalent of what Bowler described as Arumpo and Zanci units.[21] It thus straddles the Last Glacial Maximum, the period toward the end of the last glaciation when sea levels were at their lowest, glaciers and continental ice-sheets were at their maximum extent, and global climates were colder, windier and drier than at any other time during the last 70,000 years. Most of this unit comprises thin beds of alternating sands, clayey sands and clay, indicating that the lake oscillated from being at overflow level to almost drying out. During the height of the Last Glacial Maximum, circa 21,000–17,000 years BP, sediments accumulated so rapidly[22] that in some areas fine laminae[23] of alternating sands and clay, each representing an individual depositional event, are remarkably well preserved.

The final drying of the lake occurred approximately 14,500 years BP and, almost immediately, older lunette sediments were subject to aeolian or wind-driven reworking under the influence of locally more arid conditions, resulting in the build up of unconsolidated sands on the crest and lee of the lunette. The age of these sands is not yet well constrained in age, but numerous weakly developed and laterally discontinuous soil horizons indicate periods of lesser and greater humidity, resulting in episodes of greater and lesser dune stability. During the mid-Holocene, approximately 5,500–3,500 years BP, local conditions were relatively more humid, resulting in gullying of the lunette and the build-up of alluvial fans along its lake-ward margin.[24]

Activity traces are not distributed homogeneously through these strata and this provides a basis for making inferences about the palaeoenvironmental conditions that brought people to the shores of Lake Mungo in greater numbers and/or for longer periods and/or more often.[25] The greatest density of activity traces is found in Unit C, during which the lake alternated from being at overflow level to low and fluctuating. As the overflow system received water from the south-east highlands via the Lachlan River, and as Mungo had no outflow, those fluctuating lake levels reflect the input of successive flood pulses.

21 Bowler 1998.
22 Long et al. 2014: 87–88.
23 Laminae are thin layers of sediment (< 1cm thick) that result from differences in the type of sediment being deposited over short time spans. In this instance, the differences reflect alternating deposition of pelletal clays (lake level low) and quartz sands (lake full). Because laminae are thin they are easily destroyed by the biological activity associated with a stable landscape and soil formation. The preservation of laminae thus suggests that sediment accumulation was rapid and that there was insufficient time for burrowing organisms and root activity to disrupt the laminae.
24 Fitzsimmons et al. 2014.
25 Stern et al. 2013; Fitzsimmons et al. 2014.

The density of activity traces in Unit E is not as high as in Unit C, but its greater volume and the greater area of its exposure means that it actually contains the greatest number and diversity of sites in this part of the lunette. The hearths within Unit E are as abundant in the lenses of quartz sand reflecting high lake levels as they are in the pelletal clays blown up from the lake floor when lake levels were low. This suggests that it was the conditions created by the fluctuating lake levels that attracted people to the margins of Lake Mungo in greater numbers and/or more often and/or for longer, rather than high or low lake levels *per se*.

Traces of people's activities are found in relatively low density in the aeolian and alluvial sediments that accumulated after the lake dried out. There is limited exposure of sites in the alluvial fans but constantly shifting sands overlying Unit F (on the lee and crest of the lunette) repeatedly uncover and cover over heat retainer hearths, discrete sets of refitting artefacts[26] and occasional shell tools and grindstones. The lower density and diversity of these activity traces suggests a significant shift in land-use patterns once the lake dried out, with fewer people coming into this landscape for shorter periods and/or less often.

Systematic data on the distribution of sites through sediments representing different hydrological conditions and strata representing different time intervals and corresponding palaeoenvironmental conditions show the same pattern: most activity traces accumulated when lake levels were oscillating from low to high. This overturns two long-standing perceptions: first, that people were attracted to the overflow system when the lakes were full of freshwater in order to exploit their rich aquatic resources and second, that the area was so inhospitable during the Last Glacial Maximum (LGM) that people abandoned it. There is an obvious ecological explanation for the abundance of activity traces in sediments and strata laid down when the lakes were fluctuating: aquatic resources would have been less abundant and more difficult to locate during periods of sustained lake-full conditions, but when lake levels were low, aquatic resources would have been easier to find and each flood pulse would have recharged the biological productivity of the system. Furthermore, when the lakes were at overflow level, water would have abounded on the adjacent plains, removing a critical constraint on the time people could spend foraging there and the distances they could cover.[27]

---

26 Chipped stone technology is a reductive technology that creates clusters of artefacts that may contain stone-working debris as well as tool-blanks and tools. If those clusters of debris retain their integrity, despite the impact of depositional and post-exposure processes, some of the artefacts struck from the same nodule of raw material can be refitted back together, like a three-dimensional jigsaw. If sufficient numbers of refitting artefacts are available they can provide insights into the way each block of stone was worked to produce tools. For an example, see Figure 13.3.

27 Bowler 1998: 147.

Individual activity traces and the landscape palimpsest

The survey data establish when people came and went from this landscape and it provides the basic framework from which a narrative of changing patterns of land use will eventually be written. However, to gain insights into the social, economic and technological activities in which people engaged at different times obviously requires more detailed study of the activity traces preserved in specific strata. The central Mungo lunette affords an opportunity to do this for the period straddling the Last Glacial Maximum because of the diverse and well-preserved activity traces it preserves from this time interval.

Detailed investigation of these activity traces, involving studies of surface and excavated archaeological remains, has only recently begun, but it provides a springboard for highlighting some of the issues involved in writing a narrative account of people's lives in the Willandra district during a specific time interval. The most critical of these relate to the empirical structure of the record. Earlier it was argued that the record consists of a myriad of discrete activity traces representing individual events. However, all the activity traces contained within a stratigraphic unit representing a 9,000-year time interval have to be combined in order to investigate the diet and foraging strategies, technologies, or social networks that people employed during the Last Glacial Maximum. This creates what archaeologists and palaeontologists refer to as a time-averaged assemblage: the mixing together of material remains from many different and temporally unrelated events. This is the inevitable outcome of studying archaeological traces that accumulated on a landscape as it built up, because the boundaries between landforms (the lake floor, beach, dune) shift as those sediment accumulate. The resulting three-dimensional bodies of sediment are thus time-transgressive and the contemporaneity (or otherwise) of any two hearths or sets of refitting artefacts can only be established in relation to the upper and lower boundaries of that three-dimensional body of sediment.[28]

It is often assumed that the information generated from time-averaged assemblages of material will be the same as that generated from the study of all the debris from the individual events. This is predicated on the assumption that the debris contained in aggregated assemblages is an average representation of the activities that were undertaken during the time interval under consideration. There are three compelling reasons for scrutinising this assumption. Firstly, some activities generate more debris than others and though they may not take place frequently, they may nevertheless dominate an aggregated assemblage. Secondly, debris from events that take place only rarely

---

28   Stern 1994, 2008a.

may not be captured by discrete activity traces dispersed through a stratigraphic unit, unless that unit represents a sufficient length of time and unless extensive areas of that unit are exposed for study on the modern land surface. Thirdly, there are some categories of information that can be generated from discrete sets of debris that cannot be generated from aggregated samples and vice versa. In particular, aggregated samples accumulated over long time spans are viewed as a critical source of information about long-term trends and dynamics that may not have been perceived by the individuals who lived through them. The suggestion that explication of these long-term trends and dynamics is archaeology's primary purview[29] has caused a certain amount of consternation, largely because it is seen as a strategy that dehumanises the past. It is, however, a strategy that enables archaeologists to assess the interpretations they make about the past using archaeological data, rather than by reference to theories generated by ancillary disciplines drawing on qualitatively different data.

In the central Mungo lunette, hearths with associated food remains and/or stone tools are a significant feature of the Last Glacial Maximum landscape palimpsest. Some assemblages contain the bones of medium and large-sized macropods, others contain the remains of a single individual, like a bettong, or a single taxon, like a few golden perch, and a few are made up of bones representing fish, and small and medium-sized terrestrial mammals. Although hearths containing some fish remains are found throughout the stratigraphic sequence, hearths that *only* contain fish bones are found at one location in the central Mungo lunette, and they all accumulated during the height of the Last Glacial Maximum. Geochemical analysis of the fish otoliths (ear bones) suggest that the fish recovered from these hearths entered the lake when it was full of fresh water but were captured when lake waters were relatively more saline.[30] The faunal remains associated with each hearth may provide extraordinary insights into individual meals, but ongoing research needs to establish whether the sum of all of those yields the same information as the time-averaged landscape sample.

Attempts to reconstruct the stone technologies employed during the Last Glacial Maximum are confronted by similar interpretive challenges. Analysis of refitting artefacts, together with non-refitting artefacts struck from the same nodule of raw material, provide insights into specific stone-working (i.e. knapping) episodes. Establishing the relationship between those individual knapping events and the technological strategies employed during the Last Glacial Maximum is the focus of ongoing research. However, initial studies point to differences in the categories of information that can be generated from the analysis of individual nodules and refitting artefacts versus the aggregated landscape sample.[31]

---

29 Murray 1993, 1997.
30 Long et al. 2014: 88–91.
31 Spry 2014.

Towards a deep time narrative

Since the discovery of hearths, tools and burials at the southern end of the Mungo lunette in the late 1960s, Lake Mungo has been given a privileged place in accounts of continental settlement.[32] However, it is salutary to remember that those accounts are based on limited data sets as well as limited appreciation for the research strategies most productively employed to deal with discrete activity traces scattered through a vast eroding landscape made up of successive tiers of three-dimensional sedimentary units. Initial research emphasised the similarity of temporally and geographically scattered artefact and faunal assemblages, in particular the similarity of the species found in the faunal assemblages and the list of species exploited by the Paakantji (Barkindji), who lived along the Darling River during the late nineteenth century. However, at the time, limited assessment was made of how these observations should be applied to the archaeological data they were supposed to explain.[33]

Two decades later, Harry Allen offered a considered evaluation of this initial research strategy, pointing to a mismatch in scale between the archaeological record and the ethnographic and ecological models used to make sense of it. He and his colleagues argued that because study of the landscape sample involves aggregating all the archaeological traces contained in a single stratigraphic unit, the landscape palimpsest is just as readily documented from surface archaeological traces as it is from *in situ* features.[34] However, this is an approach that would fail to realise the extraordinary research potential of Mungo's archaeological record. High rates of sediment accumulation, combined with limited spatial redundancy in the location of activities, has contributed to the preservation of discrete activity traces, and the sediments encasing those also happen to record prevailing lake conditions.

This makes it possible to investigate change over time, to generate behavioural and environmental information at commensurate scales of analysis, and to investigate whether and how behavioural changes are related to environmental shifts. It also affords a rare opportunity to investigate the relationship between individual knapping events and the technological strategies, or the meals and diet and foraging strategies that characterised different time intervals and their corresponding palaeoenvironmental settings.

---

32   Mulvaney 1975: 147–152; White and O'Connell 1982: 35–39; Flood 1995: 39–55; Hiscock 2008: 5–8.
33   Allen 1972, 1974.
34   Allen 1998; Allen et al. 2008; Allen and Holdaway 2009.

Most archaeological records contain a time-averaged jumble of debris, and the traces of individual activities can rarely be separated out from that jumble.[35] This problem is particularly acute in Australian cave and rock shelter deposits that are often characterised by low rates of sediment accumulation (a few centimetres per thousand years) and sediment accumulation that was not independent of cave occupation.[36] However, it is also a problem that haunts surface archaeological records that are not derived solely from the sedimentary envelopes on which they lie, as is the case at Lake Mungo.[37] For this reason, the research potential of the Willandra will be realised largely through the study of those discrete activity traces and their contexts.

As research in the Willandra progresses, more will be learned about the way the record formed, facilitating ongoing assessment of the information that can be generated from it. However, the very existence of that myriad of discrete activity traces should enable researchers to write a narrative of the continent's early history that retains a plausible human face, even as that narrative is being subjected to rigorous empirical assessment.

Acknowledgements

This research was undertaken with permission from the Elders' Council of the Traditional Groups of the Willandra Lakes Region World Heritage Area and the Technical and Scientific Advisory Committee of the Willandra Lakes Region World Heritage Area. It is a privilege to have been welcomed into Paakantji (Barkindji), Ngiyampaa and Mutthi Mutthi country, and I am grateful to the elders for their willingness to discuss the aims and scope of this work, their contributions to the fieldwork and their ongoing support of our endeavours. This research was funded by an Australian Research Council Linkage grant (LP0775058) and an Australian Research Council Discovery grant (DP1092966) and supported by La Trobe University. I thank our industry partners, the WLRWHA Elders' Council and the NSW Office of Environment and Heritage, and my colleagues for their contributions to this research, particularly Kathryn Fitzsimmons, Colin Murray-Wallace and Rainer Grün. Paul Penzo-Kajewski and Daryl Pappin provided dedicated assistance with all aspects of the field research, and La Trobe University undergraduate students and Mungo National Park Discovery Rangers brought extraordinary commitment and enthusiasm to the fieldwork. In his retirement, Rudy Frank has been generous with his time and skills, assisting with the fieldwork and preparing the figures.

---

35   Bailey 2007.
36   Stern 2008a.
37   Tumney 2011.

Bibliography

Allen, Harry 1972, 'Where the Crow Flies Backwards: Man and Land in the Darling Basin', PhD thesis, The Australian National University, Canberra.

Allen, Harry 1974, 'The Bagundji of the Darling Basin: cereal gatherers in an uncertain environment', *World Archaeology* 5: 309–322.

Allen, Harry 1998, 'Reinterpreting the 1969–1972 Willandra Lakes archaeological surveys', *Archaeology in Oceania* 33: 207–220.

Allen, Harry, Simon Holdaway, Patricia Fanning and Judith Littleton 2008, 'Footprints in the sand: appraising the archaeology of the Willandra Lakes, western New South Wales, Australia', *Antiquity* 82: 11–24.

Allen, Harry and Simon Holdaway 2009, 'The archaeology of Mungo and the Willandra Lakes: looking back, looking forward', *Archaeology in Oceania* 44: 69–106.

Bailey, Geoffrey N 1983, 'Concepts of time in Quaternary prehistory', *Annual Review of Anthropology* 12: 165–192.

Bailey, Geoffrey N 2007, 'Time perspectives, palimpsests and the archaeology of time', *Journal of Anthropological Archaeology* 26: 198–223.

Bowler, Jim M 1971, 'Pleistocene salinities and climate change: evidence from lakes and lunettes in Southeastern Australia', in D John Mulvaney and Jack Golson (eds), *Aboriginal Man and Environment in Australia*, Australian National University Press, Canberra, 47–65.

Bowler, Jim M 1973, 'Clay dunes: their occurrence, formation and environmental significance', *Earth Science Reviews* 9: 315–318.

Bowler, Jim M 1976, 'Aridity in Australia: age, origins and expression in aeolian landforms and sediments', *Earth Science Reviews* 12: 279–310.

Bowler, Jim M 1998, 'Willandra Lakes revisited: environmental framework for human occupation', *Archaeology in Oceania* 33: 120–155.

Bowler, Jim M, Richard Gillespie, Harvey Johnston and Katarina Boljkovac 2012, 'Wind v Water: Glacial maximum records from the Willandra Lakes', in Simon Haberle and Bruno David (eds), *Peopled Landscapes: Archaeological and Biogeographical Approaches to Landscape*, Terra Australis 34, ANU E Press, Canberra, 271–296.

Fitzsimmons, Kathryn, Nicola Stern and Colin V Murray-Wallace 2014, 'Depositional history and archaeology of the central Mungo lunette, Willandra Lakes, southeast Australia', *Journal of Archaeological Science* 41: 349–364.

Grayson, Donald K 1986, 'Eoliths, archaeological ambiguity, and the generation of "middle-range" research', in David J Meltzer, Don D Fowler and Jeremy A Sabloff (eds), *American Archaeology Past and Future*, Smithsonian Institution Press, Washington, 77–133.

Herries, Andy IR 2009, 'New approaches for integrating palaeomagnetic and mineral magnetic methods to answer archaeological and geological questions on Stone Age sites', in Andrew Fairbairn, Sue O'Conner and Ben Marwick (eds), *New Directions in Archaeological Science*, Terra Australis 28, ANU E Press, Canberra, 235–253.

Holdaway, Simon and LuAnn Wandsnider 2008, 'Time in archaeology: an introduction', in Simon J Holdaway and LuAnn Wandsnider (eds), *Time and Archaeology,* University of Utah Press, Salt Lake City, 1–12.

Long, Kelsie, Nicola Stern, Ian S Williams, Les Kinsley, Rachel Wood, Katarina Sporic, Tegan Smith, Stewart Fallon, Harri Kokkonen, Ian Moffat and Rainer Grün 2014, 'Fish otolith geochemistry, environmental conditions and human occupation at Lake Mungo, Australia', *Quaternary Science Reviews* 88: 82–95.

Lubbock, James 1865, *Pre-historic Times*, Williams and Norgate, London.

Murray, Tim 1993, 'Archaeology and the threat of the past: Sir Henry Rider Haggard and the acquisition of time', *World Archaeology* 25: 175–186.

Murray, Tim 1997, 'Dynamic modelling and new social theory of the mid- to long term', in Sander Ernst van der Leeuw and James McGlade (eds), *Time, Process and Structured Transformation in Archaeology*, Routledge, London, 449–463.

Shryock, Andrew and Daniel Lord Smail 2011, 'Introduction', in Andrew Shryock and Daniel Lord Smail (eds), *Deep History: The Architecture of Past and Present*, University of California Press, Berkeley, CA, 3–20.

Spry, Caroline 2014, 'Refitting a Past: A Comparison of Late Pleistocene and Terminal Pleistocene/Early Holocene Stone Tool Technology at Lake Mungo, Southwestern New South Wales, Australia', PhD thesis, Archaeology Program, La Trobe University, Melbourne.

Stern, Nicola 1993, 'The structure of the Lower Pleistocene archaeological record: a case study from the Koobi Fora Formation in northwest Kenya', *Current Anthropology* 34: 201–225.

Stern, Nicola 1994, 'The implications of time-averaging for reconstructing the land-use patterns of early tool-using hominids', *Journal of Human Evolution* 27: 89–105.

Stern, Nicola 2008, 'Time-averaging and the structure of late Pleistocene archaeological deposits in south west Tasmania', in Simon J Holdaway and LuAnn Wandsnider (eds), *Time and Archaeology,* University of Utah Press, Salt Lake City, 134–148.

Stern, Nicola 2008b, 'Stratigraphy, depositional environments and palaeolandscape reconstruction in landscape archaeology', in Bruno David and Julian Thomas (eds), *Handbook of Landscape Archaeology*, Left Coast Press, Walnut Creek, CA, 365–378.

Stern, Nicola, Jacqui Tumney, Kathryn Fitzsimmons, and Paul Kajewski 2013, 'Strategies for investigating human responses to changes in environment at Lake Mungo in the Willandra Lakes, southeast Australia', in David Frankel, Jennifer Webb and Susan Lawrence (eds), *Archaeology in Technology and Environment*, Routledge, London, 31–50.

Stoczkowski, Wiktor 2002, *Explaining Human Origins: Myth, Imagination and Conjecture*, Cambridge University Press, Cambridge.

Tumney, Jacqui 2011, 'Environment, Landscape and Stone Technology at Lake Mungo, Southwest New South Wales, Australia', PhD thesis, Archaeology Program, La Trobe University.

Webb, Steve, Matthew L Cupper and Richard Robins 2006, 'Pleistocene human footprints from the Willandra Lakes, southeastern Australia', *Journal of Human Evolution* 50: 405–413.

14. Collaborative Histories of the Willandra Lakes

Deepening histories and the deep past

Malcolm Allbrook and Ann McGrath

In the Willandra Lakes region of south-western New South Wales, Australia, research over the past 45 years has created a vivid picture of interactions between humans and their environment spanning an immensely long period of time. The landscape provides an archaeological record of grand proportions, almost unique in its capacity to offer a complex picture of Pleistocene Aboriginal life.[1] Understandings of this landscape, and of Australia as a continent and nation, were changed by the unearthing in 1968 of the remains of a young woman who would later become known as Mungo Lady, and who is now estimated to have lived 42,000 years ago. This vital evidence of deep human history emerged due to soil erosion. As well as representing the ancient presence of *Homo sapiens*, the realisation that it was the earliest known human cremation ignited the interest of the Australian and international scientific community in the region.[2] Through scientific research, since 1968, the lands of the Willandra Lakes changed from being conceived as sparsely populated, semi-arid, marginal sheep station country, to a veritable trove of geological and cultural significance. Lake Mungo was considered sufficiently important to become a National Park in 1979, followed in 1981 with the whole Willandra Lakes region being listed as World Heritage – indeed, one of Australia's first three UNESCO recognised World Heritage Areas – and one recognised for not only the uniqueness of its natural landforms, but also for its cultural significance.[3]

This paper feeds into a larger discussion on the potential of a deepened scope and temporality for history, as well as a knowledge base that incorporates cross-cultural and population knowledges – ones with diverging experiential and conceptual time frames for historical appreciation. As a study site, the Willandra landscape has largely been the province of geoarchaeological science, an approach that is necessarily cross-disciplinary in that it combines archaeological studies with a wide range of associated disciplines, including

---

1   Johnston and Clarke 1998.

2   Bowler et al. 1970.

3   www.visitmungo.com.au/world-heritage (accessed 23 July 2014); also Douglas 2006. Along with the Willandra Lakes, the Great Barrier Reef and Kakadu were inscribed as Australia's first entries on the World Heritage list in 1981.

geomorphology, stratigraphy, sedimentology and chronology, as well as ecology.[4] However, this approach operates in the space called 'science' and does not necessarily consider history as a cognate or relevant discipline.

Already, from the 1970s, Indigenous traditional owners of the region were aware of the growing scientific importance of their traditional landscape and of the need for other knowledge bases and values systems to be brought to bear on the evidence. After the initial interventions and involvement of women and men such as Alice Kelly, Tibby Briar, Elsie Jones, Alice Bugmy, Badger Bates and Rod Smith, Aboriginal elders and members of the younger generations have steadily become a vital part of this cross-disciplinary research effort. Three traditional owner groups, the Mutthi Mutthi, Paakantji (Barkindji) and Ngyiampaa peoples, each with strong connections to the region, are closely involved in the current system of co-management of the World Heritage Area and Lake Mungo National Park. Along with heritage managers, local community representatives and scientists, they helped negotiate a system whereby any research, scientific or otherwise, in the National Park and World Heritage Area must be endorsed and supported by a Community Management Council made up of a majority of traditional owners, together with representation from the scientific community, pastoral landowners, and the Commonwealth and State governments. This arrangement has brought a high level of Indigenous involvement in research, for example in the Australian Research Council (ARC) funded Discovery and Linkage projects, including the archaeological and dating investigations of Rainer Grün and Nicola Stern, and the palaeoanthropological and DNA research of Michael Westaway and others. Research into surface archaeology and into skeletal remains continue, as do joint efforts to establish an interpretive centre and a Keeping Place at Lake Mungo, with the ultimate aim of repatriating the large number of human remains that were previously removed from the region for the purposes of salvage and research.

Despite the significance of this site to Australia's human history, before the commencement of the ARC-funded research project 'Australia's Ancient and Recent Pasts: A History of Lake Mungo' in August 2011, historians had not been involved in, or sought to undertake intensive on-site research at Lake Mungo.[5] This has partly arisen from the disciplinary schism between history and prehistory, and/or history and archaeology. Archaeologist Harry Allen's chapter in this volume already accounts for some of the history of his own discipline, especially exploring aspects of the chronological framings of archaeological thinking. We do not seek to explore such methodological

4   Holdaway and Fanning 2010. A more detailed article on the subject of the relationship between history and science at the Willandra Lakes is currently under preparation.
5   Ann McGrath is the lead Chief Investigator and Malcolm Allbrook worked as a Research Associate on this project (DP110103193) from August 2011 until January 2014.

and conceptual distinctions in any depth here, as they warrant a chapter in themselves. Nonetheless, the explanation that historical studies must rely upon textual evidence, while prehistory and archaeology rely upon digging and unearthing of material evidence, deserves to be revisited. Disciplinary divides are constantly in flux. And, as Alison Bashford has recently pointed out, the story is more plastic than any clear-cut boundaries might suggest. After all, 'in a tradition of scholarship that has long complicated "prehistory" and "history"', palaeontologists, prehistorians and archaeologists have written history, historians have written prehistory, and economic historians have attempted to tackle chronologies very different to industrialisation and wealth production.[6] Indeed, to back this argument, environmental historians such as Kirsty Douglas have undertaken research on science, landscape, heritage and the uses of the deep past in Australia between 1830 and 2003. Her subsequent book *Pictures of Time Beneath* (2007) made a significant contribution to eroding the divide between scientific and historical approaches. Her work also contributed to understanding the region, as Lake Mungo was one of three sites featured in her research. The authors' research project, 'Australia's Ancient and Recent Pasts', has added and expanded such work by bringing the methods of community historical research, including oral and filmic history techniques, biography and cultural mapping, and place-based approaches to the study of Lake Mungo and the Willandra Lakes.

Historians have been drawn to reconsider the temporal scope of Australian history, particularly the capacity to traverse the 'great divide' of 1788 – the point in time where the long, unchanging and undocumented prehistory of the continent was transformed into the well-documented 'history' of the Australian nation, based upon written, textual sources. Rapidly rising attention to Aboriginal history, and to sharp-edged political debates over sovereignty, dispossession, resistance and the stolen generations, have created the need for a continental and an inclusive history of nation which should not ignore the much deeper human histories of Australia.

Consequently, a workshop held at the 2006 Australian Historical Association conference in Canberra dwelt upon the question of whether historians were compelled to cede the ancient history of Australia to prehistory, archaeology and the sciences. Should they continue to view this long past as 'background' to narratives of human change and dynamism?[7] Participant Heather Goodall drew attention to contradictions in the 'appearance and a presentation of timelessness, which is a very important sense of the longevity of a very long set of civilisations', but which can thereby render them 'inaccessible to questions

---

6   Bashford 2013: 343. See also Mulvaney 1975; Blainey 1975; Butlin 1993; McIntyre 2009.
7   'Can we write a 60,000 year history of Australia?' Transcript of a session at the 2006 AHA Conference, Canberra.

about how change might be understood'. The vast timescales of deep time can 'awe the imagination to the point of paralysis', and can only be appreciated, even then imperfectly, by metaphor, as Tom Griffiths has noted: 'humanity as the last inch of the cosmic mile, the last few seconds before midnight, the skin of paint atop the Eiffel Tower.'[8]

Joseph Barrell, an American geologist from the turn of the twentieth century, remarked that science can show 'the flowing landscapes of geologic time ... transform from age to age'. However, he elaborated:

> the eye of man through all his lifetime sees no change, and his reason is appalled at the thought of duration so vast that the milleniums of written history have not recorded the shifting of even one of the fleeting views whose blendings make the moving picture.[9]

This consciousness of geological time has led geologists to think 'in two languages' and, as American writer John McPhee expressed it, to 'function on two different scales':

> If you free yourself from the conventional reaction to a quantity like a million years, you free yourself a bit from the boundaries of human time. And then in a way you do not live at all, but in a way you live forever.[10]

A recently published 'Conversation' in the *American Historical Review* asked four historians to address the question of how the discipline, with its 'familiar periodizations of historical training', might come to grips with such seemingly unfathomable questions of temporal scale.[11] Temporal categorisations and understandings of deep time connectedness can be reconfigured and enlivened by recognising the deep time manufacture of everyday objects.[12] Objects and technologies can play a dynamic role in creating new histories, in human embodiment and in definitions of what makes us human today and in the past.

A history of the Willandra Lakes region proceeds against the immanence of a deep human past that is vividly engraved upon the landscape. This landscape forces the historian to confront an Australian history that predates the European presence by 42,000 years. It is a place where available evidence effectively jumps over the Holocene time-bar, connecting the contemporary Anthropocene world to the human world of the Pleistocene. With its tangible evidence of the world's changing climate and the life-span of rivers and glaciers, contemporary visitors witness a dry plain with eroding sand dunes, which once teemed with

---

8   Douglas 2004: 18; Griffiths 2000: 24.
9   Joseph Barrell, quoted in Cotton 1942.
10 McPhee 1998: 90–91.
11 Aslanian et al. 2013: 1431–1472.
12 Aslanian et al. 2013: 1457.

fish and bird life, and hosted an enduring civilisation for tens of thousands of years. A history of such a cultural landscape needs to explore a land occupied by countless generations of people who, as the archaeological record reveals, left bountiful evidence of their lives and lifestyles, most potently the remains of hundreds of their dead. Furthermore, as the work of Jim Bowler and John Magee reveals, the geomorphic record provides a rich physical context for human populations which had to confront the challenges of climate change, the filling and emptying of the Willandra lake system, the Last Glacial Maximum, and transformations of the landscape through the wind-born movement of sand over the ages. Our research on Lake Mungo deals with the implications of this long human history in Australian historiography – in particular the lives and legacies of the ancient people whose interred remains, cooking hearths and tools later surfaced, serving to educate and inform contemporary Australians and international researchers into the human past.

We take up John Mulvaney's observation in 1975 about the curious reluctance of historians to look beyond 1788, thereby ceding 99.9 per cent of Australia's human history to prehistorians. The Lake Mungo history seeks to extend more recent insights into the historiography of deep time by Daniel Lord Smail, Andrew Shryock and David Christian, and a number of Australian historians, including Alison Bashford, Libby Robin, Tom Griffiths and Kirsty Douglas.

A study that is located in place, in this case the richly human landscape of Lake Mungo and the Willandra Lakes World Heritage Area, reframes the parameters of historical investigation by inviting attention to an extremely *longue durée*; a history that takes place against a backdrop of geomorphic time, climate change, environmental and climatic fluctuations, and a capacity by modern humans to respond to such changes. In a place such as Lake Mungo, there is a wealth of material for the historian to work with, including an archive of scientific literature accumulated over nearly 50 years of research activity in the region. Its archaeology, hydrology and geomorphology provides an unusually sharp record of human habitation over the *longue durée* – clear evidence that the human history of Australia began, not in 1788, but over 42,000 years ago. This demands a reframing of the chronology of Australian history. As Mike Smith's recent study of Australia's deserts explained, Australian human history is overwhelmingly an Aboriginal history, involving the 'autonomous development of the hunter-gatherer communities descended from the original late Pleistocene settlers of the "continent"'. Yet it is 'striking for its austerity', and relies just as much on 'context as on material remains'.[13]

---

13 Smith 2013: 1, 13.

The Willandra Lakes thus provides a rich setting to foreground the human, and as John Mulvaney has recently suggested, to 'humanise' the landscape.[14] Life stories and life trajectories illuminate the diverse ways in which humans over time have responded to the environment, and the ways they have been connected to and influenced by the landscape. Indigenous custodians, Parks and Heritage managers, scientists and pastoralists tell stories of connection that encompass the deep human history of the Willandra, and their contemporary relationships with this deep past, doing much to deepen historical understandings of the region. Each of the interest groups now taking part in the management of the World Heritage Area expressed these connections according to their own terminologies and worldviews. Sometimes they may be in conflict, yet diverse interests coalesce around a common commitment to manage the heritage of the area.

Over the last 50 years in particular, the Willandra Lakes has been a zone of 'deep history' contact, in which people from all kinds of backgrounds have encountered and interacted with one another. Until the first white people started to cross the country in the early nineteenth century, the history of the region was wholly Aboriginal, a place that had been occupied by the Indigenous ancestors of the Mutthi Mutthi, Paakantji and Ngyiampaa people since time immemorial. In dramatic fashion, in 1968 the (re)appearance of the burials confirmed a fact long known by contemporary traditional owners – that the ancestors had 'always' been in the land. Theirs is a connection that is personal and familiar. As local Indigenous custodians explain, Lady Mungo is like 'one of the old aunties', a person known and respected, 'a queen' for her people who has, by providing proof to a doubting Australian public of their long-standing connection, done much for their identity and sense of belonging.

To an Indigenous custodian such as Tanya Charles, the life paths of these ancient people are readily imaginable:

> It's like yesterday that our people were still walking across this country. I can't go back and say hundreds and thousands of years because everything's like yesterday to me, especially when you've still got the spirits around and you can feel their presence of them, just like this fireplace here. I could see five, six people sitting around here having a feed, leaving and then moving on and coming back again on their way to wherever they was heading.[15]

---

14   Mike Smith, pers. comm., March 2013. David 2002, 2006.
15   Tanya Charles, interview by Ann McGrath, October 2011. See also Pike and McGrath 2014.

Yet, despite this deeply felt historical connection, during the first flush of archaeological and scientific inquiry that followed Lady Mungo's re-emergence, Indigenous interests were barely acknowledged. Harry Allen was among the team who, soon after Jim Bowler had first spotted the fragmented remains of Lady Mungo late in 1968, positively identified her as human. With a sense of awe and wonder, he speaks of how the world greeted a discovery that, 'virtually overnight', expanded the human history of Australia from thousands of years to tens of thousands of years – the late Pleistocene. After the archaeological picture of the Willandra Lakes sharpened, Lake Mungo was declared a National Park in 1979, and the whole region a World Heritage Area in 1981. The research community was forced to respond to powerful assertions of Indigenous identity from a small but eloquent coalition of traditional owners. Foremost among these was Alice Kelly, a Mutthi Mutthi woman who had long been an effective advocate for her people in Balranald and who was, by all accounts, a remarkable leader. Kelly initiated contact with scientific researchers, and came to form close friendships with many of the first generation researchers at Lake Mungo, among them Isabel McBryde, Jim Bowler, Alan Thorne and Harry Allen. She played a central role in a crucial period in which archaeology and its associated sciences slowly, sometimes painstakingly, came to recognise the strength of Indigenous connection and historical attachment, and consequently, to shift research and heritage management paradigms.

In essence, Kelly and her colleagues were not surprised by the scientific evidence emerging from the lunettes and dry lakes of the Willandra, for it simply confirmed a known historical reality; they had been taught that their people had 'always been here'. However, these Aboriginal women elders were still vitally interested in the details of past lives and life paths that the archaeological investigation revealed. Archaeologist Isabel McBryde quickly recognised the strength of Kelly's arguments and also the potential for rich knowledge exchange. She had already witnessed the practical power of Indigenous people's landscape knowledge whilst undertaking work at the University of New England. McBryde saw an expanded potential for science and Indigenous knowledge not only to coexist, and cooperate, but to do so productively for all parties. However, the Indigenous custodians were increasingly disturbed about the fact that ancestral remains had been removed from their burial places, and their spirits thus prevented from resting in country. Alice Kelly continued to help mobilise other elders to lobby and campaign for a return of these remains.

Meanwhile, Isabel McBryde invited people such as Alice and Alf Kelly to witness the potential value and the actual practice of respectful research. She and other scientists interested in a more inclusive style of Australian heritage management became scientific pioneers when they offered Indigenous custodians of land the possibility of observing research taking place. Moreover, they supported their demands to gain a right of consent as to whether research would proceed. This could take place before the fact, rather than as a protest, or in the form of litigation as had occurred over the Kow Swamp later Pleistocene remains in Victoria.

In 1992, when Alan Thorne, the palaeontologist who had painstakingly pieced together and reconstructed the fragmented skull of Lady Mungo in his laboratory at The Australian National University, formally returned her remains to the custody of the traditional owners at a ceremony near her burial place, it appeared that a great moment of reconciliation was taking place. A deeply meaningful ceremony was held, and Indigenous people expressed relief that Lady Mungo's remains had finally been returned. Yet, out of respect for future scientific research, and out of the desire to ensure the remains would not again erode away, the elders remain concerned that she is not yet in an appropriate and permanent resting place.

The management structure that eventually, and sometimes with difficulty, emerged from these hesitant beginnings reflected an evolving sense of mutual recognition and respect, with many people involved in sincere efforts to carry it forward. A determined coalition of Mutthi Mutthi, Paakantji and Ngyiampaa traditional owners became powerful advocates for their country and played significant roles in its management. A crucial relationship of reciprocal support emerged with the non-Aboriginal landholders, whose pastoral interests were suddenly threatened by the declaration of world heritage, and the growing scientific profile of the Willandra Lakes. They too expressed a strong attachment to the region, born out of family history, an intimate knowledge and respect for the land and its capacity to provide a livelihood. Like the traditional owners, they shared a suspicion that scientific interests in the Willandra, supported by government, would soon come to subsume their own. In this scenario of potential conflict and suspicion, the role of a number of government officers employed by the NSW Western Lands Commission and the National Parks and Wildlife Service became central to the task of working out a solution. People today speak respectfully of the crucial role played by the late Peter Clark, a former pastoralist as well as a skilled field archaeologist and public servant, who worked to facilitate an agreement between the different parties in the Willandra. Many other government officers have played a part in the recent history of the region and, at the same time, had their life paths altered and enriched by the experience of working there. They, too, speak of the particular power and wonder of the Willandra Lakes as a place that can change life paths and bring deeper understandings, a reminder that there are many different expressions of connection, and that the human history of the region may be intensely personal.

The voices of the Willandra introduce a history that is both long and complex, and goes far beyond the written record in its portrayal of human experiences of the land, including relationships with the deep past. Extensive filmed histories recorded as part of the Australia's Ancient Pasts ARC project, as well as for the development of the film *Message from Mungo* (co-directed and produced by Andrew Pike and Ann McGrath), capture the voices of pastoralists, scientists, government officers and Aboriginal people, as they relate family stories, life experiences and histories of connection. Many have been recorded on country, at Lake Mungo and the Willandra Lakes, or in adjacent towns such as Mildura, Balranald, Wentworth and Dareton.

There is potential for a great deal more place-located oral and filmed history, including through a program of cultural and historical mapping. Oral history provides a process for re-examining the large amount of documentary, archival and photographic evidence held in diverse collecting and archival institutions around Australia, including national bodies such as the National Library, Australian Institute of Aboriginal and Torres Strait Islander Studies and the National Archives, the universities, newspapers and public media. Such engagement opens up the history of the region and provides room for many different stories and many different experiences. Alongside the defining narratives of the deep past and scientific discovery, for stories of the less-known, there are also diverse stories of more recent visitors to place, including the multicultural band of German scientists and Indian cameleers accompanying Burke and Wills on their ill-fated expedition in 1861, the pastoralists, labourers and shearers on the large runs of the nineteenth century, the Chinese labourers who are credited with building the woolshed at Lake Mungo in 1867, and for giving the Lake Mungo lunette its vernacular name, The Walls of China. Their histories connect a human history of place with a wider diaspora of human mobilities and deeper, placed-based traditions and histories elsewhere.

Oral, audio, and indeed, filmic history techniques, provide powerful testimony to a history of Aboriginal connections, including the past two centuries of colonialism, and for recent generations, the severe disruptions wrought upon culture and family life by government organisations such as the Aborigines Protection Board. Aboriginal histories are themselves diverse, some speaking of being able to stay on the land, on the stations, or moving from place to place, others with life stories dominated by institutions, reserves and missions, and forced separation as children from culture, family and kin. With its evidence of long connection and identity with country, the Lake Mungo and the Willandra Lakes World Heritage area provides a powerful unifying point for all the voices of the Willandra. Its structures have allowed conflicts over heritage and history to be played out, discussed and managed, if never completely resolved. A resolution to such a history may never be possible.

Scientific research continues, as long as Indigenous custodians agree to provide consent, and as long as they can see benefits such as useful knowledge, participation, consultation, employment and training. Perhaps there is something in the deep past of the region that motivates an impetus to compromise and respect, imperfect though it may be, and subject to an array of pitfalls and challenges. Access to archaeological sites, especially human remains, continues to be contested between the scientists and Indigenous custodians. Local and world experts frequently declare that scientific research in the Willandra has ground to a halt. At times, it has certainly done so. Excavations are restricted, but surface archaeology is being undertaken, as Nicola Stern's chapter attests. However, it is not only the hurdles of Indigenous protocols that get in the way of scientific liberty. A key obstacle can be the territorial tendencies of some disciplines, their exclusivity and repeated gate-closing. Cases where Indigenous power is exerted to block research receive far more attention than blocks created by competing academics. In coloniser states, this is one of the few areas of the law where researchers must observe Indigenous protocols. These do not necessarily mean the end of research, but they do mean a different approach to research.

As a place of deep history, Lake Mungo induces a sense of wonder at a landscape that is redolent of human meaning and occupation. Although it suggests scales of time that defy most westerners' ability to comprehend, Indigenous Australians are expert in riding this conceptual gap. If historians in the academy wish to tell the full story of deep human history in all its complexity, they may discover, like certain archaeologists, that a collaborative engagement with Indigenous understandings will enrich the practice of history, and will greatly enhance not only historical understandings of past landscapes, but also of peoples past, including those continuing peoples who persist in creating new histories in this country. Nobody would underrate the complexity of this task. But the sense of wonder may help us defeat the obstacles. After all, the human landscape of Lake Mungo and Willandra Lakes offers a model of how people living in the present manage to cross the imagined divide into deep time. It reveals how disparate groups effectively engage in meaningful ways with a long history that intimately informs contemporary individual and national identity.

Bibliography

Aslanian, Sebouh David, Joyce E Chaplin, Ann McGrath and Kristin Mann 2013, 'AHR conversation: how size matters: the question of scale in history', *American Historical Review* 118(5): 1431–1472.

Australian Historical Association 2006, 'Can We Write a 60,000 Year History of Australia?' Paper presented at the Australian Historical Association Conference, Canberra, Australia, 2006.

Bashford, Alison 2013, 'The Anthropocene is modern history; reflections on climate and Australian deep time', *Australian Historical Studies* 44(3): 341–349, DOI:10.1080/1031461X.2013.817454.

Blainey, Geoffrey 1975, *Triumph of the Nomads: A History of Ancient Australia*, Sun Books, Melbourne.

Bowler, Jim M, Rhys Jones, Harry Allen and Alan G Thorne 1970, 'Pleistocene human remains from Australia: a living site and human cremation from Lake Mungo, western New South Wales', *World Archaeology* 2: 39–60.

Butlin, Noel 1993, *Economics and the Dreamtime: A Hypothetical History*, Cambridge University Press, Melbourne.

Charles, Tanya, interview by Ann McGrath, October 2011.

Cotton, Charles A 1942, *Geomorphology: An Introduction to the Study of Landforms,* ,Whitcombe & Tombs Ltd, Christchurch.

David, Bruno 2002, *Inscribed Landscapes: Marking and Making Place,* University of Hawaii Press, Hawaii.

David, Bruno 2006, *The Social Archaeology of Australian Indigenous Societies,* Aboriginal Studies Press, Canberra.

Douglas, Kirsty 2004, 'Pictures of Time Beneath: Science, Landscape, Heritage and the Uses of the Deep Past in Australia, 1830–2003', PhD thesis, School of History, The Australian National University, Canberra.

Douglas, Kirsty 2006, 'Forsaken spot to classic ground: geological heritage in Australia and the recuperative power of the deep past', *Environment and History* 12: 269–296.

Douglas, Kirsty 2007, *Pictures of Time Beneath: Science, Heritage and the Uses of the Deep Past*, CSIRO Publishing, Collingwood, Victoria.

Griffiths, Tom 2000, 'Social history and deep time', *Tasmanian Historical Studies* 7(1): 21–38.

Holdaway, Simon J and Patricia C Fanning 2010, 'Geoarchaeology in Australia: understanding human-environment interactions', in Paul Bishop and Brad Pillans (eds), *Australian Landscapes*, Special Publication 346, Geological Society of London, London.

Johnston, Harvey and Peter Clarke 1998, 'Willandra Lakes archaeological investigations, 1968–1998', *Archaeology in Oceania* 33: 105–119.

McIntyre, Stuart 2009, *A Concise History of Australia*, Cambridge University Press, Melbourne.

McPhee, John 1998, *Annals of the Former World*, Farrar, Straus and Giroux, New York.

Mulvaney, John 1975, *Prehistory of Australia*, Penguin Books, London.

Pike, Andrew and Ann McGrath (dir.) 2014, *Message from Mungo*, Ronin Films, Canberra.

Smith, Mike 2013, *The Archaeology of Australia's Deserts*, Cambridge University Press, Cambridge.

Made in the USA
Coppell, TX
06 December 2022

87984464R00167